BAD REP

By

Tom Fynn

First Published 2013 by Abyssopelagic Publishing

Pre-Season

Lustre Productions Office, Hollywood, Los Angeles

The leather of the waiting room chair peeled noisily from her legs as she shifted, and for the second time that day Grace Willetts regretted wearing shorts. The air-conditioning hummed. A police siren blipped somewhere out on Melrose. The absurdly pretty receptionist (an actress, naturally) looked up and gave a practiced smile. She was no Julia Roberts. Too blandly attractive – one of a thousand other beautiful clones in the city. Leading ladies needed something more definitive. Hathaway's smile. Jolie's lips. Portman's eyes. Marilyn's ass.

Grace looked at her watch. Twenty minutes now. That was to show her she was unimportant. Well, OK. She *was* unimportant. Right at the bottom of the ladder and looking up. But was this meeting going to be the last rung, or the next one?

A trio of vintage movie posters lined the wall behind reception. Marlon Brando smouldering as *The Wild One*, making the t-shirt cool and the leather jacket bad. *Hey Johnny, what are you rebelling against?* Beat. *Whaddya got?* A lot of people thought he said that in *On the Waterfront*, but a lot of people hadn't seen either movie. Melvin Weitz probably hadn't seen any of the movies in those posters. Probably got a lackey to summarise them for him. Hundred words max.

A silent indicator prompted Pretty Girl on reception and she touched her ear-piece with a manicured finger. Her smile lit up – not the audition smile, not for lowly Grace – and she delivered her single line:

'Mister Weitz will see you now.'

Grace went through misted glass doors, through a vestibule with a $100 dollar fresh-cut flower arrangement in it and towards the wooden door marked with his name in gold. She paused. Should she knock? What if he was doing a line or 'auditioning' the next receptionist? A third regret about wearing shorts began to develop.

The door jerked open and there was Mel Weitz. He looked her up and down with a glance that instantly dismissed her as potential receptionist material.

5

If he lingered at all over her legs, it was only with apparent bemusement that she'd worn shorts to an appointment with him.

He flashed the professional smile. 'Grace! Come in, come in! Here, take a seat. Can I get you a decaf? Mineral water? There's a deli on the corner does an awesome guava smoothie.'

'Nothing. Thanks, Mister Weitz.'

'Hey! I'm Mel. Call me Mel. Watching your weight, I guess. Every pound counts?'

'Not really. I—'

'Anyway. Take a seat. Yeah, leather sticks to skin, doesn't it? My wife won't have it at home. But it wipes clean – that's what I like about it.'

Grace sat and folded her hands on her lap. Mel fell into his executive recliner and smiled. The pause went on too long.

'Mister W . . . Mel. I'm not really sure why . . . '

Mel held up his hands. 'Of course, of course. I told 'em not to tell you. Don't worry – you're not here to be fired. I wouldn't do that myself. I have people to do that! Tell me – how do you like working for Lustre?'

'I . . . It's a great opportunity for someone like me, you know, straight out of film school. You just can't learn film-making in a classroom. You've got to be on set. Scorcese said—'

'Yeah, Marty's got some great lines. So – you like being a production assistant? Getting coffee, handing out call-sheets, holding the walkie-talkie?'

'I don't mind starting at the bottom. It's a privilege to see the process up close, talk to people . . . learn a few things where I can.'

'Meet some stars, right? Who you met so far?'

'Well, I see them on set, of course, but I don't really get to . . . you know. It's not really about the . . . Christian Bale. Anthony Hopkins.'

'Like the guys, do you? The older guys?'

'Mister . . . Mel – I'm really confused. Am I in trouble for something?'

'What do you know about the *Corelli* sequel?'

6

'The mandolin thing? I heard it was green-lit a month or so ago, but then Cage dropped out, didn't he?'

'Yeah, he dropped out. But it's going ahead anyway with financing from some group that owns Qatar or some shit. You don't need to know that. They're in pre-production now: set-building out on that same island. Whole thing's being shot on location.'

'Then who's playing lead?'

'Craggan.'

'*James* Craggan? He's out of rehab?'

'Yeah, who knew? I thought he was dead. Turns out that Best Supporting nod last year made him niche-hot. Like Rourke in *The Wrestler*. You can't imagine the insurance we're paying. The transport guys are running a pool on him not making it through the summer.'

'But he won't . . . '

'No – he's not the money in this picture. It's more like a cameo. There've been rewrites. Schedules, casting – you know how it is. The major billings are Caro and Braddock.'

Grace processed the information. Chet Braddock: the so-called next Brad Pitt. Handsome, earnest – method all the way. He had a finger amputated on purpose for that Cherokee picture. Hannah Caro – twenty-five-year-old Monica Bellucci successor with a reputation as lurid and well-known as her body.

'Yeah, well,' said Mel. 'How'd you like to work on it?'

'On *Corelli*? I'd . . . I'd love to . . . but can I ask: why are you offering it to me personally?'

'Smart girl. This isn't a regular production assistant position. It's something a little more . . . sensitive.'

Her leg peeled away from the leather as she crossed it. 'I'm not going to "audition" if that's what you—'

'Relax, sweetie. You're not . . . Never mind. You ever met Craggan?'

'I heard he was on set here a few weeks ago, but no, I didn't see him.'

7

'Well it seems he saw you and – look, there's no easy way to say this – he's convinced you're his spectral daughter.'

'What?'

'Not an *actual* daughter. He hasn't got any kids as far as we know. But it seems he knocked up some starlet – it could be anyone; you know his reputation – about the time you were conceived. She never had it, of course, but he's got it into his head that you're the living spirit of the kid who never lived. Some guru told him – drew a picture of what the daughter might have looked like. Don't ask me how it works. His brain's so fucked by scotch and coke and God-knows-what-else I'm surprised he doesn't think he's L. Ron Hubbard. The point is, he's twisted with guilt about the scrape-job and wants to make amends. He wants you to be his personal assistant on the *Corelli* shoot. There's nothing sexual, I guarantee it. I don't think he was ever into incest. He wants to get to know you, spend some time together. Whaddya say?'

'It's . . . insane. He's insane.'

'What can I tell you? When you've lived his life, your reality is different. Think Brando or Jacko. You hear about Craggan having his favourite horse pickled by Damien Hirst? It's true – I've seen it. He's just a visitor to our world, but it looks like he might be big box office again, so he gets what he wants.'

Grace sat dumbfounded. Was there a camera on her right now? Was someone punking her? Mel's business face said not.

'But, you . . . you can't just give him a *person*!' she said. 'I'm not some *perk* you throw into the deal. What if he wants to comb my hair and buy me a pony . . . it's just sick. I'm not a shrink. I wouldn't know what to do with him. Does anyone know if he's even stable?'

'He has people. Chefs, security, drivers, PR, fucking paranormal spirit gurus . . . I don't know. Nobody's asking you to play dress-up. You'll be yourself working as an employee of Lustre. Get him coffee, take his messages, whatever. If he tries anything weird, we'll get you out of there fast.'

'What if I say no? Am I fired?'

8

'Listen, sweetie. You want experience, right? How much experience you getting now? You spend more time waiting at Starbucks than you do talking to cameras or lighting. When was the last time a director noticed you were alive? You'll get noticed when you're standing next to James fucking Craggan, trust me. Especially if he thinks you're his dead aborted kid. You'll be reading lines with him, talking shots and all that jazz. People kiss your ass when you've got the star's ear. Craggan's your passport if you want to get into the industry. Keep him happy and alive. Shit, he'll probably want re-writes. He always wants his people to do rewrites. He's famous for it. You've done screenwriting, right?'

'UCLA summer school, but—'

'You could write lines for him. You might even get a credit. How's that for your career?'

'I'm not in the writer's union. I can't get a credit.'

'Right. Now you're negotiating. Smart girl. OK, so Lustre pays your dues with WGAW. That buys you three years' membership. You got a full-length finished script from your course?'

'It's a pile of—'

'Whatever. I'll buy it for a dollar – that gives you the credits you need. Now you're a union writer.'

'I . . . '

'Think of it – a whole summer in Europe. You ever been? Rome, Paris, Venice – it's like Vegas, only bigger. There's a good crew on this movie – the kind of people kids like you could only dream of working with. You know how many Oscars they've got between 'em? The DP's got two. And Chet Braddock can only get bigger if he quits the amputating kick.'

'I . . . '

'And did I mention the pay? We're talking five times what you get for just fetching coffee. And you get a *per diem* like the talent. And you'll be staying in your own room at Craggan's villa. Use his chef. Use his limo. Use his fucking spirit guru for all I care. This is a summer that could change your life, sweetie.'

9

'You really want me to do this, don't you?'

'Me? I couldn't give a shit. Craggan wants you, and what Craggan wants, he gets. That's how it works. When you're hot, you're hot. Play the game, sweetie – that's how you get ahead. Don't they teach you that at UCLA?'

Grace looked at him leaning forward on his desk and realised that the contract had already been signed. She was a clause: part of the offer. If she refused now, would Craggan pull out and eighty-six the movie? She'd never work at Lustre again. On the other hand, they obviously *really* needed her.

Mel looked at his wafer-thin $10,000 watch. His smile strained for longevity. He held up his palms as a balance: yes or no?

The words she spoke didn't seem her own. 'There's a grad-school directing course at UCLA – it's really hard to get on to. The fees are—'

Mel smiled his great-white smile. 'You got it.'

'And . . . I haven't got the kind of clothes I'd need for summer on a Greek island.'

'You got 'em.'

'And will there be a contract . . . I mean, in case he gets weird with the daughter stuff?'

Mel beamed. 'Sure. Absolutely. Someone'll be in touch. You're flying out next week.' He stood and held out his hand. 'Good luck. And welcome to the game.'

Grace stood with a leathern sucking and gripped his outstretched hand to stop her own from shaking. She tried to leave the office on confident legs, certain that he was looking at the ugly mess of wrinkles on the backs of her thighs.

'Smart girl,' he muttered when the door had closed. But not receptionist material.

Police Office, Exogi, Kefalonia

Sergeant Nikos Petras reclined in his office chair and exhaled cigarette smoke at the *No Smoking* sign. Grinning, he held the phone receiver to his ear and picked flecks of filo pastry from his moustache.

'An intruder, eh? Is he in the house now? Is he armed?'

His eyes narrowed in amusement. He raised a plastic cup of frothy *frappe* to his lips and sipped delicately to avoid further decorating the moustache.

'A formidable weapon, you say? Is it raised in anger?'

He listened. He took another deep lungful of smoke.

'What are you wearing, *koukla mou*?'

The caller spoke at length. In fact, Maria often had an intruder problem while her husband was away at the quarry. The would-be burglar always seemed to be gone by the time Sergeant Petras arrived, but Maria would inevitably need urgent consolation. On other days, it might be the young widow Stella calling, or the language teacher Aliki, whose linguistic muscles needed to be kept flexible during the summer vacation.

'I'll be there in ten minutes. Don't change your position,' said Nikos, stubbing out the cigarette and replacing the receiver.

But as he reached for his uniform cap, the downstairs door clattered and a black shadow was cast up the stairwell from the street. Rattly wheezing announced the imminent arrival of a very unwelcome visitor.

The figure who appeared at the open door of the police office was a vision in black: black beard, black *kalimafkion* hat and a black silk cassock swishing down to black-sandalled feet.

'*Pappas* Xenomachos,' said Nikos, not standing. 'What can I do for you?'

The priest sniffed, observed the cigarette butt in the ashtray and looked pointedly at the *No Smoking* sign.

'Dispensations,' smiled Nikos. 'I understand the law also doesn't cover the use of censers in church.'

11

'You wouldn't know what goes on in my church,' said Xenomachos. 'Your childhood baptism was your most recent visit.'

Nikos indicated the cap in his hand. 'I was on my way out. Is this urgent?'

'It is more than urgent. It is matter of blasphemy and devilry corrupting our community's Christian truth.'

'That again.' Nikos sighed and tossed the cap back on the table. He thought of Maria arranged wantonly on her bed, her heavy breasts straining at a scrap of negligee.

'Do not be so flippant, Petras. The Beast is among us. *Hellenismos* – that is what they call it. The worship of the twelve Olympian gods and other Plutonian deities. *I* call it sacrilege and heathenism: pagan idolatry of the sort our Saviour died to cleanse us of.'

'What is it this time, *pappas*?'

'Signs. Irrefutable proof. An arrangement of flowers on the beach here in Exogi – left at night as an offering to some spurious ocean god.'

'That'll be Poseidon.'

'Do not mock. There was also a candle and a honey-cake left at the ancient site in Allomeros. I'm sure you remember that someone left an oil-lamp burning incense on the high rocks above the site at the last full moon.'

Nikos looked longingly at the packet of Marlboro on his desk but settled for a gulp of coffee. In his mind, Maria was now naked and below him, welcoming an intruder of an altogether different sort . . .

Xenomachos stamped a sandaled foot. 'Are you even listening? Do you know that some of us believe that site to contain the bones of a sainted Christian martyr? It is blasphemy to practise pagan rites there.'

Nikos spread his hands. 'What can I tell you, *pappas*? It's probably all just coincidence. Somebody throws some old flowers on the beach. Some kids go to the site at Allomeros for a fumble and take a candle with them. They take some of their mother's honey-cake for a snack and leave it there by accident. As for your burial site, you know that no martyr's bones have ever been discovered

12

there. And anyway, no laws have been broken even if there are some people worshipping old gods.'

'No laws broken, you say?'

'No *state* laws. I don't enforce church law.'

'Well that's where you are wrong, Petras. Anyone wanting to practise a religion other than the true Orthodox faith must make a formal application to the bishop and to the ministry. No such application has been made from this island.'

'Would you grant permission if someone applied?'

'Of course not!'

Visions of Maria began to fade. She was fiery. If he arrived much later, he'd end up in an argument rather than an embrace. He'd have to plead some formal emergency as an excuse, though it would scarcely be credible. The most heinous crime of recent memory had been a shoplifting incident the previous summer.

'Well?' said Xenomachos.

'I'll look into it.'

'Meaning what?'

'I'll make enquiries. Ask around.'

Xenomachos snorted. 'You should ask some of the women you seem to visit so often.'

Nikos glared. 'Yes, men in positions of power have secrets, don't they? You may hear things in confession, but I hear things, too, *pappas*. From parents. A lot of pretty girls here on our island, eh? Too trusting, perhaps, when speaking alone with their priest – their priest whose wife is exhausted by ceaseless childbirth. How many children have you now? Eleven, is it?'

'Outrageous!' spluttered Xenomachos. 'I would not be surprised if you are one of them: the devils in our midst.' He crossed himself elaborately and muttered a prayer against malign influence. 'See that you investigate my complaint, Petras. There's a higher law than yours and I am its agent in this village. What the state cannot enforce, the Divine Majesty will!'

13

He was gone with a furious swishing of silk and a gasping descent to the street. The door slammed behind him.

Nikos sighed and looked at his watch. He anticipated Maria's fury. Car trouble – that was the probably the best excuse. He took a blunt pencil from the desk and was about to go down to let the air out of a tyre when the fax machine below the notice-board began to whine and chug.

The police headquarters in Argostoli might have broadband, but Exogi was still strictly twentieth century. It had been so long since the yellowing machine had last spoken that the novelty drew him. He lit another merciful Marlboro and held the end of the fax paper as it emerged.

CONFIDENTIAL
POLITICAL AFFAIRS DIVISION BRIEFING NOTE
ATTENTION: KEFALONIA REGION

Our internet monitoring facility has recently recorded an occurrence of certain target words used in a web search conducted at an IP address in the village of Exogi (see below for details). The unidentified user was seeking information on the outlawed right-wing nationalist group *Filiki Eteria*, with the apparent intention of forming a Kefalonian cell of the organisation. Covert enquiries should be made by local law enforcement personnel into the origin of this search. Report any information directly to the Division of Political Affairs. No attempt should be made to communicate with the cell, which may already have made contact with the Athens HQ.

NOTE: *Filiki Eteria* is a new group currently under covert surveillance. Their aims are ultra-nationalist, seeking the expulsion of all non-native Greeks, the end of foreign tourism and investment in Greece, and a return to a pre-industrial society. They strive to recreate

14

Greece as it existed at the end of the War of Independence in 1832. They have been aligned to certain of the more extreme Orthodox bishops. They may or may not be violent.

Nikos waited for the paper to roll through and checked the IP address they had identified. It was the Kyanni Akti internet café in the village – the place where all the kids went to play on their pocket computers and phones and whatever else they were using these days. It could have been anyone.

The machine kept rumbling and a handwritten note appeared from the Argostoli office:

Nikos

Look into this, will you? It's going to be a busy summer with this movie and everything. There'll be a lot of attention on you and your village. We don't want any problems, do we? And look out for a leaflet about tourists in the post – we're all being sent one from the Tourism Ministry.

Cpt. Bastounis

He tore off the silky sheet and stood smoking as he read again the information about *Filiki Eteria*. Who on earth would want to return to a pre-industrial society? Certainly nobody in Exogi, which had become rich from tourism and money leeched out of the EU. He'd bought six goats himself when he'd found out how much he could get by calling his garden a pasture. It was probably all just another overreaction, like when that local kid had worn a heavy metal t-shirt to school and been accused of Satanism.

Still, it was something to do now that Xenomachos had ruined his other plans for the morning. He reached for the *frappe* and realised that only a centimetre of melted ice remained. So – a visit to the café was called for anyway.

15

He was putting on his cap when the phone rang. Maria calling to berate him? Or perhaps Aliki, whose husband worked on the Sami ferry. He hesitated and picked up.

'Police Office . . . A suspicious device, you say? . . . It's buzzing? . . . Where is it now? . . . When will your husband be home, *koukla mou*?'

Iliad Holidays Head Office, Athens

'Three hours he's been playing them bloody pan pipes. Three hours non-stop! Peruvian, my arse! Since when was the theme tune from *Titanic* a song of the native mountain tribes? Look at him – just look at him with the feathers in his hair and his suede bootees. It's an insult to his country and to music what he's doing down there. Give me five minutes alone with him and he'd need a colonoscopy to find them bloody pan pipes again. "My *Bowels* will go on" – that's what he'd have to call the song when I'd finished with him. God knows why they don't arrest him. There could be a proper *Greek* beggar occupying that space. Someone quieter. A gypsy fortune-teller or a cripple – that'd be good. A bloody mime artist would be better. Three hours! Makes me wish *I'd* drowned in the North-bloody-Atlantic!'

Morag Cleaver turned in disgust from the third-floor window to face the six other women gathered in the boardroom. She wasn't smiling. It wasn't clear if sycophantic laughter was required. From their expressions, more than one of them was reflecting ardently on the closing statement of her rant. The regional manager from Crete covered her face to hide a smile as she remembered a colleague's comment that Morag had once paid for family-tree research only to learn that a distant relative had been burned as a witch.

'Are we done, then?' said Morag. 'Is it drinkie time?'

Affirmative noises were made and papers were shuffled. The Peruvian piper ceased his paean to drowning and the air-conditioner's buzz was suddenly the loudest sound.

'Well, there was just one thing . . . ' said the Ionian Isles regional manager.

The rest of them paused, half-standing, half-fleeing, longingly eyeing the door.

'What is it, Donna?' sighed Morag, glancing sidelong at the bar in the street below. 'You're not getting a newer car, so forget it. That subject is finished.'

'It's not that.' Donna tried to keep the pleading out of her voice. 'It's about the rep at Exogi.'

'Exogi?'

'You know: the resort in northern Kefalonia.'

'The resort . . . ' Morag seemed distractedly to zoom in on the cocktail menu of the bar. 'Oh right, yeah: the overflow village – the pot-luck dump.'

'It's not a dump. It's probably one of the prettiest bays on the island—'

'Spare us, Donna. Just because you're married to an islander doesn't mean you have to buy any of the "traditional fishing village" shit. Never existed. We made it up – remember? That "traditional shepherd" in the Mainland brochure? He's really a drain cleaner from Pireaus – Kostas or Kyriakos somebody. Blasted my pipes back in March after the floods.'

'Well . . . ' said Donna. 'I think we need a rep there this season.'

The others remained frozen in a mid-flight tableau. They looked to Morag.

'Alright – the rest of you can go,' she said. 'Order me a Manhattan. And an ouzo. And don't let them give you any of those rancid peanuts either. I swear I've seen the same bloody nut reappear four times this week. Covered in bogies and urine and whatever. Mouse droppings. Trust me – there've been studies. A friend of mine got lockjaw from a toxic wasabi peanut.'

There were respectful expressions of awe. Morag had a friend? Then all were gone in ten seconds, none of them to the bar opposite.

'So – Exogi,' said Morag. She looked at her watch. 'Five minutes.'

'It's a new resort for us this year. And, like you said—'

'The pot-luck dump.'

'Where we send the really last-minute bookings. The problem is, there's virtually nothing there. Even the beach is only about three metres of pebbles. People are going to complain. We need someone on site.'

'They always bloody complain, Donna. Put them in the Ritz with personal servants and they'll complain. "What? Only two servants? You get *four* at the Bridlington Hilton!" If they want a choice of resort, they should have paid full price.'

'Of course . . . but the nearest rep is way down in Argostoli. There's nobody even near Exogi. If customers are going to be unhappy, we at least need someone up there to bear the brunt. And, of course, there's the *Corelli* sequel being shot there . . . we're fully booked from June.'

Morag had been staring at the street. Now she turned. 'I'm not going through all that interviews-and-training shit again.'

'You might not have to. We've had a late application: some guy who's been teaching English up near Albania over the winter.'

'Is he gay?'

'Er, what does that—?'

Morag held out a hand. 'The application.'

Donna put papers into the tanned claw and watched Morag's face turn from standard sour disapproval into something like vindictive amusement.

'He's added an extra sheet for his qualifications,' said Morag, mirth twitching at her inexpertly depilated upper lip. 'He's got a degree, by God! First class, indeed! You ever had a rep with a degree?'

'Didn't Keeley in Corfu do Drama at Warwick?'

'I meant a proper degree. Keeley's lovely, bless her, but I wouldn't let her use a pencil unsupervised.' Morag flipped the pages. 'Says he speaks Greek. Have you tested him?'

'Only on the phone. He's not bad – I suppose you could call it good tourist Greek. The thing is, almost nobody in Exogi speaks English. They're all farmers and fishermen who've cashed in their land to build apartments. I think some of them can't read or write even in Greek. Whoever the rep is up there, they'll need to know some Greek.'

Morag flipped to the last page for the 'profile' questions that were supposed to reveal applicants' true characters (according to the consultants who'd sold Iliad Holidays a fine line in HR crap). Her eyes shone and her thin lips quivered as she read through them:

Why do you want to be an Iliad Holidays rep?
I welcome the opportunity to live and work among a thriving community of island Greeks.

Do you prefer package tours or independent travel?
Only an independent traveller truly experiences a culture. Package tourism is for the bovine masses who seek nothing more than a pub in the sun and the fatuous prize of a tan to impress the neighbours on returning.

What is your idea of a perfect holiday?
One where I don't meet or even see any other English people. I would experience the native culture in its purest, uncorrupted form and be enriched by it. I understand, however, that this would not be a holiday and that contact with the English would be compulsory.

What is your favourite food/drink?

To eat: either *spetsofai* with village sausage or a traditional rabbit *stifado* with a side order of *horta*. To drink: an *ellinikos* coffee served sweet, or I might have an ouzo in the evening as a *digestif.*

Iliad Holidays is . . .

Named after an epic poem about the miseries of war. (Is this a trick question?)

Morag laid the application on the table. Her left eye appeared to flicker briefly with a seldom-seen tic that was said to appear when she delivered her notorious verbal warnings. 'Smug little shit. He's the least suitable applicant I've ever seen.'

'But . . . ' began Donna.

'Thinks he's too good to be a rep. Probably sees it as something like a shop assistant or street cleaner. He just wants a bit of money over the summer so he can go off and have more of his "experiences". If that means slumming with the commoners, he'll lower himself – but he won't pretend to like it.'

'I just thought . . . '

'You know what? I think we should give him the job.'

'But . . . Really?'

'He's got absolutely no idea. A first class degree'll be useless when he's faced with some fat, whining Brummie screaming about the air-conditioning, or some pissed-up slapper who's lost her mobile on a one-night stand. He won't be quoting Aristotle to *them* – he'll have to get down to their level and grovel for their approval if he wants his summer money.'

'I suppose so . . . '

'Yeah. Drop him in at Exogi. Let's watch him suffer. I bet he doesn't last two weeks once the first flights come in. In fact, I'll get you a newer car if he sticks it out.'

'That's very kind, Morag, but I was hoping he'd last longer than—'

'Whatever. It doesn't matter who we put there – nobody is going to like the place anyway. They'll all be complaining. He likes Greeks. Let's see how he gets on with them farmers and fishermen. They'll eat him alive. That'll be some experience for him to remember.' Morag flicked back to the first page of the application. 'Jim, he calls himself. Well, Jim Lad, I'm making you my special project this summer. It's one you'll never forget.'

Diogenes' Bar, Allomeros, Kefalonia

Diogenes Borborygmos sat smoking in his greenhouse. The glass panes were opaque to prevent sunlight from damaging the plants and also to prevent anyone from seeing the distinctive shape of their leaves. The interior effect was one of purity and peace – a divine white light that Diogenes associated with the passage from this life to the next. Not that he believed in anything as conventional as God or heaven. But there was *something* after life. Something disembodied. Like an orgasm. On opium. He'd find out one day.

'Everything dies,' he said to his plants. 'Everything has its time. You grow to maturity and then you're taken. But in your taking, you give pleasure and relaxation.' He waved the joint in illustration and blessing. 'Joyful cremation!

A morning breeze came in through the skylight and the cannabis plants nodded in seeming acknowledgment of the sermon. Yes, they seemed to say – all is finite. Nature both reaps and replenishes.

Diogenes smiled and took a sip from the tall glass of whisky he'd poured for breakfast. Chivas Regal – an octuple measure if anyone was counting, which nobody was. His eyes squinted in pleasure as the spirit went down, and for a moment there was something lizard-like about him: the goggling yellow eyes, the squamous complexion, the curiously long and pale fingers gripping the glass so that his fingerprints whorled wetly as alien calligraphy.

21

Having addressed the plants, he rose with a grunt and stepped out into the garden. The bald mountain tops of northern Kefalonia gathered round in welcome, the new day's sun descending like honey into the valleys. On the eastern horizon, a Martini glass of Ionian Sea sat cobalt in a triangle of intersecting hills. A tintinnabulation of goats passed unseen among the trees. Was there a finer life than this?

He sipped whisky and drew on the joint. Perhaps a drive into Exogi today. A coffee in the *kafenio*, a *tiropita* from the baker, a double – no, a triple – Metaxa from one of the bars that had begun to open in readiness for the summer season. He was pondering whether to opt for a seven-star or a nine-star brandy when his ginger tomcat, Socrates, trotted across the lawn and paused guiltily when spotted. A perfect disk of meat – a mottled pink hockey puck – was clamped in his mouth. It still bore the imprint of the tin it had been stolen from.

Diogenes approached with interest. Somebody's *al fresco* breakfast table? A purloined picnic prize? It was common enough for Socrates to bring home a bird, a rat, a snake and even an entire fish, but this was the first time canned goods had been presented.

'*Ti kanis, file?*' enquired Diogenes.

Socrates seemed to shrug. The meat puck made him smile.

Everything meant something. Everything was a sign. The world, time, space, fate – all were intricately connected if only one could read the signs. This disk of processed meat was an indicator: a symbol. Round like the sun – a premonition of summer itself. An unusual summer? Something odd and unprecedented about this summer?

Socrates warbled at the interruption and trotted on towards his lair beneath the rhododendron bush. Diogenes swallowed the last of the whisky. And the sun rolled honey-gold down the slopes to bathe his unlovely face.

Yes, an unusual summer. Something to look forward to.

Low Season

Exogi Resort Office, Kefalonia

ILIAD HOLIDAYS

RESORT INFORMATION FORM: EXOGI, KEFALONIA

(To be completed and returned by rep. Mark locations on map. Deadline 2 May)

1) BEACHES

(Quantity, names, variety, facilities, other comments etc.)

"Chrysos" beach is the only beach in Exogi: about 6x3 metres of large white pebbles that descend steeply into a watery abyss. Drowning seems almost inevitable for young children. It's accessed by a rusting, lop-sided iron stepladder and two uneven concrete steps, or by jumping across a metre-deep drainage ditch filled with building refuse and litter. There are no facilities, although the limestone rocks nearby seemed to have been used as an impromptu toilet. The views across the strait to Ithaca are stunning in elemental blue and white. The Greek word "Chrysos" means "gold".

2) BARS/CAFÉS

"No Name" is evidently unaware that it's one of 348 other bars in Greece that thought themselves original enough to choose the same name. It's the nearest to the beach and has utilitarian plastic chairs and tables presumably chosen to better facilitate the wiping of vomit at the end of the night. Luridly-coloured shots are a selling point.

"Kyanni Akti" is a café by day and bar by night. Candles on tables in the evening are its sole nod to sophistication – an effect minimised somewhat by the surly, pouting slattern of a waitress who seems to resent both the Lycra sheath she's obliged to wear and any customers insolent enough to take a seat. Currently, the clientele are predominantly youths using the free Wi-Fi and listening to interminable *bouzouki*-flavoured pop.

"Kafenio" is just that: a dishevelled hole at the south end of town. It's colonised exclusively by taxi-drivers, granddads and sundry other aged males who sit outside smoking and observing the passing world with wry amusement.

3) RESTAURANTS/FAST FOOD

"Spiti" is a family-run concern offering all the usual Greek staples desired by the British tourist (*moussaka, tzatziki, taramasalata,* fried squid, greek salad etc). Their menu also has some hilarious mis-translations, such as "lamp in a crock", "cock gruel" and "head cheese fried".

"Maria" is technically a *psistaria*, specialising in grilled meats and *mezedes*. It is very popular with locals, especially the local youths who seem to think that the two-wheeled hairdryers they scream up and down the seafront on are actually F16 jet fighters.

"Apicius" is a remarkable find in such a tiny place. It seems the owner also has a successful restaurant in Patras, but closes it down in summer to set up shop in Exogi. As well as the usual stuff, he does some excellent regional variations and some fancier cooking like soufflés and meat pies.

4) SHOPS

"Mini-market" just round the corner from the *kafenio* might better be termed a museum than a shop. Its entire stock is dusty, faded and past its use-by date, though the prices would seem suggest antiquation adds value. Some items have handwritten prices that have been crossed out four or five times according to inflation and currency changes. Great for curled postcards, lethal armbands, fishing nets full of dead flies, carcinogenic beachwear, easy-break sunglasses, and flick knives. Less good for anything intended for ingestion and/or pregnancy avoidance.

"Irakles" – the elderly barber has a rotating display of sunglasses outside his shop. Rudimentary inspection shows that they must be about fifteen years old and that about 80% of them are broken. He also sells bus tickets if he is in his shop (which he is for about five minutes a day).

The single bakery in Exogi is fantastic. Unlike many bakeries in tourist towns, the bread is actually baked on site by the flour-dusted baker himself. I've never tasted cheese or spinach pies like them. All of the local restaurants use it. I'd congratulate him, but I've not yet seem him awake. He sleeps in a chair in the corner of the shop while his wife takes the money.

Post office – open 7.00 am to 10.00 am.

Lotto shop – a seedy little betting shop crammed with men filling in football pools.

5) CAR HIRE

No.

6) PETROL STATION

No.

7) BANKS/CASH MACHINES

No.

8) LOCAL TRANSPORT

Two local taxis, and a bus that goes only as far as Sami once a day (departs 7.00 am, returns 2.30 pm). Tickets from the always-closed barber's shop.

9) POLICE/COAST GUARD

There is one policeman occupying a tiny office above the lotto shop. Hours are posted on the door, but he seems never to be on duty.

10) SITES OF HISTORICAL INTEREST/MUSEUMS

There's supposed to be an ancient site in the village of Allomeros but it's not well signposted and I've not been able to find it.

Jim leaned back in his chair and flicked the biro across the desk to the floor. He plucked at the neck of his official Iliad Holidays polo shirt and reached into the garish blue shorts to adjust slowly poaching testicles. What kind of travel company provided its reps with a *polyester* uniform? It wasn't even that hot yet and already he'd been forced to start buying the kind of deodorant that normally came with a prescription.

Forms forms forms. Forms detailing the resort. Forms detailing every property down to the amount of plug sockets. Forms for property owners to sign. Forms detailing health and safety concerns so that Iliad Holidays could hold him culpable when the owners refused to fix them and a toddler fell off a roof or some drunken buffoon toppled down a flight of concrete steps to be impaled on a rusty spike. The season hadn't yet begun and already it was becoming clear that the sole function of the rep was a barrier to protect the Iliad when the shit started to spray. Three more months in these shorts and he'd be infertile. He reached in for another rummage.

'Yer not gonna get away wi' that.'

He snatched the hand out and turned to see a girl wearing no less a ludicrous uniform than his own. Hers was yellow, the logo of Golden Holidays tautly distorted by colossal breasts. A vision of pale pink udders flashed unbidden into his mind and he raised his eyes to her face: gappy teeth, blow-up-doll eyes, complexion tanned to a wood-stain hue and framed by a frizzy blonde dye job.

'I'm Kelly,' she said. 'Yer name's Jim, right? I won't shek yer 'and.'

Jim blushed. 'Yeah, they told me this was a shared office. There's another . . .'

'Philippa, from Smithsons.'

'Yeah. Smithsons.' The posh holiday company.

'Exogi is the end o' the world if yer 'adn't figured it out yet. We've all got just a few rooms 'ere. There'll be lots of complaints, but at least yer won't get puked on every night.'

'That's nice.'

'Yer new, aren't yer? Yer don't look like a rep.'

'Last minute thing. It's not a career decision. I went to university. I suppose you're . . . '

'Thick?'

'No. More experienced.'

'Aye. Cyprus, Alicante, Crete, Corfu, Torremolinos – I've done 'em all. I said I'd do a season 'ere as a favour to Golden. They're sendin' me to Florida next year.'

'That'll be . . . yeah. What did you mean just now about getting away with something?'

'Yer RIF – the Resort Information Form on yer desk. They don't like jokes and they don't like big words. Just the facts. They'll just mek yer do it again.'

'Shit.'

'Where've yer got rooms?'

'Sotiris Apartments, Sunshine Apartments, the Nefeli Hotel. Not many.'

'Coolio. Yer done yer PIFs yet?'

'The property information forms, right? Not yet. I've been putting it off.'

'Hope yer Greek's good. None of 'em speak English. At least, they pretend they don't. And the owner of the Nefeli Hotel – Mister Trellos – is an absolute nutter.'

What do you mean by "nutter"?'

'A bit thick. Treats the 'otel like it's 'is own 'ouse and doesn't like visitors. Yer'll see.'

'Great.'

She pointed at the partially completed RIF. 'Sounds like yer don't like Exogi much.'

'I love it. At least, I love it now, before the tourists arrive. It's quiet. It feels real. There's a real sense of *philoxenia*.'

'Eh?'

'Hospitality. Literally: "a like of foreigners".'

'Forget yer pilloxnia – it's yer uniform they like. It means money – money for them and money for the village. I suppose Iliad 'ave told yer that yer shouldn't wear it in cafés or restaurants?'

'Because it shows favouritism and makes the locals argue.'

'Aye. Well, forget that shit straight off. If you wear it when yer're out at night, yer won't pay for a drink or meal all season. I suppose yer're sellin' the same excursions I am?'

'The Melissani Cave, the Drogarati Cave, Fiskardo . . . '

'Right. They're all organised by the same agent in Argostoli. Anyway, a lot of the locals'll bribe yer to sell *their* tours for less money. Taxi drivers live off 'em.'

'Er, thanks. Good to know.'

She looked doubtfully at Jim. 'Yer 'eard about the film?'

'The Corelli travesty? Yeah. Can't believe anyone would make a sequel after that first film. Did you see it? What a piece of shit.'

'I liked it. It were romantic. They say James Craggan's stayin' in a private villa in Allomeros. And Chet Braddock's supposed to be somewhere near. God – I'd strum *'is* violin!'

'*Mando*lin. I'm staying in Allomeros myself. Apparently, it's cheaper.'

'Iliad are such tightarses! It means yer 'ave to drive three or four miles every time yer need somethin'.'

'I like it up there. I'm in a flat above an old couple. Just goats and chickens. No internet. No landline. No TV. Iliad won't give me a mobile and I haven't got one of my own. Peace and quiet. Plus, it'll be cooler in summer.'

'Yer 'aven't got a mobile?' Her expression would have been less shocked if he'd said he'd been born without an anus.

'No. I don't like people being able to get hold of me.'

She blinked, seemingly unable to process the thought. 'There's a bar in Allomeros that the locals go to after hours. It's called "Doggy Knees" or

31

summat. Three, four in the mornin', they all go up to Allomeros and chill. No tourists. I've 'eard it's the coolest place. Guy 'oo runs it is a total nutter.'

'I've not seen it. I'll look out for it.'

She pointed at the desk. 'Are they yer worry beads?'

'My *komboloi*, yes. I bought them in Nafplio on the mainland.'

'Do yer worry a lot?'

'It's got nothing to do with worrying. It's actually—'

'Sorry, Jimbo, I'm done for the mornin' and I'm runnin' late. I'm goin' for some hot lovin' with Yianni. Good luck. See ya!'

She tripped out, dangling her keys and wiggling an arse of equine proportions. Yianni? No doubt some priapic local with hooded eyes and a perpetual scowl. One of the local *kamakia*, or "harpoons". A fast worker, evidently. Kelly couldn't have been in Exogi much more than a week. What did these guys do over the winter? Hang upside down in a cave regenerating near-toxic levels of testosterone? Anywhere but here, they'd be considered risible macho stereotypes. But add sunshine and shots, and every one of them was a Don Juan with a poet's eloquence and the earth-furrowing dong of a tyrannosaur.

Jim stood and stretched. His nascent belly tented the polo shirt and his whey-like complexion added to an overall consumptive look. His legs seemed to dangle like white ribbons from shorts he'd been obliged to hold up temporarily with a length of curtain cord. The PIFs would not wait much longer. Then there was the matter of having to buy a hundred postcards and stuff them laboriously into the "Welcome Books" for the benefit of tourists so dully unimaginative that they were unable to conceive their destination until given an A4 folder featuring views of it. Evidently, lifting their heads and using their eyes was too much effort.

He took his cheap Iliad Holidays document holder and walked down the dingy crate-and-keg strewn alley beside the Kyanni Akti café towards the sunlight. Out on Exogi's single dusty street, the view was anciently elemental: the twin humps of Ithaca bulging barren in a wine-dark sea, and the sky feathered high with cirrus. Faded litter whirled in corners while local business-owners emerged from the off-season as from a cocoon, rubbing their eyes and unrolling hoses to rinse patios. Last autumn's leaves rustled about the gutters. Palm fronds lay where they'd fallen at the base of giant-pineapple-shaped trunks. Branded parasols bloomed in the strengthening sun. Bottles rattled from the backs of vans. The obese man at the mini-market crossed out last season's prices and added his own arbitrary inflation to sun-cream and shampoo.

This was Greece without her make-up on: Greece caught unaware in her wrinkled nightie. It was not yet the "Greece" of the tourist hordes – whitewash, blue domes, *bouzouki*, souvenirs and feta – but Greece as he'd experienced it in the north: dirtier, more utilitarian, welcoming of the stranger but not fawning. The holidaymakers, when they arrived in Exogi, would be like the sudden presence of a camera, provoking ready smiles and ersatz grovelling to be sustained only as long as the summer sun shone. But for now, this was Jim's town: his kingdom by the sea.

'Nice shorts, *pousti*!' yelled an impudent youth from a flatulent passing moped.

Jim thrust out his left hand, fingers splayed, in response and smiled at the resulting abusive torrent about his mother's sexual preferences. Already, he was feeling part of the community.

His Iliad Holidays company car – the last functional Seat Marbella in Europe – was parked erratically in front of the post office but he couldn't drive it the half mile to the Nefeli Hotel because the coast road was currently a building site. Bold plans to pave it as a stately lamp-lit promenade had apparently been stalled in early spring by inevitable legal action (favourite pastime of landowning Greeks) and so the first tourists would have to carry their own luggage past earth movers, stacked sewage pipes and rubble-filled ditches. The thought made him smile as he strolled, the sun casting a balmy blessing on his post-mortem paleness.

33

The Nefeli was a two-storey concrete monstrosity at the end of the road. A broad, stone-paved patio harboured a small swimming pool that had yet to be filled. Half-a-dozen white-plastic sun-loungers had been bolted to the ground around it, allegedly because the owner didn't like the noise when heliotropic tourists dragged them about.

There was no sign of life. Here, too, the leaves and branches of the winter lay unbrushed and the pool held a half-metre of murky water in which a cat or other small mammal bobbed gaseously. Jim walked into the unlit reception area and palmed the brass bell, whose single note echoed off marble floors and walls. Waiting, he observed that there were framed pictures of animals behind the counter: cows, goats, smiling chickens. He'd seen the same thing in rural butcher's shops in northern Greece, no apparent irony intended between dismembered chunks and their photogenic donors. Perhaps these animals had been personal acquaintances of the owner back when he was a simple farmer, before he had to bolt down impertinent sun-loungers.

Nobody came. He ascended the marble staircase and walked dim hallways reminiscent of *The Shining*. He continued up to the roof, noting the total lack of door or barriers – a nice two-storey death-dive for a drunken tourist or idiot child, and another health-and-safety concern to go ignored.

'Hello! Is anybody here?' he called. Jack Nicholson, are you resident?

A rattle and a metallic clang seemed to come from the bowels of the hotel. Jim followed it and descended into near-darkness, where the fire-alarm system winked, pipes gurgled and a kitchen's steel surfaces glinted blue from a fly-extermination light. A dozen tables were laid for service and sat spectrally empty in the shadows.

'Is anyone here? Mister Trellos? I'm here from Iliad Holidays.'

A silhouette rose from beneath a kitchen surface. It was holding what appeared to be a plank.

'Mister Trellos?'

'Eh?'

'Are you Mister Trellos? The hotel owner?'

'Eh?'

Jim smiled awkwardly. How many other ways could he phrase it? He was sure he was using the correct Greek.

The figure emerged into the light of a single bulb and revealed a freakish: goggling eyes, encephalitic forehead, lugubrious mouth. The freckled pate was bald but for a few wisps of grey.

'I'm from Iliad Holidays, Mister Trellos. I'm here to complete property information forms. I think we've got rooms ten and eleven. Could somebody give me keys so I can—?'

'Eh?'

'Keys!' Perhaps the old duffer had a hearing impairment in addition to his double-figure IQ.

The compressed face twitched as if stung. He raised the plank. 'Iliad?'

'Yes that's right. We have two rooms—'

'I will murder you!' He launched himself at Jim, bringing the plank down like an axe but overreaching and stumbling into one of the laid tables so that he toppled to the floor, dragging a tablecloth and cutlery over him. There, he rolled and raged amid napkins and dessert spoons, screeching about murder and desperately trying to disentangle his plank.

'If this is an inappropriate time . . . ' said Jim.

'I. Will. Murder . . . !'

Light flooded the room and Jim turned to see a dark-haired, dark-eyed beauty of about his own age glaring at him in hatred.

'What are you doing?' she said in accented English, her voice a hollow-ground blade.

'I'm from Iliad. He fell. I was just asking . . . '

'Go! Just go!'

'But I have to . . . ' Her ember eyes forbade further utterance. By God she was beautiful – body like a sculpture, hair like . . .

35

'Out!'

He walked past her with an exculpatory shrug and inhaled her perfume. Something earthily exotic. Returning to reception, he heard her placating her insane relative:

'What are you doing, *papou*? Mice? We don't kill mice with a plank, *papou*; there are machines to do it now. A fork in your leg? Where? Where is it? Stop rolling. I'll pull it out . . . '

Jim heard the yelp as he left. No sense in coming back. He'd just ask to copy Kelly's PIF. All the rooms were probably identical anyway. No such luck with the other properties. It promised to be a long afternoon of colourful sociopathy.

Airport-Allomeros, Kefalonia

As a child, Grace had once been to a miniature park in Florida where she'd been made a giantess by the disproportionate scale. Everything had been an aerial shot. Greece – at least, Kefalonia – felt like that. Like a toy country. Like a set, in fact, that looked real at first sight but revealed itself gradually as a façade. *The Truman Show*? The roads were no bigger than bike tracks. The airport was smaller than the Greyhound station on East 17th in LA. Even the hills seemed modest. If it wasn't for the occasional road sign, it might still have been the nineteenth century.

But the light was amazing. It was like taking off a pair of old, smeary glasses and suddenly seeing the world though the clear-water brilliance of a high-end lens. It was less like reality, more like an expensive film treatment process. Colours were richer. The sky was naturally polarised. The sea was that impossible blue of paintings. What a great place for cinematography.

36

Still, she felt sick. Perhaps the twisting road was to blame, or perhaps it was fatigue after the flight, or perhaps it was just the Greek cab driver propelling his silver Mercedes at the maximum speed, one arm out of the window, the other holding a cigarette – either one only very occasionally on the wheel. She'd asked him to stop smoking but he'd just laughed and pretended not to understand. How much further? The roads were knotted and looped like unravelled wool. He'd be sorry if she puked all over his leather seats. Linda Blair in *The Exorcist*. Gary Johnson in *Team America*.

And every mile was bringing her closer to James Craggan: one of those stars so iconic – Eastwood, Ford, Connery – that you felt they were almost part of your family. Lives were measured and remembered by the milestones of their careers. The celluloid world they inhabited was timeless, immaculate. They couldn't ever die, and, by the same reasoning, they could hardly be alive in any real sense. If they became a part of their audience's world, they would surely be revealed as mannequins – the wizard behind the curtain in Oz.

She'd never been a fan of Craggan's. Not really, not consciously. He was just always there. Everyone knew his films as part of the montage of a lifetime's cinema, just like everyone always seemed to know the Beatles' work without consciously hearing it. There was his bit-part breakthrough in *Hangman's Noose*, where, like McQueen in *The Magnificent Seven*, he'd stolen almost every scene with some attention-grabbing mannerism or posture. Even then, he'd had a sixth sense about the shot and his place in it. Then there was the run of gritty cop movies in the late seventies and his Oscar nomination for *Cocaine Train*. Pity his research for that one had been so literal – the start of the slide. The stuff in the eighties had mostly been schlock, but big box-office schlock and he'd grabbed points in the biggest of them: *Kung Fu Tyrant, Mission to Pluto, Dry Gulch Stand-Off*. There'd been critical acclaim for the picture he produced himself in 1986 (*Pity*), but it had bombed. Of course it had – people didn't want to see Craggan crying unless it was because he had blood and gunpowder in his eyes.

37

Then there were the women. He was a man in the unreconstructed, pre-feminist sense: tall, broad, rugged – something animal in his underlying threat of violence. Farrah, Jacyln, Racquel, Kim, Kelly, Cindy – the list went on and on. The more wasted he got, the more attractive he seemed to be to them. Hefner put him up in the Playboy mansion for most of 1987. Jack Nicholson made that famous crack about Craggan making him look like an altar boy. Then the inevitable crash-and-burn. Cocaine might get you up, but heroin brings you down. This was the straight-to-video period, Craggan a bloated and anaesthetised parody of himself – but still with the world's beauties trying to save him. He could have retired, but stars like him didn't retire any more than the sun could be turned off with a switch. They just burned out.

So when he came back from Switzerland lean, augustly handsome and with that glint he hadn't had since the heyday, a casting agent took a chance. It was a poor film that didn't break even, but Craggan shone out of it as he had in *Hangman's Noose* all those decades before. Was he back? Last year's Best Supporting nomination seemed both a blessing and an acknowledgement. The industry loves a survivor, especially when he looks like good box-office.

And now he thought he had a daughter in Grace. Was it residual brain damage from the booze and the drugs? Or had he bought into whatever the latest bullshit Hollywood fad was? Crystals. Pyramids. Regression therapy. Aliens in volcanoes. Whatever – something you could buy. If the Christians weren't selling passports to heaven anymore, some other freaks would be happy to grant a ten-year visa. That and a new liver from an exclusive Swiss clinic. It would be weird, but weirdness was Hollywood fuel.

The cab braked hard on gravel. Grace felt her stomach lurch and looked up from her thoughts. They seemed to be on top of a hill crowned by a large white villa with terracotta roof tiles. Stony peaks rose above valleys on either side, while the sea was a deep blue plate to the east. Perhaps a dozen houses dotted the pine-forested slopes below. It was wild, but beautiful.

'Allomeros,' said the cab driver with a smoky exhalation and a grin. He stepped out and walked round to the trunk.

Grace saw a black BMW with blacked-out windows parked in front of the villa. Was Craggan in the house waiting for her right now? Did she look enough like a daughter in her jeans, sneakers and vintage CBGB t-shirt? Well, she was *somebody's* daughter.

The villa door opened and a huge guy in a dark suit came down the steps. He seemed to be a Pacific islander (Samoan, Fijian?) with elaborate tattooing covering his face and shaved head. A tiny translucent wire caught the light at his right ear. Security.

Grace got out the car and the giant approached her. She saw herself reflected child-sized in his Ray Bans.

'You Grace?' he said.

'No. Me Jane,' she said, immediately regretting it.

The giant stood immobile: an Easter Island monolith in an Armani jacket.

'Sorry. Yeah, I'm Grace. It's been a long journey.'

He nodded, paid the cab driver from a wad of notes and hoisted her giant suitcase as if weighed no more than a purse. Without further word or gesture, he walked back into the villa.

She followed, ever more aware of her appearance. Even the security guy was wearing designer. What must the other "help" think of her, strolling in with no introductions and no qualifications except her dubious spectral paternity. Did they hate her already?

Her sneakers squeaked across the white marble of the villa's reception area and into a room where a group was sitting around a large wooden table. All had obviously been anticipating her arrival. They appraised her with a collective intensity that felt like an x-ray.

She froze. The moment stretched. Nobody spoke. She became peripherally aware of the framed posters around the room: James Craggan's greatest hits. And *Pity*.

'Er, I'm Grace Willetts,' she said. 'Nice to meet you all.'

One of them stood: a boyishly attractive woman. No hips. No breasts. Obviously employed for her talent alone. 'Grace. Welcome. I know, *we* know, this must be really weird for you. I'm Granger, the AD's assistant. He asked me to come here and make the introductions.'

'Er, OK. Thanks. Nice to meet you, Granger.'

'The villa's rented. Some big shot Greek shipping magnate. Crag's got it for the duration of the shoot.'

'Is he . . . is Crag here?'

'Not yet. He's flying in this week. He's been in Grasse, France. Buying perfume. He'll introduce himself. Until then, this is Chen, Crag's personal chef. Ask him nicely and he'll cook for you, too. Strictly macrobiotic.'

The skinny Chinese guy sitting to the right of Granger stood and gave a little bow.

Granger indicated the woman beside Chen: power suit, dark lipstick, eyes like gun barrels. 'This is Penelope, PR for the production.'

'Hi, Grace,' said Penelope without warmth. 'We'll need some time together. Things to do. Things not to do. The paps are gathering. People will approach you. They'll tell you lies and trick you. Yeah, you might think you can handle it, but you can't. They'll fuck with your mind until you don't know who you are or what you're saying. They're jackals and they'll eat you alive. The only thing between them and you – between them and Crag – is me. Right?'

'Got it.'

'I'm serious.'

Grace nodded, biting a lip. First grade all over again.

'Next to Penelope is Honee . . . ' Granger's expression subtly soured.

Nose job, straightened blonde hair, Botox shine, collagen lips, tits you could rest a cup on. Fifty going on twenty.

'. . . Crag's personal assistant.'

'Hi, Grace!' twinkled Honee. 'I guess that makes me your mom!'

40

Nobody laughed.

'And you've met Lomu,' said Granger, pointing to the security guy still standing beside Grace. 'Crag's bodyguard and driver. You see anything even slightly odd, you tell Lomu.'

'And he'll kick their ass!' said Honee. 'Man's a *killing* machine!'

'Those charges were dropped,' said Penelope. 'We don't talk about that.'

'Huh? Oh, yeah.' Honee affected a chastised look and winked at Grace.

Lomu remained impassive, said nothing, wore his shades even indoors. Were there more? It seemed a pretty small entourage for someone of Craggan's fame. No astrologer? No spirit guide? No kendo master?

'You got a laptop, Grace?' said Granger. 'An iPad?'

'Yeah, here in my—'

'Great. Of course you have. I'm going to give you this.' She held up a memory stick. 'This is the shooting schedule for *Corelli*. There's also the stripboard and the latest script on here. If your device doesn't have the software, I'll get it for you. Mel said you wanted to learn.'

Grace took it. 'Thanks. That'll be really interesting.'

'Is your hardware encrypted?' said Penelope. 'We can't afford for anyone to get hold of that information. There are millions of dollars riding on this movie. People would kill – literally, I'm not exaggerating – for what's on that memory stick.'

'We can work on it,' said Granger. 'There's also your ID.' She handed over a credit-card sized plaque on a lanyard. There was a Lustre Productions hologram, a scan code, the name of the movie, Grace's name and the bold statement ACCESS ALL AREAS.

'*That's* the golden ticket,' said Honee, nodding profoundly.

'There's no replacement,' said Penelope. 'Don't lose it.'

'Look,' said Granger, 'I've got to get back to the main set. We're expecting a delivery of mandolins from Italy. Have you got any questions before I go?'

41

'A bunch, but mainly: what exactly am I supposed to do? I mean, Crag already has a personal assistant.'

Granger maintained composure. 'Honee attends to Crag's . . . *more* personal requirements. Your job is to make sure he's on set when he's supposed to be, to act as a liaison with the crew, to keep him relaxed and away from temptation. Just spend time with him.'

'There's no alcohol in this house,' said Penelope. 'The studio has rented a drug dog from the British police and she'll be sniffing round the villa weekly. It's contractual – part of the insurance. For the record, James Craggan has been straight and clean for eleven months. If you see anything to the contrary, you tell me. Only me.'

'Right.'

'That goes for you, too, Honee' said Penelope.

'Honey, what I got is more than enough to get him high,' said Honee.

Chen, the chef, giggled.

'Are the others on the island yet?' said Grace. 'Chet? Hannah?' First-name terms, like she knew them.

'Chet's in the same village, just down the hill here,' said Granger. 'I'm sure you'll see him in the villa – he and Crag are new buddies. Hannah is staying closer to the other village: Exogi. She likes to be where the action is.'

'That girl *is* the action,' said Honee.

'Shooting hasn't even started yet and already we're working our asses off to keep her out of the *National Enquirer*,' said Penelope. 'The girl's on heat.'

Grace felt an unexpected rush. She, the would-be scriptwriter/director, had promised herself to be cool about the stars. Blasé. But now Chet Braddock might now be popping by for a Coke. Hannah Caro might stumble in with all her languid, feral sensuality. And there would be Grace, sipping organic tea with Crag. Oh, hi Chet! Hi Hannah! Can I get you a macrobiotic quinoa wrap?

'Is everything OK?' said Granger. 'I know it's a lot to take in.'

'Cool. It's cool,' said Grace.

'You must be tired. Why don't you go to your room and we'll arrange to meet later. Lomu can drive you down to the main set if you feel like it.'

'Thanks. Thanks for everything, Granger. I guess I'll see you all later.'

Grace followed Lomu through the villa to a room at the back: a large, airy space with a vast window looking out over the mountains. There was a gigantic arrangement of fresh red roses in a vase on the dressing table. Their scent filled the room and made her feel faint. A hand-written note was stuck to the mirror:

Grace
I know it's weird. Go with it. Everything's gonna be fine.
Crag.

Below the mirror was a jewellery case with the embossed legend, *Martins Fine Jewellery, Rodeo Drive, Los Angeles, CA*. She looked to Lomu.

He nodded.

Curiosity and fear fought something more complex. Should she just open it? She'd done nothing to deserve it. Or would that come later? Was this her payoff up-front?

'Take it,' said Lomu, still wearing his shades. 'Man gives you a gift, it's because he wants you to have one. Values you. You don't want it, give it away.'

She picked up the box. Heavy. Not a ring or earrings. She opened it and saw only the name. Rolex. A lady's rose-gold Rolex with a midnight blue face and a diamond bezel. Her hands started to shake. It probably cost more than her school fees. She couldn't accept it. She wanted to accept it. She saw that the back of the case had been engraved with cursive script:

Grace
Thanks for coming.
Crag

'This is so . . . '

Welcome to the man's world,' said Lomu. 'You ain't never gonna wanna leave.'

Stone Hut, near Sami, Kefalonia

The isolated stone hut had withstood the 1953 earthquake, though giant cracks had rent the walls and caused the roof to sag. One day it would implode with a clatter and a billow of dust, unnoticed by the people of Sami. For the present, an entirely different kind of quake was rocking it.

Hardcore metal assailed the masonry: *Rotting Christ*'s apocalyptic track "Non Serviam" played at almost full volume on a high-end stereo system. Inside, two long-haired young men moshed and played air guitar with sweating intensity. Empty beer cans and newspapers were scattered around the single room, whose patched and mildewed furniture had originally been scavenged from their respective family homes.

A third youth appeared at the doorway and waved an envelope. He shouted, but his was voice obliterated by the music. He went over to the stereo and turned it off, watching in amusement as his friends' spastic playing continued for a few seconds. When they looked up, it was with glistening foreheads and hair streaked across their faces.

'What are you doing, *malaka*?' said Kyriakos, still holding his air guitar.

'That was the best bit coming up,' said Andreas, tuning his.

'It's here!' said Achilleus, waving the envelope: apparently a gaudy piece of junk mail announcing that the recipient had won ten million euros.

The guitars disappeared. Hair was wiped from faces.

'Shit,' said Andreas.

'Are you going to open it, then,' said Kyriakos.

44

They each took a seat, lounging with legs over the sofa arms. Achilleus slit the envelope with a thumb and took out a single piece of paper with a sky blue letterhead: a design featuring the Greek key pattern, Doric columns and the name *Filiki Eteria*.

'Read it out,' said Andreas.

Achilleus scanned it quickly and began.

Dear Friends

We welcome you to the future of a pure and uncontaminated Greece. As the word spreads and we begin to achieve national purity, new cells like yours are essential to carry the message to every border of Glorious Greece. You, like us, seek the return to the untainted nation that was ours in 1832 after our War of Independence, before the "Great Powers" forced a German king on us and signed our national destiny away. From slavery under the Turks to slavery under a foreign king, to slavery under the Judaic European Union. Immigrants, tourists, foreign landowners, industry and international money markets – all dilute the Greek nation. Even our treasures are stolen, exhibited as war trophies in foreign museums. No more! Now we will finally be free!

With this letter, you become the official Kefalonian cell of Filiki Eteria. *As befits the nature of this necessarily secret society, you must take on secret identities in all further communication and covert action. We adopt the names of great patriots from history and mythology so that we may never forget where we come from. From this day, you will be known as:*

Andreas = Kolokotronis
Kyriakos = Zorbas
Achilleus = Achilles

Now you must draw up your own action plan and report back to me using techniques that will be revealed later (do not use email – the government has been infiltrated with EU spies). How will you effect the aims of our society? How will you return Greece to her national purity? How will you rescue Greece for the Greeks and become heroes to future generations?

Be strong! Be pure! Fight to the last!

The Patriot

They looked at each other. Now it was real.

'"Judaic European Union?"' said Andreas.

'Of course,' said Kyriakos. 'Haven't you heard about the Athonite monk Philotheos? He says that the Jewish bankers run the entire EU through Germany. They run Germany, too.'

'My name's the same,' said Achilleus.

'What?' said Andreas.

'My secret identity. You're Kolokotronis. He's Zorba. *My* secret name is the same as my actual name. How is that going to fool anyone? Should I contact him and say there's been a mistake.'

'Achilles was our greatest hero,' said Kyriakos. 'Him and Leonidas.'

'I know – but it's *already* my name!'

'Perhaps it's a test,' said Kyriakos.

'What do you mean?' said Achilleus.

'You know, to see if you're going to contact him. If you do, it means you've failed.'

'Or it could be a double bluff,' said Andreas. 'Nobody would expect your secret name to be the same as your real one. It's like Epimenides. He said, "All Cretans are liars" – but he was a Cretan himself. Was he lying?'

The other two looked at Andreas.

46

'You should listen to quieter music, man,' said Kyriakos. 'It's damaged your brain.'

'Anyway,' said Achilleus, 'what's our action plan? What are we going to do to get rid of the Jews and the tourists and the immigrants and industry?'

'I've got it,' said Andreas. 'We'll go every night to Chrysos beach in Exogi and take a giant shit on it. That'll show the tourists!'

'We don't want to pollute the nation we're trying to reclaim,' said Achilleus. 'It shouldn't be anything that damages nature.'

'The movie,' said Kyriakos. 'We should do something with the movie. The world's media is watching – it's our chance.'

'But what?' said Andreas. 'Kidnap Hannah Caro and hold her for ransom?'

'How would that work?' said Achilleus. '"All immigrants, tourists, industry and Jewish investment leave Greece now or we'll kill Caro"? She's not worth that much. She'll probably overdose in a year or two anyway. And could you kill her? Really?'

'I'd stab her with my weapon,' said Kyriakos.

'She'd eat you alive,' said Achilleus. 'You'd have an asthma attack.'

'I'd have my inhaler.'

'That'd be a turn-on for her. "I'm going to stab you with my weapon, but first let me take my asthma medication."'

'*Malakas.*'

'We could make posters,' said Andreas.

'Too much trouble,' said Achilleus. 'Making them would take time, and getting them printed would give us away.'

'Graffiti!' said Kyriakos. 'Like Banksy. Stencils. That would be fast and easy. Guerrilla style!'

'That might work,' said Achilleus. 'What else?'

'Poison the tourists,' said Andreas.

'We're not killing anyone,' said Achilleus.

47

'No. There's this plant grows on my uncle's land. It gives you hallucinations and makes you really sick. He says they used to chew it when they were kids. What if we can get some of that into their food or drink? It won't kill them, but it might keep them away in future.'

'You know my uncle in Potamianata has a still,' said Kyriakos. 'He sells the raw spirit to bars all over the island. For shots. Only tourists drink that shit. What if we can get some of the weeds into it?'

'Right,' said Achilleus. 'Now we're thinking. What else? Something with the movie.'

'Hold on,' said Andreas, reaching for his phone. The screen lit his face with blue-white light. 'It's my mother. Lunch is ready.'

The other two looked at him.

'It's *pastitsio*,' said Andreas.

'Welcome to the Kefalonian cell of *Filiki Eteria*,' sighed Achilleus. 'Only the hardcore need apply.'

'At least *I've* got a secret name.'

Private House, Allomeros, Kefalonia

Professor Danae Stratigakis entered her garden wearing a long white nightdress that might almost have been the *peplos* of a classical priestess. Her silver-grey hair hung loose about her shoulders and she walked with the aid of an ornate olive-wood walking stick whose carving portrayed multitudinous intertwined serpents.

She went straight to the artesian well that had been on the property for more than a century and pressed the button on the electric winch. It hummed as the zinc bucket rose from the darkness, an eye of rippling mercury.

The water was cold enough to numb her slender parchment hands, but she rinsed them all the same, bringing the water to her face three times, not minding

48

that it ran in freezing fingers down her neck and inside her garment, bringing her flesh alive with goose bumps. With still glistening hands, she then took a lighter from a vestibule in the well's masonry and lit the wick of a small terracotta oil lamp. Immediately, the scent of frankincense came to her and she offered the hymn in a half-whisper:

Eternal Aphrodite – greetings from a sister!
Like the morning, you shine anew
Like the water, you are free and dancing
I give you praise and celebrate your beauty

She cupped her hands and drank from the bucket, allowing the water to run down her arms and down her sides.

Oh, cunning Aphrodite, hear me
The upstart religion of the Cross oppresses us
Show your power. Be with us, strong and graceful

She blew out the flame and watched the smoke curl slowly in the morning light: an arabesque of divine orthography – unintelligible to mortals, but indicative of acknowledgement. The goddess had heard.

Professor Stratigakis replaced the oil lamp and the lighter in their vestibule. She was bending to lift the bucket when the earth moved. Not one of the dizzy spells she'd been having recently when suddenly standing or bending? No – the earth was actually moving: a nauseating lateral sway accompanied by a rumbling like a distant airliner. The water in the bucket rippled.

A sign. A divine message.

The tremor was over in seconds, followed by a profound silence that seemed to descend over the island. The church bell in the campanile across the

49

valley rang once, weakly, impelled by the earth. Then the dogs started their frenetic chorus across the village.

It was surely a sign. Aphrodites' father: Zeus the Earth-Shaker?

In 1953, when almost the whole island had been levelled, an earth bank had fallen away in Allomeros to reveal the foundations of a classical site within. There had been little more than a stretch of wall and some pottery shards, but excavation had shown a century or more of votive offerings to a cult of Aphrodite. One particular discovery, a stone tablet written in Linear B and corresponding exactly to the geology of the Mycenaean plain itself, had proved utterly inexplicable. Proof of a pre-Olympian incarnation of Aphrodite? Whatever it meant, it had occupied a large proportion of the professor's career.

And now another sign: the island's abyssal caverns thundering forth divine intent even as her prayer had risen on scented smoke. But with what meaning? Disapproval at her supplication? Or acquiescence to it? Perhaps there would be some sort of longed-for visitation from the old gods!

Divination was seldom straightforward. She would have to call the others and ask what they had experienced in *their* morning devotions.

Police station, Exogi, Kefalonia

The tremor caused Sergeant Nikos to look up from the leaflet he was reading. A loose pane rattled in the louvre window above the door. The surface of his coffee shivered. Then nothing. He reached for the telephone and removed the receiver. The last thing he wanted was two-dozen neurotic old villagers calling to say there had been a tremor. Let them call *Pappas* Xenomachos – he was the authority on the world's end.

He turned again to the leaflet that had arrived by post that very morning. A publication of Greek Ministry of Culture and Tourism, it was entitled

"Understanding the British" and was a concise explanation of what caused that pale, raucous race to spend their holidays drunk, vomiting, fighting or working earnestly on varieties of aggravated melanoma. Why were 250 Britons imprisoned in Greece each summer? Why did 500 find themselves hospitalised? All the answers were apparently related within. The section on the British female was of particular interest.

The Northern European climate requires her to dress for wind and rain even during the summer months and so her skin is seldom exposed to the air. The psychological effect of her attire is a reduction of her physical sense and consequently a stifling of her natural sensuality. At home, she is a woman solely in name. Only through an excessive intake of alcohol at weekends can she release the natural urge, shedding her clothing to walk the city streets in little more than her underwear and engaging in coitus wherever she may find it.

The climate of Greece, however, encourages a sense of freedom and natural undress that awakens in her many months of suppressed libido. The touch of air and water on her skin stimulates her to great heights of sensuality, further exacerbated by excessive alcohol intake. Removed from her censorious domestic ambience and the regulating influence of family or colleagues, she acquiesces to virtually any invitation. The Greek man is her preferred target, as he understands the urgency of her need and is willing to expedite its comprehensive fulfilment. Her own countrymen are often too insensible with drink to provide the necessary relief.

Nikos nodded and lit another cigarette. It all made perfect sense. After all, was not every policeman an anthropologist in his way? He was part of his community, but also, by necessity, always external to it. Like the academic observer, he had to keep his distance in order to maintain authority through difference. Hence the uniform. Hence the baton and the gun – mere costume, really, but essential to the illusion.

He glanced across his desk to the latest edition of *Eleftheros Typos*, whose front-page carried a picture of the Hollywood actress Hannah Caro. Now there was a beauty. No chill northern woman, this one. The photographer had caught her laughing at the port of Sami, her long dress adhering to her torso in the wind and rising to reveal a well toned thigh. She seemed more goddess than mortal. Here was a creature who might truly make fools of men. In fact, hadn't Captain Bastounis in Argostoli said that the Americans would be seeking local police help with their movie? Something about liaising with their head of security?

He bent and searched in the bin for the ball of shiny fax paper. He straightened it out on the desk and wiped the cigarette ash from it, leaving sooty trails as if Miss Caro's very eyelashes had batted it.

Nikos

Any information yet on that nationalist activity? Athens is asking questions. It seems that the HQ of Filiki Eteria *has been communicating with its cells via letters disguised as junk mail – something about winning ten million euros. Does this help?*

Also, look out for someone from the American film crew. They've requested local help and I've told them you are an excellent resource. Don't let me down. And don't make me come up there again. Are you even reading this? I only send these faxes because you never seem to answer your phone.

Don't forget those nationalists – Athens seems to think they could be dangerous.

Capt Bastounis

He scowled. Everyone on the island had received that same piece of junk mail about winning ten million euros. It was utterly useless as a lead, unless *everyone* was a member of the secret society. Of course, he'd made some enquiries about the IP address, but the sullen waitress at Kyanni Akti café had been able to report nothing more helpful than that every young person in the area had probably used the internet over the winter. There had been no strangers she could remember.

Perhaps he should go to the main film set near Sami and seek out this head of security. Miss Caro herself might be there. A lurid scenario began to coalesce in his mind but was shattered by the clatter of the downstairs door and footsteps ascending to the office. Please, God – don't let it be Xenomachos come to say that the tremor was divine retribution for the pagan flowers on the beach.

The figure that appeared at the door wore no ecclesiastical garb. Indeed, the face was one that not even god could love: goggling eyes, mouth askew, a spirit-swollen and richly-veined ball of a nose.

'Mind if I smoke?' said Diogenes, already doing so.

The sergeant waved away the request and lit one of his own. 'Diogenes. It's been a while.'

'Yes.'

'Take a seat. How's Socrates?'

'He caught a tin of meat. I've been thinking about it a lot.'

'What can I tell you, Diogenes? He's getting old. Tinned prey is easier to catch. But it's really not a matter for the police—'

'No. I want to make a complaint. An official complaint.'

'If it's about the birds again, I thought we'd established it's out of my control. I can't stop them tweeting and you can't start shooting them.'

'It's not the birds. I put bread in my ears now. It's the bells.'

'The bells. The church bells?'

'Yes. They wake me on a Sunday. On other days – Easter, for example – they seem to go on all day. It's noise pollution. If I bought a gong or a steel drum and played it anytime I wanted, I'd be called a nuisance.'

'Are you planning to buy a steel drum, Diogenes?'

'It depends.'

53

'I see. You've lived in Allomeros since you returned from America, what, seven years ago? The bells have rung all that time. Are they bothering you only now?'

'I've always heard them. But only recently has it occurred to me that they're a nuisance. If Xenomachos is allowed to ring bells, why shouldn't I have a steel drum?'

'So it's a matter of fairness.'

'More one of percussion, I would say.'

'Are you a Christian, Diogenes? Are you a member of the Orthodox church?'

'Only by baptism. It's just water and oil in the end – like the bottom of a salad.'

'Look, I'll be honest – I can't tell Xenomachos to stop ringing his bells. People like it. Greeks fought and died for the right to ring bells rather than hear the muezzin's call.'

'That's a good point. Though they also fought for me to play a steel drum if I want to. If democracy means anything, it means a man can choose his own drum.'

'I understand you, Diogenes. Really, I do. But there's no possibility of stopping the bells.'

'And if I take it to the European Court of Justice?'

'You will have my wholehearted support.'

Diogenes nodded, looked troubled.

'Have you been drinking?' said Nikos.

'Since dawn.'

'And I suppose you drove into Exogi?'

Diogenes shrugged. How else would he have got there?

'Look – the tourists will be arriving soon. We can't have you running them down. How about I take you back to Allomeros. I have to go out to Sami anyway and I don't mind the diversion. Someone will bring your car up later.'

54

'Are you going to the film set?'

'I am.'

'I'd be happy to come along for the ride. I'd like to see how movies are made.'

'Do you promise not to talk to any of the Americans?'

'I'll be good.'

'Let's go.'

The sergeant took his cap, checked his breast pocket for his sunglasses and glanced briefly at his reflection to see how Hannah Caro would see him. They descended together to the street and Diogenes sat regally in the rear of the police car.

It was only as he was pulling away from the kerb that Nikos saw the fresh graffito on the side of the bakery: stark stencilled letters in black:

Fuk tourists!
Greece back to 1832

Resort Office, Exogi, Kefalonia

'A quiz night?' Jim searched for a pen while holding the phone to his ear.

'Yes,' said Donna in Argostoli. 'The revenue streams in Exogi are weaker because the guests there spend less on excursions. Get a book of questions. Charge them five euros each. And remember to rotate it among all the bars or the locals will get jealous.'

'So the five euros is towards a cash prize?'

'No. It goes behind the bar so the winners have to continue drinking there until it runs out.'

'Great incentive.'

55

'What?'

'Nothing . . . just thinking out loud.'

'Have you completed your welcome boards and welcome books?'

'Pretty much.'

'You know there might be a surprise inspection? If they're not ready by the first flight, you'll receive a verbal warning.'

'Will there be a written confirmation of that?'

Donna's end went silent. At least, only her breathing could be heard.

'Donna?'

'Are we going to have trouble with you, Jim? I was advised not to employ you. People are literally queuing to spend the summer working in a lovely Greek resort like Exogi, you know.'

Queuing where? At schools for the terminally moronic? 'Everything will be ready, Donna. I promise.'

'That's more like it. Will you be able to bring the completed PIFs down for the first flight?'

'Actually, I had a few problems with them. None of the property owners agreed to sign the contracts because they're written in English. The Sunshine Apartments are a death trap. Access is up a ten-metre concrete stairway with no handrail and with a ditch either side. He just laughed when I brought it up. The Sotiris Apartments has black mould growing on the ceiling of the rooms. He said he's going to paint it. As for the Nefeli Hotel—'

'I know about the Nefeli. We got a call. Mr Trellos said that you tried to assault him with a laid table.'

'What? The man's just a retarded yokel. He was hunting mice with a plank!'

'We don't refer to our valued property owners as "retarded yokels". Nor do we recognise the term "death trap".'

'Sorry. Is there an official euphemism?'

'Jim?'

Had he actually said that out loud? 'Sorry. It's just—'

56

'We'll send the agency lawyer up there to talk to them. Once they understand that no tourists can be accommodated without a signed contract, they'll soon sign.'

'OK.'

'And remember to wear your full dress uniform when you come down to the airport.'

Boil-in-the-bag blue polyester trousers and long-sleeved shirt. A clip-on tie that looked like vomit. 'Of course.'

Jim hung up and stared malevolently at the tower of postcards he hadn't yet stuffed into the welcome books. The welcome boards were all missing a toothsome photograph of him because he hadn't had time to go to Sami and organise some.

Enough. He left the desk a mess of materials and headed out for a coffee. The owner of Kyanni Akti was in the alley taking delivery of a giant oil drum whose only marking was an urgently crossed-out cigarette and five exclamation marks. Jim pretended not to notice the transaction.

The café was virtually empty, making the sullen waitress somehow even more lugubrious. She took Jim's order with a sigh and with no acknowledgement of his language skills. No tip for her, then, the miserable cow.

The *komboloi* dropped into his hand almost automatically – part of a ritual developed in cafés across the mainland. In Kozani, in Thessaloniki, in Lamia, at Meteora, at Delphi, in Nafplio, Sparti, Patras and Kalamata he had perfected the Hellenic coffee-drinking attitude. The drink itself was just a prop. What mattered was the company, the view, the temporal hiatus, the acute receptiveness to the moment. A coffee meant time for reflection, meditation, even epiphany. Daydreams acquired the detail of concrete plans in Greek cafés. Fantasy took on the mantle of destiny – books to be written, experiences to have, lifetimes to live.

The drink was set on the marble tabletop with a liquid clink. Jim agitated the ice with the straw but didn't drink. He let the *komboloi* beads click slowly through his fingers, marking timeless time. *This* was why he had applied for the job. A whole summer of this. Good food, good weather, native culture, a bit of money saved.

The hordes of internet-addicted kids seemed to have disappeared as soon as the temperature had risen and now there was one other customer sitting two tables in front: a girl of about his own age. Not Greek. Her hair was naturally light and her clothes too colourful for her to be a local. She was studying some sort of complex spreadsheet on the screen of an iPad. Working on holiday? What a crime.

As if aware of his gaze, she turned to look at him. An attractive girl. Not beautiful. Not exactly pretty, but with a frank gaze and clear intelligence in her features.

'Excuse me,' she said, pointing. 'What's that you're drinking?'

An American. '*Frappe*,' he said. 'Iced coffee.'

'I tried to make the girl understand but . . . This cappuccino she gave me isn't anything I recognise.'

'Ha! Well, this isn't Italy. It's best to stick to Greek coffee or *frappe* in my experience. Ask for it *metrio me gala* – semi-sweet with milk.'

'Thanks.' She smiled – polite, perfunctory, but genuine – and turned back to her iPad.

Words formed in his mind. Hey, I'm Jim. I work here. Would you like to meet up later? I could tell you a lot about Greece . . . But every passing second made it less easy to speak. She was again intent on her work and he'd just look desperate. Awkward. Inexperienced.

'Well, *that's* a blatant infringement of the rules.'

Jim looked up. He'd only vaguely noticed the figure approach his table. Her thighs struck him first: long, tanned, lissom and exhibited to remarkable effect in her brief uniform shorts. Next came the stomach: toned, flat, leading inexorably to breasts that were exactly the right size for her frame. Her hair was long and dark and drawn into a regulation ponytail that accentuated her cheekbones. Blue eyes. Full lips. A slight Megan Fox vibe. Even the uniform looked good. Undoubtedly cotton.

'Wh-what?' he said.

'Drinking in local cafés, bars and restaurants is strictly forbidden while in uniform.'

'I . . . I . . . '

She winked and gave a winning smile. 'Joking!'

Was he having palpitations, or was it the *frappe*?

She held out a hand. 'You must be Jim. Kelly told me about you. I'm Philippa, the Smithson rep.'

He took her hand – cool, slender, red-painted nails. An image flashed into his mind of her fingers grasping his engorged member and his face burned with embarrassment.

'Not much of a talker, are you?' she said.

'I'm new to the job. There's a lot to do. The first flight comes in this week.'

'Don't worry. I'll lend a hand if I can.'

He was still holding her hand. He released it.

'It's a funny place, Exogi,' she said. 'But I'd rather be here than Faliraki. I heard you met Mister Trellos.'

'Word gets around.'

'It does indeed. Village life. Did you feel the tremor?'

'Yeah. Weird. One of the locals told me I should start carrying a whistle round my neck in case the big quake hits and I have to signal rescuers from under a ton of rubble.'

'They're just messing with you. It's nothing. Did you buy a whistle?'

'Yeah.'

Was there an element of pity in her smile? 'Look, we should get together sometime: you, me and Kelly. Have a drink or a meal. Have you been up to Diogenes' bar in Allomeros yet?'

'Not yet. I'm staying there, but I haven't had time to wander round.'

59

'You should. It's cool. Have you even been to look at the film set?'

'No, I . . .'

'It's amazing! I've been there a few times trying to meet a star.'

'Chet Braddock? Get in line. Kelly says she'd like to strum his violin.'

'Not him. He's too pretty. It's James Craggan I'd like to capture. God, there's a man! *Cocaine Train, Mission to Pluto* – that's a proper leading man. His eyes! His *arms*!'

Jim peripherally noticed the iPad girl half turning as if about to speak, but she turned back just as quickly.

'Isn't he . . . well, a bit old?' said Jim. 'He must be sixty-something.'

'Experience, Jim. The things he could do with his hands . . . and the rest.'

Philippa rolled her eyes dreamily and shimmered under the imaginary caresses of James Craggan.

Jim debated whether to say that Craggan was very likely a Viagra-driven, Botox-stretched and amphetamine-fuelled zombie with bags of blood in his fridge and a syringe of clean urine for when the testers came calling.

'Look, I've got to do my rooming lists,' said Philippa, glowing almost post-coitally. 'We'll catch up again. If not here, then at the airport. See you later!'

He waited two seconds before turning to check her rear aspect . . . and was horrified to see she had anticipated it.

'Caught you!' she said, with a backwards glance, a wink and a flick of the ponytail.

His faced burned even hotter. A smile creaked across his features and he turned back to his coffee. Philippa's bottom was one he'd gladly eat from. Preferably soup. Or jelly. Did she, like Kelly, have a Yiannis somewhere? Someone with "experience". It was inconceivable that she could have been on the island for more than twenty seconds without one of the locals picking up her scent from his inverse perch in the hibernation cave. He'd be combing his chest and selecting a transparent shirt even as she innocently disembarked from the ferry.

What chance was there for Jim in such an environment? Evolution was against him – he with his sunken chest, swelling gut, thinning hair and earnest intellectualism. Girls like Philippa didn't respond well to witty quips and observations about the national culture. They wanted to be metaphorically clubbed by a hairy Neanderthal, thrown down and subjected to the relentless piston of animal lust. Feminism had barely touched the men of Greece, but it had emasculated most of northern Europe.

He looked to where the iPad girl had been sitting. She was gone. He'd probably ruined his chances with her as well now, failing to notice her once the prettier girl had arrived. It was futile anyway. If she didn't have her Yiannis by now, one would sniff her out in the next day or so, tossing her twenty-first-century technology into a bush as his trousers burst open, Hulk-like, to reveal a quivering python of . . .

The waitress appeared at his table, mutely holding a cordless phone for him to take.

'For me?' he said.

She nodded sourly. This wasn't part of her demanding job specification.

He took it. 'Er, hello?'

'Jim. If you're sitting in that café wearing your uniform, you'll receive a verbal warning.'

'Donna . . . I . . . '

'I hear everything, Jim. I see everything.'

Like the mythical hydra. Poisonous breath. Cut one head off and two more grow. 'Did Philippa—?'

'Philippa? The Smithson rep? No, Jim, I was trying to call you in the office but there was no answer. I had a hunch.'

A hunch would suit you. 'Oh, right.'

'I wanted to remind you not to mention the tremor to any guests when they arrive. It's not been widely reported and we don't want word getting out. OK? It might impact bookings later in the season.'

61

'Right. Yeah. Definitely.'

'And I'll be needing your rooming lists by the end of today.'

'Yes.'

'And I hope your welcome boards are ready, because . . . '

No longer listening. He had noticed a piece of stencilled graffiti that he was sure hadn't been there the previous day. The tourists would certainly see it, and yet it was more risible than threatening. Should he see about getting it painted over? It had a certain village charm. It might be a talking point: brief, offensive, polyglot and yet respectably concise.

No Hebrew EU tyrrania
Greece 1832!

It reminded him of a fading spray-painted scrawl on a flyover near Corinth that always made him smile: *Klinton the murderer!* Yes – let the graffito stay.

Lunchtime was approaching. Time to make a choice: finish the welcome boards, or have a *pita* at Maria's *psistaria* – a fat white-bread cone of greasy meat stuffed with soggy chips, fresh onion, tomato and *tzatziki*. His shorts were already a patchwork of oily stains from previous visits and soon his shirt would suffer. A minor rebellion against the Iliad brand, but so satisfying.

The Main Set, near Sami, Kefalonia

Lomu picked Grace up from the café, though it really had no right to call itself a café based on the evidence of that cappuccino. The whole time she'd been sitting there, all she could think of was that scene in *Mulholland Drive*: the guys sitting round the boardroom. *That is considered to be one the finest espressos in the world, sir!* Genius. She'd have to try one of those *frappes* instead – the Greeks seemed to drink nothing else.

In fact, coffee of any kind had been a mistake. If her nerves had been fluttering before, they were thrumming now. This would be her first time on set – she, the so-called spectral daughter of James Craggan. Did everyone know? Gaffers, lighting, costume, set-dressers, prop masters, camera crews, make-up – every one of them had earned their place on set by being the best at what they did, and then here came Grace – just out of film school, qualified only by the delusions of a fading star. Would they hate her? More importantly, would they hate her dress? The Greek islands had suggested colour to her imagination, but the Greek girls seemed to wear little else but black.

She stared at the back of Lomu's head, at the tattoos crawling over it like Polynesian creepers. She looked at the Rolex, turning it so that the diamonds caught the light. It felt more like a prop than a legitimate possession. Something to help her get into character.

'Paparazzi,' said Lomu, nodding at a moped driving in the centre of the road ahead.

Grace looked and saw the camera case.

Lomu accelerated, the vast BMW engine merely humming a little louder, and was almost upon the lone rider before he checked his mirror and wobbled precipitously to the side of the road, skidding to halt in the dust-cloud raised by the car.

Lomu's face smiled in the rearview.

'You could have killed him,' said Grace.

'Can't kill 'em. They like cockroaches.'

She turned to see the rider with a camera to his face. He was snapping the rear window. Just a show of bravado. He wouldn't get anything though the tinted glass. Even if he had, what would have got anyway? A girl not quite attractive enough to be a star and too brightly dressed to be a production assistant. A spectral daughter caught between sets.

The main set announced itself with a glut of trucks and glinting vehicle glass. Grace pulled her ID from inside her dress and let it hang on its lanyard. She took the iPad from her bag and opened the shooting script.

'Be cool,' said Lomu. 'You with Crag now. Anybody disses you, tell me. Nobody shits on Crag's people.'

'Thanks, Lomu.'

'Call me when you ready. I'll come get you.'

She opened the door. The film crew were too busy or cool to stare, but the locals – some of them extras in costume – watched expectantly to see if it was James Craggan himself getting out of the car. But no – it was nobody. An assistant of some kind. They went about their business.

From the outside, the main set looked like a huge plywood shantytown: all jutting struts, scaffolding, polythene and wires. Cranes and fixed lighting rigs raised their heads from inside. A work detail was unrolling two-metre-high wire fencing to stretch around the perimeter and prevent prying paparazzi eyes from stealing images of the set. All human traffic seemed to be entering to the left so Grace followed them and approached two dark-suited security guys.

'Pass,' said one of them.

She held up the ID and he scanned it with a reader. Was there a flicker of respect in his eyes when he read whatever was on his little screen? Probably not.

'Bag,' said the other one.

She opened her bag. He peered inside.

'No photography on set,' he said, pointing to the iPad. He waved her inside.

She entered a brief shadowy area where a low plyboard bridge carried her over dozens of cables and she carried on towards an open, sun-soaked area ahead. She felt like a gladiator in approaching the stadium from the cells – filmed from behind, a tracking shot following his silhouette until he entered the light and the amphitheatre's magnitude was revealed.

It was no amphitheatre. It was a reproduction of a village square: peeling façades, cracked terracotta pots, a stone fountain, a café with marble-topped tables. The real thing could no doubt be found in many places across Greece, but here it was in wood and paint – contained, controllable, transformable. The gods of cinema could make it rain here, make the earth cleave open, or destroy it all in an explosion that would cause no actual damage. It was nothing Grace hadn't seen before, but something else made it surreal.

At least twenty extras were sitting around plucking and strumming at mandolins. Surely so many mandolins been never before been gathered in once place (outside a mandolin factory). Their sound filled the air – cacophonous, but in an utterly inoffensive way. She had already found that too much *bouzouki* music brought on homicidal tendencies, but the mandolin had a much friendlier, more female tone. Still, this might have been a Monty Python sketch. There, at the far end of the square, was an artfully faded sign that explained it all: *Captain Corelli's Mandolin School.*

'Grace? Grace! Over here!'

Grace saw Granger waving from where a group of people were clustered about a camera. She'd have to walk across the whole square as they all appraised her. Should have worn jeans. On any other set, she'd be wearing jeans.

'I like your dress,' said Granger without apparent irony.

'Thanks. I'd normally wear jeans, but—'

'No problem. Let me introduce you. Mario Cacciatore, DP; Hans Welt, AC; Molly Clapham, grip; Shane Wolf, lighting. Everyone – this is Grace. She's with James Craggan.'

'But not his *personal* assistant,' said Grace.

65

Some of them smirked. She shook hands with them and wondered if it was cool to tell Mario she was a huge fan. *St Petersburg, Khe San Sunset, Indomitable, Puglian Diary* – his resume was virtually a curriculum for early twenty-first-century cinematography. But all she could say was:

'Nice camera.'

'My baby,' said Hans, stroking it.

'Grace is just out of film school,' said Granger. 'She's hoping to learn, so . . .'

They nodded. Grace blushed.

'Oh, and here comes Chet,' said Granger.

Chet Braddock. In person. Walking towards them dressed as some kind of Greek peasant. He'd grown a beard that made him look Mediterranean. He was carrying a mandolin.

'He's been in and out of character since he arrived,' muttered Granger. 'Just go with it.'

Grace watched him as he approached: rangy, limber, seemingly unconscious of his looks. She remembered his severed finger. Don't look at the finger. Don't look at the finger.

'*Kali mera sas!*' said Chet with an expansive wave. 'I am Efthimios, son of Corelli!'

She looked at the finger – or rather the absent little finger on his right hand. Not even a stump - just a gap.

He saw her looking and smiled. 'A fishing accident. I was diving for octopus and I was dragged into the reef. It was my finger or my life. I thought I would never play again.'

Grace waited for one of the others to say something. Was this a test?

She nodded at the mandolin. 'Can you play us something, er, Efthimios?'

He made an exaggerated bow of acknowledgement and took the instrument in his arms as if it were a baby. His face took on a saintly expression. He closed his eyes and began to pick at the strings with such remarkable proficiency that Grace almost looked round for a set of speakers.

The hubbub of technicians and extras in the square hushed and within moments the only sound was Chet's unaccompanied playing. It was not a tune she knew, but it was beautiful in its way. As he played, a single tear seeped from one closed eye: testament to the transport of feeling he seemed to be experiencing.

It was unreal. The cameras weren't rolling, and yet there she was in the middle of the scene. A speaking role. Everyone was going along with it: Chet Braddock playing a mandolin, dressed as a Greek peasant and calling himself Efthimios. Everyone had been subsumed into the world of Braddock's own imagining. But who were they to him? Intruders into his fictional mandolin-fisherman existence?

The final note hung in the air like a skein of smoke. He opened his eyes. Every person in the town square began to whoop and applaud so that the plyboard scenery shook with the force of it.

'My father taught me everything I know,' shrugged Chet/Efthimios.

Granger leaned close to Grace as the applause subsided. 'He's been having lessons in Italy for the last six weeks.'

'So, you're with the great James Craggan,' said Chet/Efthimios. 'I have seen his films. He is a great star.'

'I'm not *with* him exactly. I'm just a day-to-day assistant on the shoot.'

Chet/Efthimios looked oddly pained.

Should she have mentioned the shoot? If he was still in character, could he acknowledge that he was in a film? And if he didn't acknowledge it – if he really was a mandolin-playing fisherman, son of Corelli – how did he explain the cameras all around and the fact he'd soon be doing scenes with Craggan? She turned to Granger for help.

'Well,' said Granger, 'The musical director is waiting for Efthimios in the rehearsal space, so . . . '

He made another bow and walked off with a *'Ta leme!'* thrown over his shoulder.

Molly, the grip, rolled her eyes. Grace wanted to hug her.

Granger sighed. 'If it works for him . . . Look, Grace, there's not much going on at the moment. Hang around if you like and talk to the guys about what they're doing. We're not setting up any shots yet – just getting everything in place. Crag has a Winnie out the back if you get bored and want a rest. It has a dry bar. Catering restocks it daily.'

'Thanks, Granger. This is all really great. I'll just try to keep out of the way.'

Mario left immediately with Shane. Molly gave Grace a wink and went back towards the exit. Hans, the assistant cameraman, remained.

'So – James Craggan. Is this his big comeback?' he said.

'I've really got no idea. I've not even met him yet. I mean, I've followed his career like everyone has. It'd be cool for him to come back.'

'I wanted to *be* him when I was kid. Shit, I wanted to be him when I wasn't a kid. He was one of Hollywood's greatest cocksmen. The women he's had . . . '

'Yeah. I'm not one of them.'

'I figured.'

'*Thanks!*'

'No, I mean you're obviously intelligent.'

'Obviously?'

'I've said the wrong thing. Whatever. Stick around when we start shooting. Ask me anything. You used one of these before?' He patted the camera.

'I've shared one with ten other people.'

'Ha, yeah. I've been there. Look, I've got to talk to the AD. I'll see you around, Grace, OK?'

Hans strolled off. Didn't look back. Probably just being polite. At least he'd remembered her name.

She stood for a while watching scaffolding rise, lighting rigs wired and final touches put to the set. Her lack of function was palpable. Perhaps she would go

68

to see Crag's Winnebago. After all, this would probably be the only time in her life she'd ever get inside one.

There were a few of them parked at the rear of the set: the director's, Crag's, Hannah Caro's, Chet's. All were identical except for the signs on the door. She wondered if Chet's had been treated by the art department to look like a fisherman's cabin inside. There was no security barring her way, so she walked straight to Crag's and reached for the door handle.

It was only then that she became aware that the whole thing was moving. Somebody was inside. Crag unexpectedly back from France? She paused, not ready yet. She'd rehearsed a first meeting and this wasn't how it was supposed to go.

There was a muffled cry and a thud from inside. The Winnebago rocked. She had a vision of Crag rolling on the floor, arm tied off and an overdose heading for his heart. Or Crag unconscious with a thirty-year-old bottle of Scotch slowly killing his brain.

She pulled open the door and stepped in.

Large leather recliners, fresh flowers, giant plasma. No body. She walked on thick-pile carpet towards a door that stood ajar. Another grunt. A moan. She pushed the door.

Hannah Caro was sitting on the edge of the bed, her head thrown back, her luxuriant hair across her face, her perfect mouth open. Her naked legs were open and a male head was working busily between them. Not Crag, but a young man with short, dark hair.

Grace froze. Neither of them had noticed her.

'Daddy! *Oh Daddy!*' sighed Caro.

Grace was paralysed. Her hand remained on the door. Her feet refused to move. This shot would make her rich for life if she were a paparazza. A 60mm lens would do it.

'*Oh! Oh Ah! Uh-huh! Uh-huh!*'

Still, they hadn't noticed her. Why would they?

69

She had to move. She willed her feet to lift. She pulled the door back towards her, praying it wouldn't creak. She tip-toed through the seating area and was just stepping down from the Winnebago as Hannah Caro reached a prolonged and very vocal climax.

Penelope was waiting outside the door. Her arms folded and her face a mask of accusation.

'I . . . I had no idea—' began Grace.

'Is it Hannah?'

'Yes.'

'That girl. Who's she with?'

'I only saw the back of his head. Dark hair. Short . . . the hair, I mean.'

'If it's another goddamn extra we'll have to . . . never mind. Do *not* tell anyone about this. And don't worry – I'll make sure Crag's stuff is professionally cleaned. God knows why she chose his Winnie. I should be grateful she didn't do it right out on the beach.'

'Should I go?'

'Yes. Go. Any pray that Crag's still on the wagon.'

Grace walked numbly back towards the set. Could she put any of this in an email? Would anyone believe it?

The Church, Exogi, Kefalonia

It was not the church Pappas Xenomachos would have chosen. There were older and more beautiful churches – churches with honey-coloured campaniles and Venetian stonework; churches with carved Byzantine iconostases and gilded icons rich with the patina of two centuries' faith; churches with cool, musty crypts and serried reliquaries glinting with the promise of sanctified anatomy; churches, moreover, with fading seventeenth-century frescoes of martyrdoms to challenge those of Athos or Mystra (griddles, pitchforks, arrows, cauldrons and beds of nails, the figures' eyes gouged out by superstitious Ottoman occupiers). *They* were churches to inculcate a healthy fear of God – sanctuaries of a spirit as palpable as censer smoke. A church like that would help him in his battle against the pagans.

But he hadn't had the choice. He had this church instead. A pre-fabricated church delivered on a flat-bed truck and lowered into place by crane. A wood-framed church with fibreglass panels and dome. A church whose benches, icons, brassware, and iconostasis had been selected from a catalogue with mock-Byzantine fonts and shipped from a giant ecclesiastical warehouse on the Corinth-Patras highway. This was orthodoxy in the twenty-first century.

What next, mused Xenomachos. Blessings by email? Baptism by post? Confession vouchers free with margarine? Whatever it might be, the monks of Athos were probably already working on it. They had the churches they wanted – the best churches around. Miracles happened in their churches. Not so much these days, admittedly, but one never knew with Athos. Just as a seismic line passed under Kefalonia, so a miraculous fault seemed to support the Athonite peninsula. They got all the best miracles and left none for anyone else.

Thirty two people looked back at Xenomachos in his pulpit (a proper, carved wooden pulpit – he had been quite adamant in arguing for this one). The pause in his sermon had now stretched into the realms of awkwardness. Sundry coughs punctuated the silence. What had he been saying? Something about . . .

'Pagans!' he continued.

Was there a collective groan?

'Pagans!' he said, slightly louder. 'They walk among us here on this island. Yes. I am not referring to Catholics, Evangelists, Jehovah's Witnesses and Jews – though they, too, are bound for the fires of hell – but those who follow the pseudo-faith they call Hellenismos. You have heard of it. Sixty-thousand practitioners in Greece according to our bishop's estimate! Sixty-thousand! That's almost the population of Kalamata.'

The congregation stared at him, apparently with little sense of fear or wonder.

'Oh, I know that some of you think it's harmless – just a group of eccentrics worshipping the old gods. We all studied it at school: Zeus and his lightning bolts, limping Hephaestus, Artemis and her bow, feather-footed Hermes . . . how could such comic-book characters possibly be a threat to the realm of our redeeming Christ, you may ask? Well let me remind you that Zeus raped Leda while disguised as a swan! Not just rape, you understand, but bestiality at the same time! You'll remember that Europa faced a similar fate: raped by Zeus the bull, much as Europe today is being violated by . . . well, never mind that. I ask you, what kind of god does such a thing?'

The congregation seemed unmoved.

'And let me be quite clear about this. It's not only the so-called twelve Olympians they worship. No. It's also the gods they call "chthonic" – gods of the darkness and underworld, gods of the moon, of dreams and of darkness. Pluto: lord of Hell. Persephone: his bride. Hekate: the witch. Devil worshippers! Have we not all seen the signs? Little shrines on the beach. Offerings at Allomeros, where we believe a true Christian martyr's bones may lie. These people still believe in sacrifice! Would you like your child to go strolling in the village and find an animal carcass bearing its guts to the sky? The acolytes of darkness are among us! What will you do? What will you do?'

A long pause. Was it a rhetorical question?

'Avoid going to Kalamata?' said someone.

Splutters were hastily disguised as coughs.

Xenomachos glared.

'Keep away from swans?' muttered another.

'Who said that?' said Xenomachos.

Silence crackled.

A reggae-flavoured ringtone started somewhere in the congregation.

All heads turned as if directed by a sudden breeze.

It was Diogenes Borborygmos, his face illuminated by the pale light of his phone. The ringtone now changed to a classic guitar riff . . . now to a *bouzouki* workout . . . now to a classic hit by Nikos Karvelas. People began nodding to the beat.

'Diogenes! What are you doing?' shouted Xenomachos. 'This is the house of God!'

The Karvelas song continued to play. More people were nodding or tapping out the beat.

'Diogenes!'

'Noise pollution,' said Diogenes. 'It's a terrible thing, isn't it? A man seeks peace, but his concentration is disrupted by unwanted noise. It seems the law can't do anything.'

'Stop that music at once!'

Diogenes pressed a button and the song ceased. There was a quiet groan of disappointment from the congregation, but then a new song began: *Pyx Lax*'s hit "Monaxia Mou". A ripple of pleasure passed through the people.

'This is blasphemy!' screeched Xenomachos. 'I know what you are doing, Diogenes. I know what this is about. Leave! Leave now!'

Diogenes stood, grinning. The song played on and he strolled down the aisle to the door, improvising a few shambolic dance moves as he went. He had made his point.

The door banged and the nave was returned to awkwardness. Somebody humming the ringtone stopped abruptly.

'I have had a vision,' said Xenomachos. 'A visitation, I should say, from Saint Athanasios himself – he who had the power of casting out evil spirits, and who retains that power still through his holy relics on this island. It came to me just after the tremor.'

He let this fact settle over them. Saint Athanasios was taken seriously on Kefalonia, even if his priestly intercessors in this world were not. Plus, a tremor was always a good opportunity for a vision.

73

'Yes, it was he – the sainted martyr. He told me that we are saturated in sin here in Exogi. We have been polluted by the tourist hordes, lured away from righteousness by the money they bring. And now this film, whose so-called stars are agents of sin. Drug addicts. Drinkers. Fornicators and adulterers.'

He glared at the three married women he suspected of sharing their beds with Sergeant Nikos Petras and saw that they were unashamed. The widow he was seeing actually appeared to smirk!

'And Saint Athanasios told me that I should lead a stand against this poisoning influence. I should lead my flock in saying no to the foreign tourist, shunning his pieces of silver and turning him back. No more public exhibitions of near nudity! No more fornicating on the beach! No more pools of vomit on our pleasant streets! We must stand together. Who will walk with me and Saint Athanasios in this crusade? Who will say no to the foreign tourist?'

The congregation – hoteliers, shop-owners, bar-owners, deckchair-renters, restaurateurs, and tour leaders – responded stonily. Nobody spoke. Some looked at their watches.

Xenomachos sighed. This was what happened when you had a prefabricated church with mail-order icons. No spirit.

There was one in the congregation, however, who had been moved by what he had heard. His heavy-metal t-shirt was hidden under a sweater, but he had started to see how the church might be of some very practical benefit.

Airport, South Coast, Kefalonia

'Take your sunglasses off, Jim.'

'Seriously? The sun's like an atomic flash in this car park.'

'It's part of the Iliad Holidays dress code – which you should have read. It explicitly states that no sunglasses may be worn when interacting with guests. They need to see your eyes so they know you're being sincere.'

'It'll take more than that.'

'Pardon me?'

'Nothing.'

'And what's that around your waist? Is it . . . is it a curtain cord?'

'These trousers are two sizes too big. They don't sell belts in Exogi.'

'You're a disgrace, Jim. If we didn't have people coming in for Exogi today, I'd send you home.'

'Yes, Donna.'

'Your coach will be dropping people off all the way back to Exogi. Tick them off on the manifest before letting them on. See that everyone finds their room before you move on to the next place. Have you been practising your arrival speech and welcome meeting?'

'Religiously.'

'Right, let's go inside. The others are waiting.'

They went through automatic doors into a dim sanctuary of air-conditioned cool. Immediately, Jim saw a cluster of Iliad skirts and blouses. He was the only male rep.

'All right,' said Donna. 'We've got five minutes. This is Jim – he's the new rep up in Exogi.'

They offered greetings of varying insincerity. He was neither hairy nor muscular enough to warrant their serious attention. Plus, he looked like a fancy-dress flight attendant in the heinous polyester uniform. Donna introduced them in turn and Jim filed them away in a folder marked "Irrelevant":

Shania – ludicrous mahogany tan, Shetland-pony legs, village-idiot face.

Britney – blonde frizz, love-bite on her neck, mouth-breather.

Jackie – leering, lip-sticked, probably highly promiscuous.

Sharon – talcum-powdered, enormous.

Other reps from other companies were also waiting at the arrivals gate, each segregated according to their own sense of quality or prestige. The Golden reps – Kelly, winking – looked like a hen party before a big night. The Smithson reps – Philippa, pert and fluttering – represented a higher level of evolution: taller, thinner, pony-tailed and subtly made up in contrast to the war-paint of the Golden girls. Was that linen they were wearing? Then there was the sole rep of Hellenic Club: a gentleman in his forties wearing a Panama hat and a linen-silk mix blazer. The bastard.

'As queer as the scoutmaster's sling-backs, him', opined Shania.

'You look nervous, Jim,' said Jackie, leaning so close that her zeppelin breasts squashed against the back of his arm and her perfume scratched at his tonsils. 'Don't worry – I'm sure there'll be some lovely guys for you!'

'I'm not g—'

'Everybody smile!' said Donna. 'Here they come!'

The doors slid open and Jim saw his tourists for the first time.

They ambled like cattle, gaudy in shades and styles they would never wear in England. New trainers, new sunglasses, new tops and trousers that would all be re-packed in two weeks, stained with sun cream, olive oil, vomit, blood. They moved like sleepwalkers, mouths agape, sacrificing themselves totally to the reps who would tell them where to wait, where to get off, where to stay. The very fact of being in a foreign country had begun to work its magic on them during the flight, initially cowing them through theft of language, then beguiling them with Mediterranean light before later robbing them of their native inhibitions so that every night would become Friday night. They were pale, flabby, sickly-looking – unexotic insects that seemed to have crawled from under something to emerge blinking into a polychrome world. Greece, to them, was a theme park rather than a nation. If people spoke differently here, it was just an anomaly – a compulsory part of the show.

This was the parochial, insipid, crass and unimaginative Britishness Jim had yearned to leave behind and excise from his self. Now it was his job to protect it

76

from too much foreignness while introducing it to rapacious tourist Greece – an arranged marriage in which six-year-old Britain put its pale little hand into the grizzled palm of a sixty-year-old Greece. But who was corrupting whom?

He held up a card with his destinations and they approached him with grudging deference combined with a vague resentment of his very existence. To each of these shuffling, waddling, luggage-trundling people he repeated the mantra, 'Coach number three, left outside the doors . . . ', occasionally modifying it for those of especially low IQ: 'Yes, yes – a big blue coach . . . a number three on the front . . . wheels, internal combustion engine . . . '

And all the while, there was the dread of the impending welcome speech gnawing at the base of his stomach. This was his audience. These were *his* tourists.

'Right – off you go!' said Donna when the last bewildered soul had come through.

The car park was full of them, standing beside the coaches even though the doors were open and the inside blissfully air-conditioned. Nobody had actually told them to get on; they hadn't got on. The coach driver, Kostas, sat in the driver's seat smoking. He hadn't been told actually to load their luggage; he hadn't loaded their luggage.

'What kind of service is this?' said an elderly man with a head and neck like a tortoise. 'It's baking hot out here! My wife has almost fainted twice!'

Jim turned to the wife, who looked like she'd been embalmed a couple of years previously. She nodded sourly in verification.

'It is surely better *almost* to faint than to faint,' said Jim with exaggerated Wildean intonation.

Tortoise-head gaped. 'I beg your pardon!'

Jim imagined the gummy mouth working on a lettuce leaf. He jerked his head at Kostas: get out and do your job, you lazy git.

'Leave your luggage, ladies and gentlemen. Kostas will see to it. Please get on board and we'll soon be at your delightful accommodation.'

He stood by the door, squinting in the blinding sun, nodding and smiling like a moron as they filed past him, all moaning *sotto voce* about the level of service, about the heat, about the in-flight sandwiches and how rude the airport toilet attendant had been.

Meanwhile, Kostas tossed and kicked the luggage beneath, grunting at his work but not relinquishing his precious nicotine lifeline.

Finally, the doors sighed closed, the air-conditioning went up a gear, and Jim took his seat beside Kostas. Now for the worst part.

He reached for the microphone headset and put it on, immediately becoming a call-centre drone. Kostas smirked and Jim offered him a covert middle finger. There was no escape. He turned on the headset and heard his own oddly nasal tones come through the coach's PA system:

'Ladies and gentlemen – I'm Jim. May I welcome you on behalf of Iliad Holidays [because I personally couldn't care less] to the beautiful island of Kefalonia. As you can see [so why mention it?] the sky is blue [some high cloud actually] and the weather is hot, hot, hot! [hot enough to almost faint]. Our journey today will take us along the south coast of the island to Argostoli and then north to your delightful accommodations [erroneous plural], which have been hand picked by Iliad Holidays for their charm [their cheapness], their wonderful views [of each other] and their comfort [if you're just out prison, as some of you appear to be] – real homes from home [if you're from the Third World and have a high tolerance for black mould]! My job is to ensure [by force, if necessary] that you enjoy the golden [tissue-strewn, pebble] beaches, the crystal-clear [lethally shelving] ocean and the glorious sights [over-priced excursions] of this unique [one of about five-hundred very similar] Greek island. If you have any questions, [keep them to yourself], save them for tonight's welcome meeting [Nuremburg-rally-style hard-sell] or catch me [literally, see if you can] at my appointed visiting hours, as detailed on the welcome boards at your accommodation [in fact, still incomplete and at the resort office in Exogi]. It's [really not] my greatest pleasure to be your host and I hope you go home [immediately] with fond memories of Iliad Holidays [probably a cast on your leg, a sexually-transmitted disease and/or third-degree burns].'

Jim pulled off the headset and tossed it on the dash. There was a patter of applause – probably the same people who clap when their plane lands safely.

'Bravo!' muttered Kostas.

Only three more months to go. Could it really be that bad? Just think of the money. The accommodation in Allomeros was free, the car was free, even the food and drink was free if he prostituted the Iliad uniform to best effect. In three months, he could save enough to take him through the winter. Istanbul beckoned. Cairo was close. Perhaps a permit to visit Athos. There was a whole world of experience out there.

A figure appeared at Jim's side: a tremulous middle-aged man wearing a new sunhat and with factor seven-hundred sun-cream on his nose. 'Excuse me,' said the man. 'Do you think you could stop the bus? Those awful sandwiches on the plane . . . My wife is going to be sick.'

Can't she use your hat? 'Yes, sir. Right away.'

Kostas – whose coach was an extension of himself – jerked the vehicle to a crunching halt by the side of the road and Jim watched as Mr Sunhat led his wife into the scrub for a good heave. The other tourists tutted at Jim for the state of the sandwiches they'd all been forced to eat on the plane.

And creeping sense of omission came to him. Donna had mentioned something about ticking a manifest as the people boarded. It was there in his gaudy Iliad Holidays file. Unticked.

The Ancient Site, Allomeros, Kefalonia

Professor Stratigakis walked with two others down one of Allomeros' steep, jasmine-scented streets. The moon cast silver-filigreed shadows at their feet.

79

House lights flickered as false constellations up each side of the valley. They spoke quietly as they strolled, the professor's stick tapping on the asphalt.

'Me, too,' said Magda, a woman of about the professor's age who had retired to the island to paint. 'The smoke seemed to behave oddly after my supplication. Then the tremor.'

'It's clearly a sign. There's no doubt,' said Niki, a schoolteacher in Sami. She might have been the daughter of one of the older women. 'Zeus speaks through the earth and the sky. Thunder and lightning is his preferred sign, of course, but a tremor can't be discounted.'

'Yes, yes,' said the professor, 'but it doesn't help us. Poseidon, also, is a great bringer of earthquakes and we didn't pray to him either. It's Aphrodite we addressed. Was it she who replied? Or was it one of the others?'

'The gods do speak in riddles,' said Magda.

'And yet we're their priestesses,' said Niki.

'It's so frustrating,' said the professor. 'I know that there are rooms of tablets from Mycenae that have yet to be studied. They're just sitting there, crumbling and ignored. But they won't let *me* near them. Where would be the benefit for them in letting *me* make a discovery from *their* tablets? It's so small-minded and parochial. Our history belongs to all of us. And then there's the Church. We all know that no ancient martyr was buried here. There's absolutely no proof for it. They can't even agree which martyr it might be.'

'The gods will have their way,' said Magda, 'even if it takes another two millennia.'

They walked on, further into agricultural land. The scent of pine and the river-bed came hot from the valley floor. A lost goat clanked in the darkness. The bald mountaintops were frosted in lunar illumination.

'I got some work as an extra on the movie,' said Niki.

'Really?' said the professor.

'Well, there are no classes until September. The money isn't anything special, but I thought it might be fun.'

'Have you seen any stars?' said Magda. 'James Craggan?'

'No, I've only seen Chet Braddock. He walks around playing his mandolin and calling himself Efthimios. I think that must be his character. He even speaks a bit of Greek. But I'm hoping to meet Eleni Skouras – she's playing Corelli's wife, er . . . '

'Pelegia,' said Magda.

'Yes, that's it,' said Niki. 'Eleni is just wonderful! I might try to get her autograph.'

'Ha! You two make me feel out of touch,' said the professor. 'I know James Craggan, but I've no idea who this Craddock is.'

'Braddock,' said Niki. 'The new Brad Pitt.'

'Who?'

'Think of a young Brando,' said Magda. 'Only with fewer fingers.'

They walked the rest of the way in silence, passing a sign for the "Sanctuary of Aphrodite" that had been defaced with Christian crosses. The site itself was little more than a number of trenches, a stretch of ancient wall and a rectangle of drooping, rusty barbed wire. Faded placards forbade public access.

'Let's stop for a moment,' said the professor.

'Is it your leg?' said Niki.

'No. Just listen. Look around.'

They spread out, walking quietly. They had come on the only road passing the site, but the crazy priest Xenomachos could conceivably have asked one of his congregation to keep a look out. At this hour, and in this light, they were undoubtedly safe from any long-distance observer with binoculars.

Finally, the professor nodded and held the wire up with her stick. Niki and Magda ducked under and helped her through. All were reverent now – on sacred ground – and each had a duty. Magda took terracotta lamps from a bag, filled them with oil and incense, lit them and distributed them about the ancient altar. Niki took a bottle of water and a large earthenware bowl from her bag. She sprinkled some water over the altar, muttering 'Oh, Aphrodite, turn away evil,' then filled the bowl for ritual cleansing.

When all had washed their faces and hands, they stood hand-in-hand in a circle before the altar.

'Let no-one speak an ill-omened word,' said the professor.

'We come in honour and sisterhood,' said the worshippers simultaneously.

'Hear us, Aphrodite and receive our sacrifice with joy.'

'We praise only you.'

'Make clear your intent, oh Beautiful One, and clarify your sign.'

'We pray earnestly for this.'

The professor released the others' hands and bent to her own bag, removing a live wild rabbit. It was small, brown and frozen with trepidation, its eyes glistening black beads. She sat it on the altar and it made no attempt to flee. Next, she took a long, thin kitchen knife from the bag and felt along the rabbit's spine for the right place.

'Receive this sacrifice in your honour, oh Aphrodite,' she said.

'And only in yours,' said the worshippers.

She inserted the knife decisively. The rabbit twitched. Its head fell forwards. There were a few more twitches and it was still. She waited a few more moments before rapidly slitting open its belly, flinging the entrails into the bushes and artfully arranging the carcass on the altar.

Magda stepped close and used one of the oil burners to scorch first a patch of fur and then the flesh so that two kinds of smoke rose pale into the moonlight.

Niki filled a silver cup from a hipflask, took a sip and passed it on until the three of them had drunk.

'Receive your gift and rejoice,' said the professor.

'We worship you and delight in your beauty,' said the worshippers.

Magda blew out the candles and Niki tipped the rest of the flask on to the altar

A smell of brandy rose, commingled with the scented smoke of the oil burners. They looked at each other. The rabbit hadn't seemed to suffer unduly.

'I think someone's coming!' whispered Niki.

They scrabbled urgently about the altar, taking back the lamps, bowl, flask and cup. The professor again held the barbed wire with her stick and they were on the other side of it when a figure strolled whistling from the darkness.

It was a man, completely nude. The tinny sound of music revealed that he must have an mp3 player somewhere about his person. A cigarette illuminated his face as he puffed at it: Diogenes Borborygmos, out for his evening constitutional.

Becoming aware of the women, he stopped and nodded a greeting. He thumbed a device in his right palm and the music ceased. He seemed utterly unembarrassed by his state of undress. His nostrils twitched as it picked up the brandy fumes.

'Metaxa. Seven stars,' he said, evidently impressed. Then he turned the music back on and continued walking until his pale buttocks disappeared into the night.

The women shared bemused glances.

'Did you see the size of that joint?' said Niki.

Private House, Near Sami, Kefalonia

Andreas worked with the scalpel, cutting out the letters of his latest graffiti stencil. Achilleus stood over him shaking his head.

'There's a "c" in "fuck". I told you before. You're making us look like a joke.'

'At least I know the difference between "Hebrew" and "Jew",' said Andreas, jabbing the scalpel into the table top so its handle quivered.

83

'We should've got some English person to check them before we used them,' said Kyriakos, idly looking though a pile of death-metal CDs.

'Yeah, imagine that,' said Achilleus. '"Excuse me, mister tourist – would you mind checking the spelling on this radical anti-tourist graffiti before we deface the town?". Why not just ask Miss Niki or Petras the cop?'

'We could ask one of the British holiday reps,' said Andreas. 'There's a guy working in Exogi.'

'The homo?' said Kyriakos.

'Yeah. I've heard he hates tourists almost as much as we do. He might help.'

'Are you two even listening?' said Achilleus. 'We're supposed to be a *secret* society. We can't go about asking people for help – especially not the enemy.'

'Well we're not doing very well with the action plan so far, are we?' said Kyriakos. 'Most of the graffiti was painted over immediately, and people are just laughing at spelling mistakes in the ones that are still around. I've seen tourists taking pictures of them.'

'What happened with the doctored alcohol?' said Achilleus. 'Nobody's got sick yet.'

'It was delivered to different bars, but they've probably still got some left from last season. The tourists are only just arriving, so . . . '

They ruminated glumly.

'I got a job as an extra on the movie,' said Andreas.

'What?' said Achilleus. 'When did we decide that?'

'It's not for the cause; it's just for a bit of money. And I might get to be in some scenes with Hannah Caro. I've seen her on set.'

'Is she as hot in real life?' said Kyriakos.

'Smouldering. You'd need an industrial asthma inhaler if you saw her.'

'*Malakas.*'

'Miss Niki is also working as an extra. She plays a peasant girl.'

'I'd bang Caro so hard she'd wake up in a different era,' said Kyriakos.

'I'd make her come so many times that she'd go into a coma.'

84

'A coma wouldn't put me off. I'd bang her until she woke up. They'd call it a miracle.'

'Stop!' said Achilleus. 'Wait a minute. We could do something with this. We've infiltrated a Hollywood movie with real stars in it. The world's media are watching. We need to think how to use this.'

'So I finally did the right thing?' said Andreas, showing Kyriakos a middle finger.

'Accidentally, but yes.'

'Actually, I had an idea, too,' said Kyriakos. 'I went to church on Sunday.'

The others paused and exchanged glances. They observed his long black hair and his t-shirt with the inverted cross and pentagram design. He was absently rolling a joint.

'Why?' said Andreas.

'The church stands for Greece, right? All through the Turkish occupation, it kept our language and culture alive. To be Greek is to be Orthodox. Remember I mentioned the monk Philotheos before? He's just one who's against Europe. I wondered if Xenomachos might be the same. It turns out he hates tourists. He started to say something about Europe but stopped himself. I think he could be an ally.'

'What exactly are you thinking?' said Achilleus, wary. 'You know the church has its own agenda.'

'I know, but I think our aims might be generally the same. The church was strongest before industrialisation and foreign investment and tourists and the EU, right? If we achieve our aims, the church will be pleased to be powerful again. Greece will look more like it did in 1832.'

'So, what? We invite Xenomachos into our cell and give him a secret name?' said Andreas.

'No, *malakas*. I go to confession and tell him our plans. I ask him if he's willing to fight with us for a pure Greece. And the best bit is that he can't tell anyone else because it's a confession, right? If he tells anyone, he goes to hell. Anyway, everyone knows he hates Petras – he'd never go to the police.'

Achilleus tapped a brief air-drum solo. 'It might work. We need to get our action plan going somehow.'

'I could do something in the film,' said Andreas.

'What could you do?' said Kyriakos.

'I . . . I could slip hidden messages into scenes so that the film becomes a propaganda vehicle for us.'

'What hidden messages? Are you going to mime "No foreign investment" in the background as James Craggan plays his violin?'

'*Mand*olin,' said Achilleus.

'No,' said Andreas. 'I could . . . I could talk to Chet Braddock and get him on our side. He already believes he's Greek. He's a star. He could get the script changed to suit our purposes.'

'Changed how?' said Kyriakos. 'Changed so that Corelli uses his mandolin to play all the Jews and tourists out of Greece? So that Hannah Caro gives a speech about the EU? Maybe they could change the name of the movie to "1832".'

'Hey!' said Achilleus. 'Come on! Let's stay focused. Andreas is thinking along the right lines – just not very realistically. We need to take advantage of this in the right way.'

'How about some inspiration?' said Kyriakos, aiming a remote control at the stereo.

Classic *Metallica* blasted from the speakers and they each took up their air instrument: Achilleus on drums, Kyriakos on bass, Andreas on lead guitar.

James Craggan's Villa, Allomeros, Kefalonia

A small hand-bell tinkled advance warning that lunch was about to be served. Lying on her bed, Grace folded the corner of William Goldman's *Adventures in the Screen Trade* and rested it on her chest with a sigh. She was hungry, but living in the villa had become increasingly like a bizarre reality TV show: *Para-Celebrity Big Brother*. They were all employed by a star, but the star was absent. So were the cameras and sound gear, and yet they all determinedly played their roles, those of them who knew what the role was supposed to be. It was a luxury sanatorium. A five-star Bedlam. It would probably make a good script. Who could play Grace? Scarlett? Could she do "mad" like Brad Pitt in *Twelve Monkeys*?

'Come on, Grace!' cried Honee. 'Ding-a-ling-a-ling!'

She sighed again and went to the dining room, where Chen was laying out platters of macrobiotic stuff. It smelled great, but she knew she'd be hungry again half an hour after eating it. Honee was already seated, her tanned, sculpted breasts poised to escape from a minuscule halter top. She'd been losing weight in preparation for Crag's delayed arrival.

'No cheese burgers today, Chen?' said Grace.

The chef giggled on his way back to the kitchen.

'You don't wanna eat that stuff,' said Honee, nibbling at a bean sprout. 'Goes straight on your ass and hips. You'll look like barrel when you're thirty.'

But I won't have brittle bones and bowel cancer from faddy dieting. 'Just one wouldn't hurt.'

'That's how it starts, honey. Gotta look after the goods. You think I hooked Crag with my *brain*?'

Honee did a little shimmy but her breasts were too perfectly engineered to fall out. It was all top-quality work. The teeth, the cheekbones. The nose, too? It was so difficult to tell these days. The work had gotten *that* good.

'How did you two meet?' said Grace, filling her plate.

'It was so romantic! I was doing promotion at a car-racing thing in Vegas and he asked if he could take me for a drive. We did it on the hood and I burned my ass.'

'True romance.'

'Yeah. What's the deal with you, hon? No offense, but why d'you dress like a geek? We're in Greece! Show a little more thigh! Where's that midriff? You pierced?' Honee stood to show a diamond dangling from her own navel.

'No . . . I suppose I want people to appreciate me for what I do or think instead of how I look. I mean, I'm not an actress.'

'Hey! Neither am I! You think I'm a whore or something?'

'Absolutely not.'

'All I'm saying is: people won't notice what you think if you're just a little mouse.' Honee nibbled at her bean sprout. 'Look at me. I'm next to Crag. I talk to him about his scripts and stuff. He tells me about directors and all the insider goss. You think *I've* got a Masters in anything?'

'I never thought that.'

'There you go.'

Lomu strolled in: a dark Armani monolith clutching a *pita* stuffed with oniony meat and fries.

'Where did you get that?' said Grace. 'It doesn't look very macrobiotic.'

'Call-out,' said Lomu. 'I pay a kid ten dollars to ride 'em here on his bike.'

'Just your little secret, eh?'

Lomu winked. 'Get ready – Crag's on set. Man wants to meet you.'

Honee shrieked and leapt to her feet, jiggling and shimmying and waving her arms. 'My baby! My baby's back! How do I look? Wait – I've just got to re-apply—'

'Not you,' said Lomu. 'Just Grace.'

'Huh?'

'You'll see him later. Shootin' today – man needs his technical people around him.'

The food seemed stuck in Grace's gullet. Of course, she'd studied the shooting schedule she knew that shooting began today. But there was always a chance – a hope – that Crag would be late, injured, relapsed. She stood on unsteady legs.

'How do I look?' she said.

Honee snorted and stuffed a handful of bean sprouts into her mouth.

'Man don't care how you look. Only what you think and do.'

Honee appeared to choke, her face becoming red.

Grace grinned and debated whether to plant a kiss on his adamantine jaw.

'Let's go.' Lomu screwed up the grease-paper from his *pita* and lobbed it four metres into a trash can.

Grace ran to her room and grabbed the iPad. When she got outside, Lomu had already turned the car around and had the passenger open for her.

'I get to ride up front now, do I?' she said. 'I guess I passed the test.'

He smiled, sphinx-like in his Ray Bans, and set off down the valley.

'Talk to me, Lomu. I'm nervous about meeting him.'

'Don't be. Man's cool.'

'What's your story? How did you get the bodyguard gig? You with an agency?'

'Did a favour for Crag and he paid me back.'

'Do I want to know what kind of favour?'

'People were botherin' him. Bad people – bringin' him down, feedin' his weakness. I made 'em go away.'

'Permanently?'

'Man's back to himself now. Healthy. Gonna be big again – takin' us all with him.'

'Okaay . . . What's your favourite Crag film?'

'*Kung Fu Tyrant*. That part where he wastes everyone in the hotel with an M60. Says that cool line at the end.'

'"Now ya got lead poisoning!"'

'That's it.'

'Classic cinema. Truffaut never thought of that.'

'You don't like the man's movies?'

'I suppose they're OK with some popcorn and a beer. I prefer *film* to movies.'

'Wait . . . you drink beer?'

'This has been a great talk, Lomu, but you should concentrate on your driving now.'

He actually smiled.

'Careful,' she said. 'People might think you're getting soft.'

Even from a distance, the set seemed busier. The number of trucks was the same, but there were more extras standing about, more cars and definitely more mopeds as the paparazzi buzzed around for a glimpse of star. At least two TV wagons were present, their dish-transmitters extended on stalks, and there was a rush towards the BMW as it stopped.

'Good luck,' said Lomu. His UV-protected eyes gave nothing away.

She nodded, mouth dry, and stepped out to a barrage of questions and camera clicks that faded immediately when they saw she was a nobody. Everyone turned away – everyone apart from one rodent-faced British guy who pushed a greasy card into her hand and muttered, 'Any insider info. I'll make it worth your while.'

Grace passed through security almost at a run.

Penelope was waiting inside. 'Did you tell him anything?'

'Who? The guy who gave me this card? No. Nothing.'

Penelope took the card distastefully between fingertips. 'Kevin Slate. I'd wash your hands if I were you. He's scum.'

'Oh, OK.'

Something crashed and voices were raised from within mock town square. The director, Tony Brass, strode past with his assistant running behind.

'The atmosphere is a little tense at the moment,' said Penelope. 'We've had some bad news. The Corelli author – Bernie something – is saying we can't use the name. The art department's got to repaint the sign. The script will have to be amended. Also, Chet's causing problems.'

'Really?'

'Method shtick.'

'Right. Does any of this affect Crag? His character changing name, I mean.'

'It's your job to make sure it doesn't affect him. The last thing I need is him snorting half of Peru because he's upset. Trust me, there are people who'll give it to him if he asks.'

Grace forced a smile. She was just the spectral daughter – what was *she* supposed to do?

'Anyway . . . things to organise.' Penelope stalked off towards the security guys at the gate.

Grace walked towards the town square, which was being prepared for the first shot of the movie. Two dozen child mandolin players sat around on benches, all dressed as rustic peasant kids. A guy on a ladder at the rear of the square was amending the sign to read *Captain Cornetto's Mandolin School*. Chet Braddock was among the mandolin kindergarten, wearing a cap with a large feather protruding from it and gesticulating urgently in discussion with the AD.

'There's absolutely no reason why Efthimios would wear a feathered cap,' said the AD. 'This isn't Robin Hood. He's a fisherman for Christ's sake, not Baron von Trapp!'

'I can't tell you *why*,' said Chet. 'I just *feel* he would wear the feather. It's a metaphor for his exuberance, a quill to write his destiny.'

'I'm sorry, Chet. The feather's got to go.'

'Get Tony back here now. I want to hear it from him.'

Grace saw Hans, the assistant camera operator, and wandered over to talk.

'How's it going?' she said.

'It's not. We'd just blocked the shot and locked off when Braddock turned up in the feather.'

'Right. So tell me about the shot.'

'It's a crane shot. We start with the master shot and then move in for the close-up. Tony likes to keep the action going as much as possible. It's better for the actors, too.'

'Can I look at the monitor?'

'Sure. But don't touch anything.'

She made a sarcastic face and stepped behind the camera to observe the screen. It was magic – almost exactly the same view she'd had before, but now framed from above and rendered through the camera's digital brain. This wasn't reality; this was the shot. The shot was greater than reality.

'It looked better,' said Hans. 'When everyone was in position. Before the feather.'

Grace watched transfixed as Tony Brass returned and spoke quietly to Chet. There was some brief resistance, but then the feathered cap was taken away by someone from wardrobe. Granger appeared in shot. She conferred with Brass and there was some nodding.

'Five minutes!' shouted Granger.

The ladder was removed. Extras took their places. Lighting and sound technicians got into position. Wardrobe and make-up made last-minute adjustments to the extras while a continuity girl took photos on a digital camera.

'We're on,' said Hans.

'Oh, yeah. Sorry.' Grace moved out of the way.

The principle camera operator stepped up and Grace watched the shot coalescing before her.

But something seemed wrong. She was doing nothing. With a swelling sense of dread, she snatched the iPad from her bag and jabbed at its screen in search of what she already knew was true. Crag was in this scene. Her job was to manage Crag. Where was Crag? She looked towards the rear and the exit to where the Winnies were. Would it be unseemly to run?

A hand settled on her arm: Granger.

'Don't worry, Grace. He's been told. He came straight here from the airport and said you might not be here for the shot. To be honest, I think he just wanted your first experience of him to be a set-piece: Crag doing what he does. Shall we allow him that little vanity?'

Grace could only nod. She stepped back into the shadows, away from the cameras and the technical crews. She watched Tony Brass take his seat and his assistant hand him a hand monitor so he could view the shot. Everyone seemed to be in place. He nodded and the lights came on.

Someone held an LED clapperboard in front of the camera.

'Action!'

The mandolin children struck up and began to play a piece. Chet sat among them, featherless, but with a discernibly larger instrument. The noise was excruciating, but would be dubbed with soundtrack later. There'd also be a voiceover, according to the shooting notes.

She caught movement at the corner of her eye and felt the atmosphere on set change. It wasn't a sound. It wasn't the light. It wasn't anything anybody did. It was just a sense of something extra – some indefinable element – being in the space.

The tall figure almost brushed her as it passed. She caught a scent of remarkable cologne and watched spellbound from behind as he strode into the scene. Though affecting an old man's gait for the character, his physical presence – those shoulders, those hands – was magnetic.

He walked until he hit his mark and then turned to sit at the centre of the playing children. James Craggan. Craggan of *St Petersburg*. Craggan of *Kung Fu Tyrant*. Craggan of *Cocaine Train* and *Hangman's Noose*. To see him live was to see a rapid montage of his scenes – a face previously known only from a screen.

A toothsome child handed him a mandolin and he began to play along with them, exuding beneficence and good will – he, Captain Cornetto, *pater familias* of a world-leading mandolin academy.

'Cut! That'll do it,' said Tony Brass.

Immediately, the children left their instruments and began to file from the square. Tony Brass strode towards Crag and they shook hands like old friends. Others, too, gathered round, back-slapping, laughing. And Grace realised that the cameras might as well still be rolling. It was a scene written by Crag himself – choreographed in collusion with the director – in order to present himself to her, to establish character and tone. Any moment now . . .

Yes – there it was: the tight close-up. He caught her eye through the crowd of admirers, letting her know he knew she was there and that, amid all the adoration, his thoughts were with her. It was cynical. It was artificial. It worked more powerfully than she could possibly have expected.

He came towards her, sloughing off the others as if emerging from water. Even dressed as an Italo-Greek mandolin instructor, he was uncompromisingly James Craggan – the kind of star (Connery, Ford, Eastwood) who really only ever portrayed himself.

'That was quite a performance,' she said.

His eyes crinkled in mirth. 'They told me you were smart. I knew you would be. I always knew.'

'Always?'

'It's a long story. Look, shall we go to my Winnie while they set up the next shot?'

Grace saw that many people were urgently trying to disguise their interest in this pseudo-father-daughter pair. 'Yes. Let's.'

People parted before him as they walked to the rear exit. Granger nodded some kind of approval. Chet offered a pinkyless wave.

'That's a nice watch you're wearing,' said Crag as the neared the Winnebago.

'It's beautiful,' she said. 'And terrible.'

94

Inside, Crag took two bottles of mineral water from a mini-fridge and waved her to the huge pale leather seats. He passed her a bottle and a glass and sat opposite her as if to study her.

'Well, this isn't awkward,' she said.

'Why is the watch terrible?' he said, leaning back in creaking leather.

'It's not just a watch, is it? It's what it represents. Accepting it is like agreeing to something, but I'm not sure what I'm accepting.'

He sighed. 'I know it's weird. You're young; you have other concerns. When you've lived as many years . . . when you've lived a life like mine, you open up to other things. You begin to understand that there must be more than *this*.' He dismissed the luxury with a gesture. 'I've done bad things, Grace. I can't undo most of them. But some of them I can make right.'

He reached inside his costume and took out a picture about as big as a passport. He skimmed it over the table to Grace. It was a hand-drawn sketch of a girl that looked almost identical to her. The hair was a little longer, but the resemblance was remarkable.

'That was drawn before I ever saw you in LA,' he said. 'It was done during a spectral regression session in New York – a difficult session. We were working through some things, getting in touch with people who got lost along the way. That picture represents the soul of a daughter I never had. And sometimes souls find a way back as the image they *would have* had. Something like reincarnation. So when I saw you on set, I was amazed. The coincidence . . . the resemblance! Sometimes you just have to believe, you know?'

'Look . . . I've got to be honest: I don't believe in any of this.'

'You don't have to. A soul doesn't ever know what might have been.'

'I have parents.'

'Of course you do. But I'm not talking about *actual* parentage. This is beyond that. All I'm asking is that you stick around for the shoot. It's good for me. I need it. Can't we just be buddies for a couple months? Whatever you want to see or learn, I'll make it happen.'

95

'I . . . just don't want to feel owned.'

'Hey, tell me about it! Don't you think the whole world thinks they own *me*? They come up to me like I'm their best friend in the world. They've "known" me for years. What's employment if it isn't ownership? You take your money and you do your monkey dance. It's all about respect in the end. I respect you. I hope you can come to respect me.'

'Do you actually rehearse this stuff?'

He grinned – the same grin as the final shot in *Cocaine Train*. 'How are you getting on with Chen and Lomu?'

'Chen needs to add burgers to his menu. Lomu's a sweetheart inside a granite pillar. You didn't ask about Honee.'

He shrugged, spread his hands and offered an expression that said some habits died harder than others. He raised his glass to drink.

'That *is* water, isn't it?' she said. 'I'm under instructions to check stuff like that.'

He leaned forward and switched the bottles. 'Try it. I'm clean. I'm coming back, Grace. I've wasted too much time.'

'Are you sure *Captain Cornetto's Mandolin School* is the right vehicle?'

'You think it'll be a turkey?'

'I don't know. . . It's got the right cast and crew, but I've seen the script.'

'See? I knew it was right to have you here. You're a fresh perspective. People always tell me what they think I want to hear, not what I need to hear. That's why I have Lomu. That's why I wanted you. Tell me about the script.'

'You haven't read it?'

He shrugged and gave her that star twinkle – a practised close-up.

'Well, where to start? How about the Nazi treasure buried under the mandolin school . . . '

Jim's Apartment, Allomeros, Kefalonia

Jim sat in a white plastic patio chair on his first-floor balcony. He sipped from a tall glass of iced ouzo and swung the worry beads lazily in his other hand as he watched his landlord – a toothless but amiable hunchback – raking at a patch of barren earth. The mountaintops around the village were incandescent against the blue sky. Goat bells clanked and an ethereal wind played about the pine tops in the valley. Peace. Finally.

The few days following the tourists' arrival had been some of the longest and most wretched in his life. As expected, the welcome meeting had been the stuff of nightmares – a highly-nuanced ritual humiliation beginning with some insincere spiel about the island before segueing into a series of gushing lies about the excursions. The Melissani Cave: second only to the Grand Canyon in terms of depth and beauty. The Drogarati Cave: eighth wonder of the world. Myrtos Beach: makes Bondi and Copacabana look like rubbish tips. Fiskardo: a fishing village of such picturesque charm that some people (clinical morons) had been known to faint merely by glancing at a postcard of it.

It had seemed to go reasonably well, apart from the cynical stares, scoffing snorts and sneering superiority exhibited by any Briton faced with a uniformed lackey. Someone at Iliad Holidays – clearly someone with no knowledge of popular culture after 1950 – must have thought that the script was the latest thing in subtle persuasion. Goebbels would have found it laughably obvious. The Q&A session afterwards had been proof enough of that.

Portly slattern: 'OK, so the excursions are fifty euros each. How much is the local bus fare? There's a stop just by the café, isn't there?'

Jim: 'Er, it's two euros . . . but it's been known to crash. Very often. Terrible head injures. And there's no guide.'

Red-faced bigot: 'I've been to the Melissani Cave before. A rip off – not even a proper cave. It's just a hole in the ground with water in it.'

Jim: 'Crystal-clear, fresh water from deep in the island's mountains. You've never seen such remarkable, er, blueness.'

Hatchet-faced pub landlady: 'Is there another beach? This one's a joke.'

Jim: 'Actually, the lovely Chrysos Beach has won an award.'

Scouse stereotype: 'What? "Smallest Buildin' Site"? "Most Used Bog Roll"?'

Jim: 'I think it was something like "Best View".'

Double-chinned half-wit: 'Where's the best place to get fuckin' smashed?'

Jim: 'All of the bars serve alcohol. Although you should be aware that the free shots they offer are often made of raw spirit.

Scouse stereotype: 'Bring it on!'

Querulous pensioner: 'Where's the best place to eat, young man?'

Jim: 'I'm not really supposed to recommend particular places but [clutching the fifty euros pressed on him by the owner of "Spiti" five minutes before the welcome meeting] "Spiti" is an excellent choice.'

Brummie racist: 'Our accommodation is shit. Can we move to one of them lively resorts with a beach on the south coast?'

Jim: 'Alas, no. When you selected the last-minute, no-choice, low-budget option, you consigned yourself to this remote outpost for the duration of your holiday. Serves you and your bulldog-faced wife right for being so tight, you tattooed prick. And don't forget, it's quiz night on Thursday!'

Or words to that effect. The real complaints had started next day when he'd stopped at each accommodation for his visiting hours. Evidently, the tourists had been studying the hastily-affixed (and still incomplete) welcome boards well in advance and had put aside some hours to work themselves into the requisite apoplectic frenzy. During the subsequent spittle-flecked tantrums – most of them containing the ludicrous threat to sue – Jim had offset the impotent humiliation by mentally compiling a top ten complaints list, which he planned to perfect in coming weeks. So far, he had:

1) No kettle. (Because the critical thing on arriving in a new and exotic place is to have a nice cup of tea, just like at home.)

2) No sink plugs. (Who would have thought that the inability to fill a sink would reduce a grown man to weeping?)

3) Lightbulbs broken. (A perfectly legitimate complaint, but one that would only be remedied by the tourists going to the mini-market and buying bulbs themselves.)

4) Beds broken. (Might be the joints, might be the slats, might be the headboard. Usually all three. Just don't turn the mattress over.)

5) Black mould on ceiling. (Natch.)

6) No wheelchair access. (None of the tourists has or needs a wheelchair.)

7) No shower curtain. (The bathroom is a marble box – get over it.)

8) Mosquitoes. (Might as well add "heat" and "Greeks".)

9) No bank, car hire, petrol station, ferry, regular bus service or good shops. (But look at the lovely beach!)

10) The taxi drivers go too fast. (A bit esoteric, this one. May slip out of the top ten)

Then, of course, there had been the issue with the Pearsons, the insipid couple on Jim's coach who he'd turfed out at a grim Communist-style block on the way to Exogi. If he'd bothered to tick his passenger manifest, he would have known that their hotel was actually in Argostoli. Apparently, they'd waited for hours before flagging down a local bus and making their own way to the right place. Their phone call to Donna had been ill-tempered. Hers to Jim in the resort office had left him partially deaf in one ear. It was his first verbal warning.

But now that was all in the past, like the Holocaust or the Native American genocide. Today was for relaxation. A cool drink, a stroll around Allomeros to find the ancient site and this bar that everyone kept talking about. Later, perhaps a nap and some quality self-abuse while fantasising about Philippa. In the evening, he'd put on the polyester clown costume and blag a free meal from

Apicius, then maybe a free Metaxa at Kyanni Akti. Philippa might come by, swishing her ponytail, and suggest popping into the resort office for some animalistic sex.

The ice rattled at the bottom of his glass. Myrtos Beach was only a ten-minute drive. Perhaps he'd go there first and have a swim. There was supposed to be a vicious rip current according to a guy he'd spoken to at Maria's *psistaria*, but he'd just avoid that part of the shore. Drowning would at least give him a good excuse to avoid the impending quiz night.

A car crunched over the gravel of the driveway. Jim stood to see who it might be. It was the policeman from Exogi.

The landlord hobbled over and exchanged a few words with the policeman. The landlord's wife – gold teeth, some sort of congenital deformity – emerged from their flat, handing the policeman a bunch of fresh herbs and some newly-laid eggs. He seemed to ask a question and all three looked up to see Jim standing on the balcony.

Jim waved, immediately feeling like an imbecile, and the policeman strode for the staircase up to the flat. Please let it be a tourist fatality rather than the occasional drunken drive back from Exogi in the company car.

'You are Jim?' said the policeman in English. 'With Iliad Holidays?'

'Yes?'

The policeman studied him quite casually, seeming to assess his footwear, his clothing, his build and his general level of grooming. All the while, his moustache twitched in apparent amusement.

'Is there a problem?' said Jim.

'Some of your tourists are sick.'

'Trust me, they're all sick.'

The policeman didn't smile. 'You must come with me to the health centre in Sami.'

'It's OK – I can drive there.'

100

'But you have been drinking, no? I can smell it. Do you regularly drive after drinking?'

'Never. No. Can't I go tomorrow? It's my day off today and . . . '

'They are very sick. You don't care?'

Jim sought an expression of professional concern, but it was beyond him. Back to lies, then: 'I care. Of course I do.'

'I will wait in my car. You will get dressed.'

Jim looked down at his oil-blotched shorts and the t-shirt with a Jackson Pollock of chocolate sauce down it. What was he *supposed* to wear at home – a smoking jacket and a silk cravat?

The policeman nodded in approval when Jim emerged wearing a clean shirt and long trousers. He opened the passenger door beside him and Jim settled into the smoky interior.

'You don't mind if I smoke,' said the policeman.

'That wasn't a question, was it?' said Jim.

The policeman merely smiled and swung an arm behind Jim's seat to reverse the car. A printed icon dangled from the rear-view mirror and the foot wells were littered with paper bags from the baker's in Exogi.

'He does a great *tiropita*,' said Jim, pointing to the bags.

'You should try the *loukanokopita* or the *zambontiri*.'

'Your English is good.'

'Good for Exogi. Good enough. Tell me – are you a homosexual?'

'No . . . no, not even a little bit. What are people saying?'

'It is not people. It was a report. It says English men are mostly homosexual. They are afraid of women and must drink to approach them. It says that English men prefer the dog position so they can think about boys. Is this so?'

'What report? Is it a joke?'

'Not a joke. It is to help us understand our British guests. You have a very problematic culture. Is that the right word?'

101

'"Problematic"? It might be better to say we have no culture – just alcohol and TV. But I don't think you can say most Englishmen are gay. It's probably about the same percentage in every country.'

'Not in Greece.'

'Are you serious? You virtually invented it! I've seen the ancient vases.'

'Not in Greece.'

'Right.'

They passed the *kafenio* in Exogi and all the old men looked up from their coffees. Great. In thirty seconds the entire village would know that Jim had been taken away by the police. In a minute more, Kelly from Golden Holidays would know and the nearest mobile mast would be thrumming with her gossip bulletins. In five minutes, Donna would know and would begin to speculate on the possible reasons.

The policeman seemed to be sulking. Time for some hearty heterosexual banter? 'What do Greek women go for? I mean, how can I make myself interesting to them? No, really . . . Why are you . . . ? I'm serious.'

The laughing fit went on for some seconds before the policeman was able to speak. 'First, you should pretend to be German or Scandinavian. All Englishmen are gay, remember?'

'I see.'

'Have you heard of the *kamakia*?'

'The vampires who descend on tourist towns for the summer to prey on female tourists? Of course.'

'Not vampires. You should watch them and learn. They have a different woman every night. Sometimes two.'

Jim brooded. If the only way of getting laid was to affect unironic machismo to a sociopathic degree, his prospects didn't seem good. And yet, perhaps there was something in it. Look at all the Yiannises. Beneath every woman's demand to be taken seriously as a sapient and equal human being was

102

also apparently the desire to be subjugated by an ape. It was a thought to worry over as they approached Sami.

'Why is this a police matter anyway?' said Jim. 'I mean, tourists end up in hospital all the time. Drinking. Sunburn. Moped accidents. Suicide attempts. Sometimes all at once.'

'We will see. I need your help. Some of them speak a kind of English I don't understand.'

The police car slipped into a parking space with a wheelchair painted on it and they got out. At reception, the policeman flirted outrageously and at some length with the classically beautiful girl who didn't seem to notice Jim.

'This way,' said the policeman, finally, having proved his masculine credentials beyond all doubt.

They went along a corridor to a ward in which three people lay in beds. Jim immediately recognised the Scouser from the welcome meeting. Now, however, the man's face was burned a radioactive scarlet except for the pale and finely delineated outline of a pair of sunglasses. He looked like a superhero. The Goggler. Captain Dickhead. A saline drip fed into his forearm.

The patient beside him was the double-chinned half-wit who had asked about the best place to "get fuckin' smashed". Unfortunately, her intention had proven more literal than she expected. Her entire face was swathed in bandages so that only her eyes and a pineapple-like effusion of frizzy blonde hair revealed her identity. *The (Single) Mummy Returns.*

In the third bed lay the Brummie racist. Only half of his face was hideously sunburnt, but his left arm was in cast and the unburned part of his face showed road-rash where he'd evidently come off a moped. Or been run over. Or perhaps fallen from a balcony.

'It's not fuckin' funny!' growled the Scouser.

'This one,' said the policeman in Greek. 'What language does he speak?'

'What's he sayin'?' said the Scouser.

'Mf hmmff m hmmfff n nfff!' said the bandaged slapper.

103

'I'm gonna sue Iliad Holidays so badly I'll own you!' said the Brummie.

'And this one, too,' said the policeman. 'I recognise only some words.'

'Calm down, calm down!' said Jim, avoiding the Scouser's chemo-glare. 'Who's going to tell me what happened here?'

'Hnff n hfff mf ffnnuf fnnnn!'

'Not you,' said Jim.

'Someone poisoned our shots!' said the Scouser. 'They were handin' 'em out like sweeties and so we all 'ad a few, like. It were 'arsh stuff but it did the job. Only, it all went mental after that. I thought me hands were meltin' and I . . . I shat meself.'

'I got on a moped to go back to the room,' said the Brummie. 'I thought I was flying a Spitfire. I thought I was in a dogfight with them spaceships out of *Independence Day*. I crashed in a field and woke up next afternoon.'

'Did you also soil yourself?' said Jim, all solicitude.

'You little bastard! If I wasn't in this bed . . . '

'What does he say?' said the policeman. 'Is it English?'

'I passed out on the beach and woke up about two in the afternoon,' said the Scouser. 'With me face burning red like a fuckin' tomater and me shorts all full of shit. The flies were terrible!'

'What happened to her?' said Jim. 'Does anyone know?'

'Someone made her laugh while she was lightin' a fag,' said the Scouser. 'She sprayed a shot out her nose. Fireball like fuckin' Nagasaki. Her face's like a burger under all that.'

'Mf hnnn mfuhununa hmf!'

'This is all very . . . ,' said Jim.

'What's *he* doing here?' said the Brummie, pointing at the policeman.

'What does he say?' said the policeman.

'He's asking why you're here.'

'A number of reasons,' said the policeman. 'This man stole the moped he crashed. He rode it while drunk and then destroyed it. There will be a fine.'

104

'I see.'

'What's he sayin'?' said the Scouser? 'Why don't you speak English?'

'This one,' said the policeman. 'He did not pay for his drinks.'

'Hmm. A matter of an unpaid bill,' said Jim to the scouser.

'My 'ands were meltin', man! I'd shat meself!'

'This is not a normal reaction to drinking shots,' said the policeman. 'Even with the British. The alcohol may have been contaminated. Blood tests are being done. I ask you not to tell them this until we have results.'

'Why?'

'It is not good for business if people go to a lawyer because they had poison in one of our bars. It is better for them to believe it was their own fault for drinking too much.'

'I absolutely agree.'

'What are you two talking about?' said the Brummie. 'Don't you know it's rude to talk in a foreign language if we don't understand! I'm gonna sue you so hard that I'll own the shirt on your back!'

'Can this one be sedated?' said Jim to the policeman. 'And given a saline enema?'

'That is not medically necessary.'

'As a favour to me, then. Say it's a detox or something.'

'As you wish.'

'Is there anything else I can do here, or can I enjoy the rest of my day off?'

'Do whatever you must. These people will not be released until they have paid whatever they owe. The woman may be here until her holiday is finished. I will call you if I discover anything more. Do you mind taking the bus back to Exogi?'

'I suppose not. I might try a *zambontiropita* at the bakery.'

The policeman gave a slight bow and a smile.

'What are you two bloody saying?' said the Brummie, quite unaware of the impending rectal invasion.

105

Mini-market, Exogi, Kefalonia

Sergeant Nikos had spent a good half hour talking to the receptionist at the medical centre, getting her mobile number before returning to the mini-market in Exogi. Now he stood before a dusty shelf of home-improvement materials and studied them carefully. There were tins of paint whose contents must surely have solidified; there were bathroom sealants and adhesives long past their optimum usefulness; there were sundry tools imported from China, many of them already broken. Prices in drachmas had been crossed out and appended with prices in euros. The exchange rate was highly unfavourable.

More importantly, there was a row of spray-paint cans. They were faded and featured images of outdated supercars. Circles in the dust indicated where two of the cans had recently been removed.

He walked around the store pretending to look at other things, knowing that the owner Evangelos was watching him carefully in the convex mirror above the checkout. The presence of his uniform here was like the scent of a fox to chickens, and these people of Allomeros and Exogi were all chickens in their way – all hoarding their secret eggs from authority as they pecked humbly away at their grain. Nothing to see here, Mr Fox. No illegal still, no greenhouse full of cannabis, no shed of tobacco smuggled from Albania via Corfu, no cash-only transactions because the till had been regrettably broken since 1992.

Still, Greeks will be Greeks. The fox and the chicken must play their game. Even a policeman had to accept that. As long as an acceptable level of order could be maintained, there was no need to bring the law into it. What was the law anyway except a loose set of guidelines? Interpretation was the thing. Everything was an interpretation in the end – otherwise, one might as well be living in Germany.

He picked up a child's mask-and-snorkel set. The rubber in the mask had perished and a mummified spider was lodged in the tube. At least the price was up to date.

106

He went to the checkout, where Evangelos was ostentatiously attempting to fix the receipt roll in the till, tutting and clucking his impatience that he was unable to give his customers the proof-of-purchase they so ardently desired.

'I was hoping to buy some black spray-paint but there's none left,' said Nikos.

'Oh? Did you look on the shelf?'

'Of course.'

'Well, I'm not really expecting new stock for quite a while . . . '

'I need only a little. It's for a scratch on the police car. Do you remember who bought the last cans? Maybe they'll let me have a quick spray of theirs.'

'No . . . no I can't remember.'

'Do you sell many cans of spray-paint?'

'Not so many . . . ' Evangleos fiddled nervously with the till.

'Whoever bought them must have done so recently – you can see the circles in the dust. I'm surprised you can't remember. Shall we have a look at your till roll for the last few days? I'm sure there'll be a record of the purchase.'

'The till roll? I . . . oh, I remember now. It was one of the kids.'

'From where? Exogi? Allomeros? Makryotika?'

'I didn't recognise him. He must have come from somewhere else.'

'Describe him.'

'They all look the same, don't they? Long hair, dark clothes – some kind of design on his t-shirt . . . a star? A cross? Something from the zodiac maybe.'

'Did you hear him leave or arrive on a moped?'

'A motorbike. One of those with the knobbly wheels. I saw the back of it.'

'Did he buy anything else?'

'One of these.' Evangelos pointed to a dusty rack holding blister-packed scalpels with extra blades.

'Is it good to be selling these to kids?'

'Eh, I'm a shopkeeper, not a schoolteacher. I blame computer games.'

'Naturally. Well, I wish you good luck with your till.'

Nikos strolled towards the main street. The owner of No Name was serving beer to an English couple with frighteningly red faces. On glimpsing the uniform, he looked up with unconvincing pleasure.

'Sergeant Petras! Welcome! Will you have a drink? On the house, of course! Here – sit here in the shade.'

'It's OK. I'll stand at the bar.'

The owner offered a fractured smile and scuttled back behind the bar.

'What will you have, sergeant? A cool beer? No – a whisky. Johnnie Black, eh? Only the best for our policeman!'

'I'm on duty. I'll have a frappe, *sketo.*'

'Right away.'

The owner busied himself with the coffee and electric whisk while the sergeant's eyes ranged over the bottles behind the bar. It was all the usual things: garish coloured liqueurs for cocktails, a dusty bottle of cognac, something with a floating abomination that might have been a chilli pepper or a worm. And one oversize bottle fastened to the mirrored wall in an optic bracket. There was no label and the contents were clear, albeit with an apparently oily residue. It was half full.

'Maybe I will have a quick shot,' he said. 'What's that one on the end?'

'Ha! You don't want that, Sergeant. We use it in the "special" cocktails. For tourists.'

'What is it? Vodka?'

'Vodka, yes. Something very like vodka.'

'A shot wouldn't hurt. Just squirt one in a plastic cup for me. I don't want to dirty your glasses.'

'I really wouldn't recommend—'

The sergeant's stare was uncompromising. The owner reached up to the optic and passed the plastic cup across the bar. His expression was one of earnest exculpation. He wouldn't answer to any consequences.

Nikos sniffed and recoiled. It was like petrol or white spirit with a tarry, oily note that remained unpleasantly in the nose. 'I think I won't drink that.'

'Excellent choice, Sergeant.'

'But I will take it with me. I need to clean some tar spots off my car.'

'Ha! Yes, yes – that's probably the best use for it.'

The sergeant sipped his *frappe* and watched the English couple order more beer. The woman looked miserable. Her clothes did nothing for her figure. Rather, her flesh was pulled tautly into rolls and pouches and lumps by the ill-fitting swimsuit and sarong. She drank the beer with no evident pleasure in its taste or coolness. Only the alcohol seemed to matter. Why not just inject a couple of shots into a vein and be done with it? Her husband looked even more morose, drinking as if it was his duty.

'Why do they sit here drinking?' he said to the bar owner. 'Why don't they go to the beach?'

'I don't know, Sergeant. I don't care. They sit here until two and they come back at seven, staying until midnight. It's good for business.'

Nikos shook his head. Such were the mysteries of national culture.

'I heard you've been helping the movie people,' said the bar owner.

'Where did you hear that?'

'You know – just around. Did you hear about Hannah Caro?'

'Go on.'

'They say she picked up a young guy in a bar in Sami and took him back to her place. By the time she'd finished with him, he needed medical attention. Dehydration, exhaustion and chafing, they say.'

'Fantasy. She probably had one drink there and went home alone.'

'If you say so, Sergeant.'

He brooded. Captain Bastounis had apparently had a meeting with the production company's head of security and a fierce woman called Penelope. They were having problems with the paparazzi and wanted to know if the police could help. The land on which the main set was constructed was privately

109

owned, they said – could intruders be charged with trespassing? Might some of the paparazzi be guilty of riding their mopeds without a helmet or applicable licence?

It was an awkward position that Captain Bastounis had put him in. There was only one cell – really just a room with a lock – at the police office in Exogi and the paperwork involved in any such minor charges was just too tiresome to bother with. It was basically state-sanctioned bullying so that Bastounis could be invited to celebrity parties and meet Hannah Caro. Besides, there were many more important things to do. Adulterous affairs to be maintained, *zambontiropites* to be eaten, the delicate local equilibrium of petty rivalries and minor crimes to be maintained. The movie was a nuisance.

'*Opa!* Here's comes the *pappas!*' said the bar owner, disappearing into the back room.

The sergeant looked up and saw Xenomachos swishing towards the bar with great purpose. He was carrying a plastic bag.

'Greetings to you, *pappas,*' said the sergeant. 'Will you have a *frappe?*'

'Forget *frappe*. The devil is among us.'

'At the No Name bar? What does he drink?'

Xenomachos furiously rustled the plastic bag. 'Laugh now, Sergeant, when you see the instruments of evil!' He emptied the contents of the bag on to the bar: a small terracotta oil-burner and a stiff rabbit corpse with ants crawling over it.

'What are you doing, *pappas?* You can't bring dead animals into a bar like this.'

'This was found at the site in Allomeros: gutted and laid out in ritual posture. The oil-burner was in the long grass to one side – obviously dropped. Do you understand what this means, Petras? *Sacrifice!* They are now sacrificing animals to their heathen gods! See how the fur is charred? Smell the burner – there is incense in it. What is next? Will children begin disappearing from our homes?'

110

'Wait,' said Nikos. 'Isn't it possible that you've misunderstood the signs?'

'No. A man, a hunter, does not shoot a rabbit only to leave it gutted inside the wire of a closed-off ancient site. There is no bullet hole or trap marks on this rabbit – only a mark where its spine was cut. See?' The priest stuck the end of his little finger into the hole.

'What do you want me to do, *pappas*? Rabbit murder is not a crime. If people want to burn aromatic oil, they can.'

'That is not the true crime here and you know it. Have you made further enquiries since the last time I came to you?'

'I've turned up nothing.'

'What enquiries did you make?'

'I don't ask you about the mysteries of *your* profession, *pappas*.'

'You did nothing, didn't you?'

'Would you have me camp at the ancient site with night-vision equipment? Or perhaps you'd like me to visit everyone in Allomeros and ask if they've worshipped an Olympian recently.'

'Not everyone – just those who don't attend church.'

'I think you overestimate the purity of your congregation.'

'Do not imagine you can win with these clever words and evasions, Petras. There is a higher law. There are men with vision who understand the mortal threat we face.'

'Which men?'

'Never mind which men. I know where they are and I will contact them.'

'That's your right, *pappas*.'

'Yes, yes it is. And what are you going to do about the tourists?'

'The tourists? What do you mean?'

'Have you not seen them vomiting and drunkenly fornicating on the streets at night?'

'They can't help it, *pappas*. It's their culture, their psychology. I've read a report on the subject.'

111

'You will be first into the fires of Hell, Petras! You and your whores!'

The priest departed in a gust of agitation and midnight silk.

'You forgot your pagan rabbit!' called Nikos.

The bar owner appeared from the backroom and frowned at the furry corpse. 'Heathen sacrifice? That's a new one.'

'He's insane,' muttered Nikos. He took the oil-burner and sniffed it. There was some sort of fragrance – something exotic that he couldn't quite place: earthy and somehow floral. He wrapped it in napkins from the bar and put it in his trouser pocket. 'Thanks for the coffee.'

'Aren't you going to take your rabbit?' shouted the bar owner as Nikos left.

'Keep it. The gods have smiled on it.'

'Eh?'

Nikos walked back to the office, being careful not to spill the raw alcohol in the plastic cup. A friend in Patras would be able to tell him whether it might be related to the recent accidents. In the meantime, there were a few more calls to make. The ferry had only recently left Sami and Aliki would be home alone.

The rabbit ended up on the specials menu at Spiti.

Exogi Main Street, Kefalonia

Jim left the hated Seat Marbella parked at an angle, unlocked and with the windows open. He was contractually obliged to have it washed once a week to maintain the pristine reputation of the Iliad brand, but he'd been somewhat remiss. The left-hand wing mirror was missing (knocked off by a lamp post someone had put in the wrong place), Allomeros dust coated the paintwork, and the windscreen was splattered with a vast eruption from some passing seabird. He'd put the Iliad "How can I help you?" window sticker on upside-down – a puerile gesture, but satisfying nonetheless.

So this was Exogi in its full tourist splendour. Bars and restaurants all along the main street cast light and music into the night: *bouzouki*, throbbing Euro-techno, strobes, neon, and flickering strip-lights illuminating photographic menus in which every dish looked like an illicit vivisection shot. People strolled or staggered – red-faced and gaudily-attired – through gauntlets of restaurant wranglers who sidled and whispered identical mantras of '*tzatziki*, Greek salad, *moussaka*, *taramasalata*, octopus, feta, olives, *soutzoukaikia* – good food, please, please . . . '

The air was full of grilling meat and fish, cigarette smoke, holiday perfume, after-sun lotion, fresh-washed hair, moped fumes, beer and saccharine liquors. Laughs, shouts, revving engines and the ever-plashing sea played beneath it all. Women bared bounteous cleavages and pinkened thighs to the darkness and to lurking *kamakia*. Men wore their tattoos as tribal markings and flexed scorched muscles with atavistic impulse. It was an anthropological case study playing out simultaneously across the Mediterranean – the northern peoples heading south to see what light and life was like.

But not for Jim. In his jester's garb of Iliad shirt and shorts, *he* was required to chair the inaugural quiz night at No Name. His hope that nobody would be interested had been proved wrong and fourteen people had paid money to replicate the experience they were used to having at home in Manchester or Liverpool or Wigan. Well, this wouldn't be quite what they were used to.

They were sitting in a circle, their tables pushed together and loaded with drinks. The owner flashed a capitalistic wink from the bar and nodded his approval. Jim fought the same sort of nausea he'd felt at the welcome meeting and waved a greeting to the tourists.

''Aven't yer got 'andouts?' said a man with a lacquered comb-over.

'You've got to 'ave a picture round!' offered his wife (or brother).

'No, no,' said Jim. 'This is strictly low-tech – Greek rules.'

113

Translation: I didn't want to drive to Argostoli on my day off to spend my own money on a book of quiz questions, so I've made some up instead. Quizzes are for morons, anyway.

'What's the prize?' said a glassy-eyed girl who – Jim knew, *everyone* knew – had already been through most of the town's *kamakia*.

'It's on the ticket, yer daft cow!' said her friend, who was less promiscuous only by dint of her remarkable corpulence. 'It's a tab at the bar.'

'*Woo-hoo!*' cheered the group.

Jim pulled out a chair beside a young man who'd come on holiday alone and who smelled of antiseptic. 'Right – here are the rules. I'll read out a question. First person to put their hand up gets to answer. If you just shout out, you lose a turn.'

'That's not how it works!' said the hatchet-faced pub landlady. 'You have to have handouts!'

'I might have mentioned a few seconds ago that there are no handouts in this quiz—'

'And a picture round!' said the wife/sibling.

'So – let's begin,' said Jim, taking a folded piece of paper from his shorts pocket. 'Hands at the ready!'

They grumbled among themselves.

'Question one! What's the name of the Platonic dialogue in which the philosopher relates the trial of his tutor Socrates?'

Silence.

'No? Bit of a tough one. Anyone? No? OK, I'll give you the first one. It was *The Apologia* – not to be confused with the modern meaning of our word "apology".'

They looked at him.

'Never mind. Question two: Hercules kills a number of mythical creatures in his twelve labours. One was the Nemean lion. Can you name another?'

Silence.

114

'A mythical creature . . . ?' he prompted.

'The sphinx!' said Antiseptic Boy.

'You didn't raise your hand,' said Jim. 'You lose a turn. And it's wrong anyway.'

Hatchet-faced woman raised an eager hand.

'Yes?'

'That woman with snakes instead of hair . . . er . . . Oh God, it's on the tip of—'

'Medusa?' said Jim.

'Yes! Yes! That's her!'

'Wrong. Perseus killed *her*. I think I'll have to tell you. There was the Lernaen hydra, the Stymphalian birds, the Erymanthian boar—'

'What kind of bloody questions are these?' said Comb-over. 'Where's the sport and TV questions?'

Muttered assent went round the table.

'Sport and TV?' said Jim. 'Right. Let's see . . . Ah yes. Question seven: what was the name of the fighting event in the ancient Olympics? Something like mixed martial arts these days.'

Silence. They looked at each other. They looked at Jim.

'It helps if you think etymologically.'

Antiseptic Boy thrust up a yearning hand.

'Yes?'

'Insects!'

'You're thinking of *ento*mology. And "insects" is hardly the name of an Olympic event, is it?'

The rest didn't look like they were seriously considering the question.

'OK. I'll give you a clue. The prefix *pan*– means "all" and the term *kratos* is the same as in "demo*cracy*". It means "strength". So the event was called . . . anyone? Anyone? It was the *pankratia*. *Pan-kratia*. See?'

'This is shit,' muttered Comb-over.

115

'OK, OK – I've got a TV one,' said Jim. 'On the second of October 1925, the first television transmission—'

'John Logie Baird!' shouted Hatchet Face.

'Let me finish . . . was made by John Logie Baird. But how many pictures per second were scanned on to the rudimentary thirty-line vertical image?'

Silence.

'Are you taking the piss?' said Unattractive Friend.

'Eighteen million,' said a man whose nose was sun-burned almost to down the cartilage.

'You didn't raise your hand.'

Kamaki-comforter raised her hand. 'Eighteen million.'

'No. You were almost there. It was five pictures per second. Bad luck.'

'Are they all like this?' said Comb-over. 'This isn't *Mastermind* – it's a pub quiz.'

Jim scanned the questions. The categories were all somewhat esoteric. The tourists were staring at him. Would it be a bad idea just to make something up on the spot?

'OK – let's try some easier ones,' he said. '*The Naked and the Dead* was the debut novel of which American writer?'

Fourteen angry faces looked back at him.

'Dan Brown?' said Hatchet Face.

'Yes! That's right!' said Jim as Norman Mailer tossed and writhed in his grave.

A weak cheer went around the table. Better keep the momentum going.

'Next one. Which notable moustache-wearer featured in the famous First World War recruitment posters?'

A pause. A longer pause. Too tricky?

'Adam Woodyatt!' shrieked *Kamaki*-comforter.

'I'm not sure I can accept . . . '

'Ian! Ian Beale from *EasterEnders*!'

Jim scanned the faces around the table. Surely *somebody* was going to contradict her? Did any of them really think that soap actor Woodyatt was more than a hundred years old?

'Yes – it was Ian Beale,' he sighed as Lord Kitchener wailed across the abyss of history.

'But Ian hasn't even got a moustache anymore!' said Burned Nose.

'He had one in the First World War!' said *Kamaki*-comforter. 'Isn't that right, Jim?'

'Y-yes. That's right. Back when he was an aristocratic army general . . . before he became an actor.'

Hatchet Face stood. 'I'm going. This is a bloody joke. Everybody knows it was Churchill in those pictures. You're just making these answers up. I'm complaining about you.'

Comb-over stood. 'Me, too. I'll be writing a letter to your boss.'

Jim shrugged, earnestly apologetic. You can write?

'I want a refund,' said Burned Nose.

There was a chorus of 'Me, toos.'

'You'll have to ask the owner about that,' said Jim. 'He's holding the money behind the bar. I'm sorry you didn't like the quiz. We might have to postpone them for the next few weeks while I research some questions about football and reality shows.'

With that, he made a dignified but precipitous exit from the bar, using palm trees for cover as he headed for Apicius at the end of town. The cacophony of raised voices from No Name soon faded and he left the lights of the main street to venture along the promenade building site.

The electricity for the street lights had been turned off and the pot-holed road was a health-and-safety assault course. Bags of cement lay solidified on pallets; mounds of sand were rut-riven by rain and tyre tracks; stacks of marble blocks spilled into trenches; earth moving machinery squatted idle and rusting. As he picked his way through, the percussive gasps of hurried coitus came to

117

him from the bushes and he peered into the shadows to see thighs splayed either side of a standing male: a *kamaki* making his first conquest of the evening. Call him Ishmael.

Jim walked quietly so as not to disturb the rutting couple. Or, rather, to avoid having to make eye-contact with either of them. The lights of Apicius now appeared round the corner – a prize for those gourmands who were willing to risk the trials of the building site.

And the smells. The smells! Garlic in olive oil, meat and fish grilled over charcoal, octopus in red wine sauce, frying calamari, fruit in syrup, fresh-cut cucumber and tomato, barrel-aged *feta* and *graviera* cheeses, caramelised sugar, hot chocolate sauce, brandy flambé, the anise tang of ouzo. Jim's stomach gurgled in anticipation of epic gluttony and he hurried his step through cracked puddle beds.

'*Herete!*' said the owner on seeing Jim emerge from the darkness. Portly in his kitchen whites, his eyes played lovingly over the branded uniform and he sat Jim directly beneath a light that illuminated the large Iliad Holidays logo across the shoulders.

Human billboard Jim had no need of the menu. 'I'll take some *horta*, fava, *soutzoukakia, kolokythokeftedes* and . . . the *kalamarakia*.'

'*Malista*. And to drink?'

'A big water. Zagoria if you've got it.'

'*Amesos!*'

The owner raised his voice just slightly so his tourist clientele might notice that no lesser a personage than the official Iliad Holidays rep had chosen to eat here.

The Zagoria water came chilled and perspiring in its glass bottle, drawn from mountain springs in the wild north-west of the country. The *horta* – steamed spring greens – was served with slivers of garlic and a generous dousing of olive oil. To this, Jim added a good squeeze of lemon and forked the leaves dripping into an intemperate mouth. The pureed fava beans came next, topped

118

with fresh-diced onion, sprinkled paprika and a deluge of oil. Jim stirred the dish and alternated mouthfuls of this and the *horta*, stopping only to tear off hunks of bread and soak them in the pools of peppery green oil. If this wasn't heaven, then heaven wasn't worth seeing.

He'd virtually licked the plates clean when the *soutzoukakia* – meatballs in tomato sauce – arrived with an accompanying mound of steaming rice. Jim called for more bread and slid the plate closer to savour the seasoned beef. The courgette balls and fried squid followed in rapid succession and so began the frenzy of greedy-eater's roulette. A mouthful of meat, a mouthful of squid, a mouthful of rice, a dab of bread, a fork of *horta*, a scrape of fava, a jostle of courgette ball and meatball – one in each cheek like a feeding hamster. His shirtfront was marbled with stains and smears. His chin glistened. The table was littered with crusts and drops of oil and tomato sauce.

Barely twenty minutes later, he leaned back in his chair, lightheaded from the rush of blood to his bowels and clutching his stomach like a woman in the latter stages of pregnancy. The owner strolled over and offered an indulgent grin. Here was a customer who enjoyed his food – not like those faddy northern European diners who put health above pleasure and asked about calorie counts, gluten and nuts.

'Dessert?' he enquired.

'I think . . . I'm going to haemorrhage,' said Jim.

'I have an excellent chocolate pudding with brandy double cream.'

'I . . . I can't say no to that.'

The owner nodded and the plates were cleared. Jim slumped under the weight of his indulgence. An ouzo, perhaps? Something powerful to act as a *digestif?*

'Breaking the rules again?'

He looked up and saw Philippa standing beside his table with Kelly. Both were dressed in civilian clothes: Philippa in skin-tight satiny trousers and a form-fitting blouse, Kelly in a Lycra-based dress that barely withheld her boulder breasts.

Great. And here was he: sweating with greed and covered in food.

'Looks like yer need a bib!' said Kelly.

'Looks like you need a doctor,' said Philippa.

'I enjoy my food,' he said.

'We 'eard about your quiz night!' said Kelly. 'Classic!'

'Classics,' said Philippa, an ironic smirk playing about her gorgeous lips.

'Would you like to join me for a drink?' he said.

'Are yer suggestin' a threesome?' said Kelly.

Philippa cocked an eyebrow, not discernibly shocked or surprised.

'No! I didn't mean that . . . but, you know . . . if, well, you know . . . go with the flow. That's what I say.'

Kelly nudged Philippa and laughed throatily. 'Got a sweet tooth, have yer, Jimbo?'

The owner arrived with the hot chocolate pudding and laid it before Jim. It was swimming in a heart-clogging sauce.

'Ooh, I love chocolate!' said Philippa. 'Can I?' She took his spoon and sliced a half-moon of dark matter, raising it to an ardent mouth and welcoming it with a tongue that emerged languorously to cup the convex curve of the spoon. 'Hmmm! Hmmm! *Hmmmm!*'

Jim felt a vital stirring in his Iliad shorts. He jealously regarded the spoon's handle quivering as Philippa – eyes closed – worked it inside her mouth. Don't faint. Don't faint.

Kelly laughed like an end-of-the-pier comedian doing smut jokes.

Philippa returned the spoon, shining clean. 'Sorry, Jim, but we're meeting friends. She nodded to a corner of the patio and he turned to see two Greeks, one of them presumably Yiannis – hulking, hirsute, Hellenic – and the other apparently a professional athlete. Probably had a torso like bodybuilder. Six-pack. Biceps like thighs. A vast penile anaconda furled in his Calvin Klein briefs. *His* shirt wasn't covered in stains.

'Bon appétit, Jim!' said Philippa. 'We might be going to Diogenes' bar up in Allomeros later if you want to have a drink.' She touched his shoulder and glided across to her date.

He nodded, but she hadn't seen. Did the "we" include the gorilla twins? He watched Philippa's satiny buttocks catching the light and felt a resurgence of hunger. Thank god for the chocolate pudding.

Should he request a new spoon? Or should he rest his own tongue where hers had been? The thought set his shorts a-tremor once more. Had she done it on purpose? Was it flirtation, or had the two of them just been mocking him? Why would she mention Diogenes' bar if she had no interest?

He set about the chocolate pudding, making cunnelingual love to the spoon with every mouthful. A large ouzo followed, then a sweet Greek coffee. All the while, he covertly turned to see whether Philippa was laughing at the sparkling wit of her date, or fellating *his* spoon.

When he waddled back towards his car, it was with the ballast of the meal weighing his every step and the ouzo soothing the periphery of consciousness. The next day was his day off and the night was still young. Perhaps a trip to Diogenes' bar was in order.

Allomeros, Kefalonia

Grace walked carefully along dry earth path and knew for certain that she shouldn't have worn the sandals. She bent to pick another stone from under her sole.

Tonight had been designated "private time" for Crag and Honee. The staff had been told to take the evening off. Chen had gone to gather some sort of

121

aromatic night flower he claimed had medicinal properties, while Lomu had gone into Sami to fill up on pizza and *souvlaki* with some of the other security personnel. She would have liked to hear their gossip, but it was strictly a guy thing, apparently.

And so here she was: wandering the village in search of this bar they'd told her about. It seemed that, at any moment, she might come across a crumbling cliff that fell away into a steaming void: the actual, literal end of the world. How could anyone live here? Still, it was pleasantly surreal in its way – the kind of place the Coen brothers might dream up. Like reality, but with a hysterical subtext.

She had to smile every time she thought of it. Even now. She was living with James Craggan. In a luxury villa. In Europe. Sitting with him at breakfast, riding with him in the BMW, talking about the script with him . . . watching him when she thought he wasn't aware and reminding herself who he really was. But he always seemed to catch her – always seemed to be aware when he was being watched, what his angles were, what lens was being used. When he drank. When he ate. When he stood at the doorway, turned and winked. Everything was a shot to him. Was she, too, part of the shot? Or was the camera only on him? Perpetual close-up – the actor's dream and nightmare. What had they said about Marilyn? She made love to the camera because it gave her the pure, unconditional adoration no human ever could. All it wanted was her beauty.

Of course, there were imperfections. The James Craggan of the movies didn't slurp his orange juice and worry about what he ate. The guy in *Cocaine Train* wouldn't have let anyone see him checking his eyebrows in a mirror. And then there was Honee: silicone-enhanced, Botoxed and cellulite-free Honee – his guilty pleasure now that his body wasn't allowed anything stronger. However much you wanted to respect the man, his choice of woman would always disappoint. Call it a generational thing. Steve McQueen probably never bought into feminism either.

122

Her wanderings had brought her to a house: the only house on the road. She stopped and listened. There was definitely music coming from inside, but no exterior indication it was a bar. The patio out front had no chairs or tables, and only one person was visible through a window: an old man sitting asleep in an armchair. The Exogi-Myrtos road that went through the village seemed empty for miles in either direction. The chirrup of crickets and the occasional clanking goat bell made for a scene of rustic desolation.

The door opened and a man with an oddly compressed face appeared in a cloud of smoke. He was wearing a Hawaiian shirt and neoprene scuba-diving leggings. His stomach showed beneath the shirt, teetering over the waistline. 'Can I help you, my dear?' he said in heavily-accented English.

'Someone told me there was a bar round here . . . '

'You're an American.'

'Yes . . . ?'

'I worked in America many years. I am Diogenes. You are welcome to my bar. Enter, please.'

'Oh, OK.'

She followed him into a long, stone-paved room that seemed to be part of his house. A mirrored bar occupied one end and the rest of the space was filled with a jumble of mismatched chairs and tables. The only other customer was the old man she had glimpsed through the window. He snuffled in his sleep and passed wind with a long vibrating note.

'I apologise for Memo,' said Diogenes. 'He would not normally produce gas when a lady is present.'

'It's OK . . . but is the bar actually open? I . . . ' she gestured at the gaping emptiness.

'Open? I am always open. What will you drink? Bourbon? I have Wild Turkey and Maker's Mark.'

'Bourbon? Yeah, why not. Whichever's good.'

He nodded his approval. 'Ice?'

123

'Uh-huh.'

He filled a half-litre glass almost to the brim with bourbon and dropped in a couple of ice cubes so the spirit ran over.

'Whoa! What kind of measure is that?'

'The measures in Diogenes' bar reflect the harshness of the world and the burdens we must carry.'

'Okaay.'

'Would you like to get high?' He took a metal box from the bar and flipped the lid to reveal a row of ready-rolled joints.

'Maybe later. You're high yourself, though, aren't you?'

'Since 1997. Shall we go to the garden? The others are out there.'

Grace slurped bourbon from the brimming glass so she'd be able to walk without spilling more. She smiled at his theatrical gesture and at his ludicrous clothes. Wasn't neoprene a bad choice in the heat of summer?

Outside, half a dozen people were sitting in mismatched patio furniture. Candles burned in bottles and some kind of Greek jazz – clarinet and splashy cymbals – played quietly through speakers. Everyone present was clearly a local: dusty-looking men in work boots, grey old men wearing clothes that seemed three decades old – villagers who recognised no other world than the two square miles from this point. Worry beads clicked in the candle light. At least two people were smoking joints.

'Welcome a friend,' announced Diogenes to his guests. 'She is American, like me.'

'Grace. I'm Grace,' she said.

There were mutters of welcome. A chair was pushed out to her and she sat, simultaneously bemused and amused by this place. It could be a scene in the movie.

'Why you make war in Vietnam?' asked one of the old men who, in the dimness, seemed to be wearing a classic Mao suit.

'It wasn't me,' she said. 'Though *Apocalypse Now* is one of my favourite movies.'

'The director's cut?' said Diogenes.

'No, I thought that was too indulgent. The whole French colonial thing . . . The original studio cut was sharper.'

Diogenes nodded. 'You are working on the movie here?'

'I'm an assistant, yeah.'

'That Caro girl,' said a giant man with earth-stained jeans and work boots. 'She is nymphoman?'

'I couldn't say. I guess it's possible.'

'James Craggan. *He* is a star,' said another. '*Cocaine Train.*'

The man in the work boots spluttered and said something Grace didn't catch. Within a second, an argument erupted with all of them shouting and waving. Only the occasional word made sense.

'What are they saying?' she said to Diogenes.

'They are discussing if Craggan could kill Connery in a fistfight, or whether Eastwood could take them both. In 1987 – not now. Another drink?'

'I still have about eight measures in here. I'm feeling a little . . . I'm not really used to . . . '

Diogenes waved away her excuses and took the still half-full glass back into the bar.

She looked up at the mountain-tops, pale against a brilliant sky. Who could have guessed, six months ago, that she would be here, in Europe, working on a movie, living in James Craggan's villa, drinking a pitcher of bourbon in a garden full of village lunatics? This wasn't real. It was a screenplay by Charlie Kaufman.

Go with it. If this was a montage, how would it look? Begin with her, Grace, sipping her bourbon and musing . . . fade into Crag spending the evening alone with Honee, no doubt in some athletic and debased karma-sutric work-out that only movie stars engaged in . . . fade into Chet Braddock with his surrogate Greek family, working on pronunciation and plucking technique against the

125

handicap of a self-severed finger ... fade into Hannah Caro, naked, perspiring and in the throes of another uncontrollable ecstasy with some unwitting guy who'd spend the rest of his life measuring every other woman against this wild goddess ... and back to Grace, glassy-eyed with bourbon.

Diogenes reappeared and put the refilled glass on the table in front of her. He'd brought another customer with him: the holiday-company guy from the café the other day who'd told her to order *frappe*. He was still in his uniform, though now it was heavily stained with food.

'Everybody – meet our new friend Jim,' said Diogenes. 'He's English. He hates tourists and loves Greece. He had nothing to do with Vietnam.'

Muted greetings were offered. Jim put his half-litre glass of whisky on Grace's table and sat beside her.

'English?' said the old man in the Mao suit. 'Why you abandon Poland in the Yalta Conference?'

An immediate chorus of derision followed and the old man sat muttering to himself.

'Hello again,' said Grace.

Jim seemed to notice her for the first time. 'Ah, yes. The café. Have you tried a *frappe* yet?'

'A couple. It's still not real coffee, though, is it?'

'*I* like it.'

'Did you meet Memo?'

'The old guy inside? He must eat a lot of pickles. Just don't light a match in there.'

'I'm Grace, by the way.' She held out a hand.

He shook it and nodded to her drink. 'He takes his drinking seriously, doesn't he?'

'No kidding. I'll be under the table if I drink all of it. So, can I ask you a question? Why are you working for a holiday company if you hate tourists?'

126

'I just want to make some money over the summer. I've never had a job I actually enjoyed, so this one didn't seem any different. It's just a case of tolerating them and trying to enjoy myself when I can.'

'How do you enjoy yourself?'

'Good food. Relaxation. Swimming. Trying to absorb a bit of the culture. That's why I came here, to this bar. You've got to admit it's different.'

'That's one word for it.'

'Are you working on the film?'

'I'm an assistant, yeah.'

'Then let me ask *you* a question. A Corelli sequel? *Why*? Wasn't the first one an absolute disaster?'

'It wasn't a disaster exactly. OK, so it's got an IMDB rating of about five and Cruz won a Razzie for her performance, but everyone knows she's better in Spanish-speaking roles. It did make a profit worldwide. Not much, admittedly, but a profit is a profit. People forget that it had a great director in John Madden and a brilliant DP in John Toll. If you're going to blame anything, blame the screenplay. It didn't capture the epic scope of the book.'

'You seem to know a lot about it.'

'I studied film.'

'I suppose what I mean is: what else is there to say in a sequel?'

'Well, you know, Corelli is back on the island and he's set up Europe's pre-eminent mandolin training school.'

'Seriously?'

'Yeah. But there's a twist. His daughter, who's Greek-Italian, falls for a boy who's German-Italian and it stirs up memories of the war. I can't give too much away, but it turns out there are still some Nazis living in secret on the island and they have an interest in Corelli's daughter not winning the World Mandolin Championship.'

'I'd like to thank the Academy . . .'

127

'I know it sounds lame, but it's got a fantastic crew. Tony Brass directing, Mario Cacciatore on cinematography. It's got Braddock, Caro, Craggan. The screenplay is by Scott LaBrava. Did you ever see *Flora*?'

'That silent film about the guy who has sex with flowers?'

'That's it. A big hit at Cannes.'

'No. But this sounds like a sure-fire blockbuster.'

'The truth is, you just never know. Look at *A Countess from Hong Kong*, 1967. Directed by Charlie Chaplin, starring Brando and Sophia Loren. Should have been massive. Total disaster. You know the rule in Hollywood: "Nobody knows anything."'

'William Goldman, right? I've read him. He and Joe Eszterhas have written good books about screenwriting.'

'Hey! You're a cinephile?'

'I studied literature. I'm interested in writing. I don't know anything about the technical side of filmmaking. Wait . . . I've got a quote for you. Do you know what Mel Brooks said the hardest thing about film-making was?'

'Go on.'

'Punching all the little holes on the side of the film.'

'Yeah, right.'

They both drank. She appraised him over the top of her glass. Not especially attractive. No immediate charisma. But it was funny how he wore his uniform off-duty and let it get covered in food. He was a mess, but he didn't care.

'You know, Jim, this is the first proper conversation – I mean, with a normal person – I've had since I arrived in Greece.'

'I'm flattered you think I'm normal.'

'You know what I mean. Everyone on the movie has . . . I don't know . . . an agenda.'

'Yeah. To be honest, it's nice to talk to someone who doesn't want to make a complaint or sue me.'

'What's your favourite film, Jim?'

'Ah. Now you're going to judge me on my taste.'

'No – I'm just interested.'

'OK. Well, I'm a big fan of Steven Seagal's early-nineties work.'

She gave him a deadpan stare.

He grinned. 'I suppose I'm more interested in scripts. I liked *Being John Malkovich* and that one with George Clooney: *Up in the Air.*'

'Good movies. Although I prefer *Eternal Sunshine* if we're talking Charlie Kaufman.'

'Pretentious. Wilfully over-complicated. I don't think it would have got made if *Malkovich* hadn't been a hit.'

'How about Nicholson in *Chinatown*?'

'Overrated.'

'*The Good the Bad and the Ugly*?'

'Too long. Good music.'

'*True Romance.*'

'Great story. Tarantino should only write, not direct.'

'*Rear Window.*'

'Classic. Pure storytelling.'

'*Alien.*'

'The best of the series. Masterclass in suspense.'

'*Goodfellas.*'

'Epic. Great narrative drive.'

'*Apocalypse Now.*'

'One of my favourites. But not the director's cut.'

'You're wasted at Iliad Holidays,' she said.

'Tell me about it. I've got a first class degree. I suppose you like the more arty stuff – Fritz Lang and the rest.'

'Lang was a pioneer, but so was Chaplin in his way. I'm a big fan of Antonioni and Fellini. But I'm not a film snob. Spielberg deserves *some* credit.'

'I think I missed the Fellini stuff. Van Damme wasn't in any of them, was he?'

She smiled. They both drank.

'I want to make films, Jim. I want to direct. What do you want? What's it all about for you?'

'Why are we alive, you mean? No reason. Use the time however you like. There's so much to see and experience. That's what I want – just to live. If that means having to dress like a moron and tolerate small-minded people for the summer . . . '

'The meaning of life!' sang Diogenes. 'We are atoms in a cosmic soup – connected by spirit! There are higher levels of being beyond what we see. Our bodies are shells, but the mind can be free.'

Some of the regulars jeered. Others seemed already to be free of their imprisoning shells.

'He told me he's been high since 1997,' whispered Grace.

'I like him. He's an original.' Jim put his glass down. 'I think . . . I think I'm going to pass out if I have one more sip of this whisky.'

'Take it easy, Jim.'

'I could live in this village, you know. Get a job as a shepherd or a carpenter or something. Simple food. Fresh air. That's the way to live.'

'You don't think it's just running away? You'd be hiding from that big world of experience you were talking about.'

Jim was staring into his whisky. Had he heard the question?

'Life!' sang Diogenes. 'Live is life!'

'Will you excuse me a moment?' said Jim, tight voiced. 'I've got to throw up.'

He staggered urgently into the shadows of the garden and let forth a great gurgling retch. The regulars cheered.

A loud *thunk* and clatter caused Grace to turn. Diogenes had passed out on his table, the joint extinguished by his cheek and his glass of brandy knocked over. He seemed to be smiling, even the depths of his intoxicated oblivion.

It was probably time to head back to the villa.

Donna's House, Argostoli, Kefalonia

The phone illuminated and *Zorba the Greek* began trilling over the vibration. Donna groped in the darkness of her bedroom to locate it and squinted at the caller ID. If it was one of the reps, she'd be down their throat like . . .

It was Morag Cleaver.

'Morag? Hello. Is there an emergency? It's half-past—'

'What's going on with the rep in Exogi, Donna?' There was a slight slurring of the voice. Live *bouzouki* music was playing in the background.

'You mean Jim? I . . . Morag – do you know what time it is?'

'I'm seeing a lot of complaints on Twitter – eight of them just tonight. It seems the quiz night was a disaster.'

'Really?'

'Yes, "really". He was asking them impossible questions about philosophy, the smart-arsed little shit.'

'I . . . I told him to buy a book of questions.'

'Well, he didn't. Do you know we had three people in hospital over there?'

'Yes, yes I know. There was some contaminated alcohol. The local policeman is looking—'

'A Mr Thurrock was given an unnecessary enema. Do you know why that might be?'

'An enema? No, I didn't—'

131

'And what's happening with excursions? The Golden and Smithson reps have been selling them fine, but Jim is way behind. I don't need to tell you that we're hardly making a penny from that resort. We. Need. To. Sell. More. Excur. Sions. Do you understand?'

'Yes, Morag.'

'How about a Greek night? Get him to organise something. Music, food, whatever. Frankly, I don't care if people end up in hospital as long as we make a profit. If anyone sues, we'll pin it on Jim Lad.'

'I'll tell him . . . about organising it, I mean.'

'We've had five letters of complaint about him so far. Five.'

'That's no *so* bad . . . '

'We're only at the beginning of the season, Donna. We're barely into June. This is his first batch of guests. One of them – Miss Jenson at the Nefeli Hotel – asked him what to do about her sunstroke. Do you know what he said?'

'Did he recommend after-sun lotion, drinking plenty of water and staying in the shade? That's the official—'

'He told her anyone who gets drunk and lies in the sun all day deserves to be hospitalised. He said that if people want to get burned, they might as well save some money, stay at home and have a chip-pan fire instead of going on holiday.'

'He actually said that?'

'There were no witnesses. It's unlikely she'll be able to sue. I've sent her some vouchers and an Iliad pen.'

'I'll talk to him, Morag. I'll be quite clear.'

'Yeah. I'm thinking about giving him Tripa.'

'But . . . I thought Jackie had Tripa.'

'Well, it's a long way for her to drive from Argostoli. And you know that *nobody* wants to be there.'

'But it's even further away from Exogi and—'

'He's got a car, hasn't he?'

'It's just that . . . you know, the guests at Tripa tend to be—'

'Give it to him. I'm pulling Jackie out.'

'Right, Morag. And I'll give him a written warning about the guest with sunstroke.'

'No. Not yet. It's too early.'

Donna heard a cackle and ice rattling in a drink. Or was it a cauldron?

Morag slurped and gulped. 'I think I'll send the secret tourist up there to observe him.'

'A written warning would be—'

'No. That's what I'm going to do.'

'Yes, Morag. Is that all?'

'That's all, Donna. And don't call me again at this time of night. This is my personal time.'

'But I didn't . . . '

The line had gone dead.

Donna's husband rolled over. 'What's going on?'

'Nothing. Just the witch. Go to sleep.'

The phone light went off and she lay in the darkness. Tripa – the place they sent any guest who absolutely insisted on being transferred to alternative accommodation. It made Exogi look like Las Vegas.

High season

8.00 a.m, Police Office, Exogi

Sergeant Nikos took the mobile phone from his shirt pocket and read the text he'd just received: a brief but laudably explicit message from Maria. So she had forgiven him for his recent lack of attention. The phone buzzed and pinged again: a photo this time. He opened it and saw Maria arranged uncompromisingly in her bathroom. A pair of his handcuffs. A blindfold. It was necessary to turn the screen diagonally to fully understand what he was looking at.

Time to make a personal visit. Official police business. The office would be closed for the remainder of the afternoon. He felt for his uniform cap on the desk top.

The phone began to ring. He smiled and answered it immediately:

'*Ela, koukla mou. Ena leptaki, endaxi?*'

Silence, though there was evidently someone on the line.

He removed the phone from his ear and checked the number. Not Maria's.

'Hello?' said a female voice. 'Hello? Is this Sergeant Nikos Petras in Exogi?'

'Who is this?' he said.

'This is Penelope. From the movie. Listen, I—'

'How did you get this number?'

'I get numbers, Mister Petras. That's my job. A small matter has arisen and I require your assistance.'

'I was just leaving on urgent police business – a suspected robbery at a private house.'

'Of course, but this concerns Hannah Caro.'

His eyes moved to the notice board and the newspaper picture of the actress arriving at Sami.

'Go on,' he said.

'Some items of hers have been stolen from her trailer at the set and she's very upset. She feels unable to do her scenes. I realise that there's no possibility

137

of recovering her things, but it might make her feel better if she thought something official was being done. Do you understand me?'

'You want me to come in my uniform, perhaps ask her some questions and then do nothing about it. She is a star – she must have what she wants.'

'Excellent. How soon can you be here?'

He looked again at the newspaper photo. He thought of Maria in her bathroom. There were few harder decisions for a man of natural passions.

'Give me fifteen minutes,' he said.

He used the siren until he was on the fast stretch of road towards Sami. Once on the straight, he checked his moustache for crumbs in the visor mirror and tried different angles for his cap. He should be dashing but remote: an authority figure to slightly intimidate yet also provoke attraction. A Greek Gregory Peck or Clarke Gable.

The woman Penelope – attractive, but apparently unhappily celibate for a long time – was waiting for him at the set and ushered him through security, through a mocked-up village square and into a car park at the rear. She was talking the whole time.

'OK. Good. Right. Here's the deal. Someone went in her Winnie and took some of her clothes – a dress, a pair of shoes, a hairbrush. Nothing really expensive. Nothing *intimate* – no knickers or sex toys. It's not the cost, you understand, but rather the principle. It's an offense to her status. Nobody else was robbed. It looks like we care less about her. At least, that's how she sees it. So, you know, just ask her some police questions and make notes or something. Whatever it is that you normally do. Keep her happy. Am I talking too fast? Are you getting all this? Do you have any questions?'

'Sex toys?'

'Never mind. Right, we're here. Serious face. Do you mind if I stretch the truth a little when I introduce you?'

He shrugged. 'Public relations.'

'Exactly.'

138

Penelope knocked one the door: three quick knocks and two slow ones.

'Come in!'

Nikos felt an unprecedented flutter in his guts. The voice of Hannah Caro. The voice to animate the photograph. He took off his cap and put it on again. He took it off and put it under his arm

They stepped inside.

'Hannah – this is Commandant Nikos Petras of the Serious Crime Unit,' said Penelope. 'He came as soon as he heard. You must tell him everything he needs to know and these thieves will be hunted down.'

And there she was: Hannah Caro, reclining on a large leather sofa. She wore her long, dark hair tied back. She wore some sort of tracksuit that sheathed her body and revealed just a hint of cleavage. If she was wearing any make-up, it wasn't clear to Nikos – she appeared fresh and clean and scented as if she'd stepped from the shower just five minutes previously. And he knew – knew with the certainty of his long and varied experience of women – that here was a woman who might make slaves of men. She knew her power over them and would exploit it until she ruined them, herself, or both. She seemed to sense his understanding of this and held his eyes, appraising him and smiling with ambiguous appreciation.

'Commandant Petras?' prompted Penelope.

'Yes. Yes. I am sorry about your losses, Miss Caro.'

'Call me Han.'

'Han . . . it makes me think of honey . . . the way we Greeks pronounce it.'

'I like the way *you* pronounce it, Nikos. Do you like honey? Do you have a sweet tooth?'

'Tooth? No, I think with honey I must use my tongue.'

Caro giggled and reclined further on the sofa. Her body seemed ready to burst from its covering like a too-ripe fruit from its skin.

Penelope rolled her eyes. 'Why don't you tell the policeman what was stolen? He's very busy.'

'A dress. A pair of shoes. Nothing really.' She toyed with the zip down her front.

'A favourite dress?' said Nikos, talking a notepad from his rear trouser pocket.

'I wore it when I arrived at the port. Perhaps you saw the pictures?'

'I did. A very beautiful dress.'

'You liked it?'

'The way you wore it. I envied the wind that day.'

She glowed with the compliment.

Penelope coughed. 'And there was also a brush, isn't that right? Tell him about the brush.'

'Yeah, a brush. From the bathroom. I thought, maybe, it was some pervert, you know? Wanted to use my hair? Some guys are into that.'

'Hair on a brush is not the same as hair on a body,' said Nikos, doodling nonsense in his notebook.

'You won't find a hair on *my* body,' said Caro. 'Except on my head, I mean.'

She twirled a tendril, fed it to an incisor and gave Nikos a look that he felt like a punch.

'Excellent!' said Penelope. 'So – the commandant will follow up these leads and get back to us. Is that right, Mr Petras?'

'But I have not asked the young lady about—'

'Mere formalities. Miss Caro is due on set in twenty minutes and wardrobe is waiting. Perhaps you can come back later, Commandant, and tell us how your investigation is progressing. Would you like that, Hannah?'

'Uh-huh. A *lot*.' She was still twirling the hair and reclining languorously.

'Thank you for your time, Commandant,' said Penelope, pushing him towards the door. 'Thank you. Now let's leave Hannah to the wardrobe people.'

'See you soon, Nikos!' called Caro as they stepped down from the Winnebago.

'Jesus!' said Penelope as they walked back to the exit. 'There should be a bucket of iced water outside just in case. If I hadn't been in there with you, she'd have probably jumped you.'

'I was thinking exactly the same.'

'Well, the main thing is that she might do her scene now. Thanks so much for coming.'

'I will need descriptions of what was taken and details of when if you want this to look like a real investigation.'

'Of course, of course.'

She led him to security and waved him off, stalking straight back inside to solve whatever other minor crises had occurred. There was a woman, he reflected, who carried her own bucket of iced water within her. If only she'd left him alone with Caro. He might at least have got a phone number. Would it be worth going into Argostoli and buying an expensive hairbrush just to have an excuse to visit again?

He sat in his car and turned on the air-conditioning. What a mystery was woman! The old, the young, the in-between – each had their special allure. Fire, women and the sea: the three great dangers for man throughout all of history. Even he – even Nikos Petras – might be brought to his knees by a woman like Hannah Caro. Han, like honey. But what a consummation it would be! To die upon her, within her, would be a worthy death. A hero's death.

He sighed. It was now too late to go to Maria's and work off the accumulated passion. He looked again in the visor mirror and his eye was caught by the mail he'd collected earlier from the post office and tossed on the back seat. Perhaps work would focus his mind.

The uppermost envelope was another of those junk-mail promises of immediate wealth. Did that mean the so-called nationalists had also received another communication from Athens? Too late to do anything about it now, although another urgent fax from Captain Bastounis was probably already on the way.

141

The second letter was postmarked Patras. He ripped this open and read the brief note within. The results of the alcohol analysis were as expected, apart from one exotic botanical element that would require a little further investigation. Nikos knew a man in Allomeros who was just the person to ask. Perhaps that information would be something to send Captain Bastounis.

The third was addressed by hand, although in a barely-literate and deeply-indented pencil scrawl. It had the familiar look of an anonymous threatening letter or denunciation – one of the half-dozen he received every week condemning a neighbour, informing on a business competitor, or simply railing against the government. The contents, however, were more serious than expected.

Petras

I know about you and Maria. End it now. Don't tell her why. If I ever catch you, you're dead.

He ran his fingers over the letter. He sniffed. He licked. Stone dust – gritty with quartz. A letter from a quarryman? Maria's husband.

Now here was a delicate situation.

9.00 a.m. Resort Office, Exogi

To whom it may concern

I would like to congratulate you on employing such a ~~sterling~~ remarkable rep as Jim at Exogi. Seldom in all my ~~miserable existence~~ life have I met such a helpful, intelligent, insightful and ~~professionally attired~~ well turned-out individual. He has

142

made our holiday a ~~sojourn of almost orgasmic bliss~~ *true pleasure and we would urge you to give him* ~~a fat bonus~~ *some sort of reward for his* ~~slavish subservience~~ *hard work.*

If I may give just one example of his excellence. My wife Valerie had ~~stupidly staggered into the sea while pissed~~ *decided to go snorkelling and hurt her foot on a sea urchin. Quick as a flash, Jim offered* ~~to urinate on it~~ *run to the pharmacy in Sami some ten kilometres away and buy some* ~~rat poison~~ *a soothing balm with his own* ~~meagre pay packet~~ *money. Of course, we declined his* ~~sarcastic insult~~ *generous offer and instead offered* ~~our only daughter in virgin sacrifice~~ *him a considerable cash tip, which he* ~~grasped with lightning speed~~ *modestly declined.*

Jim is a ~~living saint~~ *fine young man and deserves credit for his* ~~loathing of~~ *dedication to Iliad Holidays. Please thank him from us and give him a bonus of some kind.*

Yours

David and Valerie Dangleberry

Jim threw the biro across the office and crumpled the scrap of paper to join three others on his desk. If he could keep just the bitterness out of these letters, he might finally be able to complete one and counteract the increasingly negative attitude building within Iliad Holidays.

Kelly – God bless her massive udders – had just got back from Argostoli and had tipped him off, having overhead a phone call between Donna and her boss concerning the growing pile of complaint emails and letters being sent to the Athens HQ. Apparently, there was some sort of allowable quota of complaints before a rep was immediately fired. Only a balancing quantity of favourable reports could stay the executioner's blade. It was merely a matter of creating a false email address in the name of certain genuine guests and sending

143

enough letters of praise to save his job – this job he hated but which would pay for many months of pleasure in future.

The coach horn bellowed outside.

He glanced at the wall clock. Shit!

He raced down the alley to the main street, where Kostas was gesticulating madly from the driver's seat. Didn't Jim realise that there were eight properties they had to collect from between here and the south coast? Didn't Jim remember that it always took longer than expected? Wasn't Jim aware that the flights would not wait for him?

'Yeah, yeah,' said Jim, getting into the seat behind Kostas, thinking that the airport took longer only because Kostas refused to put down the cigarette while loading luggage.

First stop: the Sunshine Apartments, so named because they faced north into a hill. The tourists stood with their luggage on the road outside, bleary-eyed at this hour of the morning and glowing red from one last day's carcinogenic roasting.

At the sight of the coach, they shuffled into an instinctive queue. At the sight of Jim in his formal uniform (now with a cardboard belt), they scowled and muttered imprecations in which the words "sue", "letter" and "complaint" predominated.

'Good morning!' said Jim as the doors sighed open. 'All ready to go home? I checked the weather back in England and guess what? It's raining!'

They dumped their luggage for Kostas to abuse and filed past Jim on to the coach, taking the same seats they'd occupied on the inward journey. He counted them on, ticking them off on the manifest he'd remembered to bring this time. But someone was missing.

'Ms Grockle?' he called. 'Ms Grockle. Has anyone seen Ms Grockle?'

'She's still in her room,' called someone from the back, evident satisfaction in their tone.

'I heard her shagging in the night,' said another.

144

'I heard her puking,' said another.

Great. He sprinted two-at-a-time up the concrete stairs of death and banged on the door of room number four. 'Ms Grockle! Ms Grockle. Time to go home! The coach is here and everyone is waiting for you. You're going to miss the flight!'

Not only her. Everyone. His next warning from Donna would be a four-minute warning.

'Ms Grockle? Make some sort of noise if you can hear me.'

There was a crash of breaking glass.

He pushed at the door and was surprised when it opened without hindrance. A piece of adhesive tape had been put over the latch to allow unfettered access, presumably to any passing *kamakia*. The scene within was horrific.

First there was the smell: stale sweat, cigarette smoke, fruit-scented alcohol, and vomit. Clothes were strewn across the floor and piled on furniture: swimming costumes, socks, stained underwear, stained t-shirts, stained dresses. At least four used condoms were visible – shrivelled anaemic slugs lying wherever they'd been flung. And at the centre of the trash heap was Ms Grockle herself, sprawled facedown on the bed, her stained nightie ridden up and her much-exercised genitals bared in all their shameless detail. Her pillow was wet with vomit and, consequently, her hair. The bedside lamp was on the floor, shadeless and with the bulb shattered across the marble. It must have been that she'd knocked over to signal her existence.

'Ms Grockle – you've got two minutes to pack.'

She groaned. She made no attempt to conceal her vulva.

'Would you like some help? Look – just get dressed. I'll pack for you.'

He dragged her purple suitcase from the top of the wardrobe and opened it on the floor. Two-handed, he scraped up whatever clothes lay around and tossed them pell-mell into the case. The underwear, he flicked in with a foot. Open bottles of sun cream and shampoo followed. A travel hairdryer, female emollients and unguents, a sticky vibrator that he retrieved from the bedside cabinet with a handful of tissue. The rest, he kicked under the bed for the maid to throw away later. Ms Grockle would be home (or in A&E) before she'd miss any of it.

By now, the girl had managed to pull a sundress half on. She was sitting on the edge of the bed with it over her face, one arm trapped upwards in a sleeve. Jim tugged it unceremoniously down over her splattered nightie. He fitted pair of flip-flops between her chipped-pink toenails.

'Right!' he said. 'Ready to go! You look as fresh as a daisy!'

She looked like the Medusa after a fourteen-hour gangbang.

'Gonna puke,' she mumbled.

'Well, just do it down your front. It won't matter much.'

'Need a . . . need a wheelchair.'

'I'd like to see you go down those stairs in a wheelchair, but we haven't got one. So you'll just have to walk while everyone on the coach judges you.'

'Need to brush my . . . need to *bleeeeeuuurrrrrgh . . . heurrrrrgh . . . a-urrrrrgh!*'

Vomit jetted wetly across the marble floor.

'You had the calamari? Good choice.'

'*Heuuuuuuuuuurgh a-a-a-euuuuuuaargh oh god!*'

'I'll carry your case. If you're not immediately behind me, you'll be paying for your own flight back.'

Grim-faced, he carried the half-full case down the steps. She followed, flip-flops flapping and eyes downcast under the condemnatory onslaught of the faces at the coach windows.

Kostas seemed about to leap up in protest against allowing her on one of his seats, but Jim wearily waved him down. 'Leave it. Just take us to the Sotiris Apartments.'

Another po-faced clutch of tourists stood less than a mile further on, herding their luggage like sheep. Kostas single-armed their bags under the bus while Jim ticked them off on the list, pausing only briefly to help Kostas lift a case that appeared to contain anvils.

One name remained unaccounted for.

'Mister Tickell? Mister Tickell?' Jim called into the coach.

No answer. Only malevolent glares.

Kostas nudged him and pointed at the parking mirror above the windscreen. Two tanned legs protruded from under the coach.

Jim's bowels loosened. 'Kostas – did you run him over?'

The driver spluttered smoke. 'Did you see me run him, *re*?'

They got out together and stared down at the legs of Mr Tickell: thin, sparse with hair, tanned to the hue and general appearance of Twiglets. They were not moving. Kostas kicked a foot as if it were a softening tyre.

'Ow!'

'Mister Tickell?' said Jim. 'Are you OK? Are you hurt?'

'Tell him I never run you!' said Kostas to the legs.

'I'm not moving until I get my refund from the cave excursion!' came the sub-vehicular voice. 'I told you I'd do this and I am doing it! I'm a man of my word!'

'What? What refund?'

'You told me the Melissani Cave was more wondrous than the Grand Canyon, more beautiful than the Taj Mahal! It was a bloody hole with a puddle in it!'

'It's my job to sell things, Mister Tickell . . . '

'False advertising! I'm going to sue you so badly you'll have to change your name! I'll own it!'

Kostas shrugged. He lit another cigarette. *His* name was safe.

'You can't have a refund just because you didn't like the excursion, Mister Tickell. It's not as if you can give it back. You've had it now. What if everyone said they didn't like it?'

'Everybody *did* say that!'

147

'Well, *I* liked it. It moved me to tears.' Of boredom.

'I'm not arguing with you, young man! Just give me my fifty euros or I'm staying here for the rest of summer. I'm a man of my word.'

'How will the other passengers feel if they all miss their flight because of you?'

'I don't care!'

'For the sake of fifty pounds? How will Missus Tickell or the little Tickells feel if you spend the rest of the summer under a coach in Kefalonia?'

'I don't care!'

Mrs Tickell sat at a window eight seats back, her face a lined and dimpled mask of humiliation. Someone had put an arm round her.

Jim turned to Kostas and spoke in Greek. 'Can you just reverse it and go round him?'

Kostas exhaled Marlboro smoke. 'And if his clothes get hooked under? Or his hair?'

'He's bald.'

'You'll take the blame if I drive over him?'

'You can maim him – just don't kill him.'

'Stay here. Tell me left or right.' Kostas got back in the driver's seat and set the engine rumbling.

'I shall not be moo-oo-ved!' sang Mr Tickell.

The coach began to reverse. There was no rip of clothing or fearsome scream. Jim kept waving Kostas back and the torso of Mr Tickell emerged, followed by a face that was red with excessive ultra-violet exposure and apoplexy.

'Swine!' he spat from his prostrate position.

'Now,' said Jim. 'You can get on the coach, or you can lie here and pay for your own flight home. Is it worth it for fifty euros?'

Mr Tickell stood, stamped his foot like a petulant child and walked stiff-legged towards the coach door. There, with one foot on the step, he turned and stared with squinting rage at Jim.

'I'm going to sue you so badly you'll be paying me back from heaven.'

'Thank God I'm an atheist, then,' said Jim beneath the diesel engine.

Next stop: Sami and the Blue Sky Apartments.

Jim fell into the navigator's seat and picked up the microphone headset from the dash. Kostas chuckled and received a splayed palm in response.

'Right – listen up, you morons,' he muttered.

'We heard that!' came a voice from behind.

He snatched at the headset and saw that it was on. His bowels liquefied once more.

Kostas reached forward and turned on some frenetic *bouzouki*, filling the coach with trills and Zorba-flavoured joviality.

'Thanks,' said Jim, slumping.

They drove for ten minutes without incident, Jim fabricating letters of praise in his head, Kostas smoking contentedly, the tourists complaining audibly – but not formally – about the smoke and the *bouzouki* music. It was almost possible to pretend that they didn't exist.

Until Kostas' phone rang. He fumbled for it, driving with his knees. He answered, grunted and passed it to Jim. 'For you.'

'Jim? It's Donna. Look, Sharon over in Ithaca has fallen off her moped and she can't see her guests on to the ferry at Sami. You won't be coming to the airport today. Get off the coach at Sami. There's a load of people already waiting at the quayside. Make sure they all get on the ferry to Ithaca, then just go back to Exogi and get on with your duties. OK? Kostas will bring the rest of your people to the airport. Now give the phone back to him and I'll explain it. Is he smoking?'

'No. He's not smoking.'

Kostas coughed a gust of Marlboro.

149

'Good. Good. I've got some extra duties for you, but I'll tell you about them after the transfers. Don't let me down. The Ithaca guests are used to a premier service. Right – give me Kostas again.'

He handed the phone back. *Yes!* No airport duty! He could spend the afternoon slacking off while everyone else was busy on the transfers. A nice swim, an indulgent meal, a bout of Onanism using a photo of Philippa he'd nicked from one of her welcome boards. Just a head shot, but it would do.

A thought flashed unbidden and unexpected: what would Grace say about his theft and abuse of the photograph? It had been a few days since their meeting at Diogenes' bar and his memories of it were admittedly hazy. She'd been easy enough to talk to, but then it was always the case with girls that didn't engender instant priapism. If only he could talk to Philippa the way he'd talked to Grace. Did Philippa like films, too? Or just hot, gymnastic sex with anatomically perfect males?

'Sami,' said Kostas, pulling over. '*Kali tychi, file.*'

'And *kali dromi* to you. See you next week.'

Jim stepped down on to the baking tarmac of the port car park. No need to tell the tourists why he was getting off. Let them worry for the next fifteen minutes why they'd seen him standing there waving as the coach pulled away. Kostas wouldn't tell them anything.

The Ithaca-bound tourists were waiting at the quay where their coach had dropped them. The ferry was already about a quarter mile offshore and turning round to reverse. He wandered over, the polyester trousers roasting his crotch and virtually sparking with static.

'Hello. I'm Jim, I'll be—'

'Where's Sharon?' said a woman wearing a hat that looked like fungus. 'They told us someone called Sharon would meet us.'

'I'm Jim. I also work for Iliad Holidays. I promise I'm not an imposter.'

'But what happened to Sharon?'

'She contracted dengue fever and was rushed to the tropical diseases unit in Argostoli. Now listen – when the ferry backs in, just grab your bags and walk up to the passenger ramp on the right. Don't try to walk up the vehicle ramp or they'll blow their whistles at you. And let everyone come off before you get on. I won't be coming with you, but someone will be waiting there to collect you. Any questions?'

They gaped.

'Should we worry about the dengue fever?' said a pale man of about eighty. 'I haven't had injections for that.'

'He was joking, Wilfred,' said Fungus Hat.

'Eh?'

'There's no dengue fever!' said the woman.

'There is!' he said. 'In Africa. Mildred caught it in 1947. Don't you remember?'

Jim put his sunglasses on. The ferry was churning water on its final approach. The doors had started to descend. Soon he'd be free. Swimming. Food. Philippa's graven image.

'Ohh – I left me handbag in that café,' said a woman with an aluminium walking frame.

He followed the direction of her finger. The café was at the other end of Sami, shimmering in the heat.

Jim eyed the docking ferry. 'Don't worry. I'll have it sent on to your hotel.'

'No! My Pills! My heart pills!'

'Couldn't you miss a day or two?'

'Run and get the lady's handbag, Jim,' said a man wearing a straw boater.

He eyed the ferry, cars and people about to start streaming off it. He looked at the café in the distance. 'OK, look. As soon as you get the signal, get on board. If the ferry is gone when I get back, I'll have the bag sent on.'

And he sprinted, cursing them with every step, around Sami bay towards the café. Not since that fated 100-metres race at school had he exerted himself to

151

such extremes. Within seconds, sweat was dripping into his eyes. The polyester trousers seethed and sparked. The polyester shirt clung to his unhoned torso. A quick glance back – the ferry was still there.

'Quick!' he panted at the waitress. 'Did someone leave a bag here?'

'What?'

'A bag! A bag! A handbag! Here!'

'Oh – the old lady . . . ' The waitress ambled back inside to fetch it.

He turned. The ferry was still there, its effusion of people and vehicles now just a dribble.

He stared madly into the café and saw the girl chatting to a colleague.

'*The bag!*' he screeched.

She strolled sloth-like towards him, holding what appeared to be a brown faux-leather bowling-ball bag.

'Thanks!' He snatched it and ran.

Sweat filled his eyes, blurring his vision. But the ferry was still there. Its doors were still open. He picked up his pace, one breath chasing another. Thirty more seconds. Were the ferry doors closing? Twenty more seconds. Were they . . . were they casting off the ropes? Ten more seconds.

He arrived gasping and sweating to see the ferry doors closing and the great ship about two metres free of the quay. Newly-arrived people were making their way into the town. Cars were leaving the car park.

And there was his group of tourists.

Still standing exactly where he'd left them.

Staring dumbly between him and the departing ferry.

His brain rebelled. His trousers crackled. 'What happened? Why didn't you get on?'

'Nobody gave us a signal,' said Straw Boater.

Jim gaped. 'A signal?'

'You said someone would give a signal for us to get on.'

'The fucking signal was the door opening and everyone else getting on! The signal was the doors closing and the ferry leaving without you!'

'No need to swear,' mumbled somebody.

Jim numbly handed the bag to the woman with the walking aid.

'Oh no, dear. That's not my bag. My bag is red.'

'*Cheerleading Christ!*'

'What did he say?' said Wilfred.

'I'll be writing a letter about you,' said Fungus Hat

The next ferry to Vathy wasn't until the following morning.

He would have to call Donna.

'Look,' he said. 'Wait here. I've got to make a call. Don't move from this place.'

'Sharon wouldn't have caused this much trouble,' said Fungus Hat.

'What about my bag?' said Walking Aid.

He went to a payphone on the main street and fed coins into the slot. He dialled the number. His mind raced. His heart stuttered. What had Hitler said? People will always believe the big lie. Lie big. Lie big.

'Hello?'

'Donna – it's Jim. Slight problem with the ferry transfer.'

'Tell me they're on their way to Vathy.'

'No. They're not.'

Silence crackled over the line.

'Donna – it was like this. There's a really old woman in the group. She has a heart condition. Just as the ferry was coming in, she had some sort of seizure. A heart attack, maybe. A stroke, I don't know. Anyway, I was forced to perform CPR on her at the quayside. Saved her life. But the ferry wouldn't wait and the other guests wouldn't leave her.'

Silence crackled.

'Donna?'

'Did you really save her life, Jim?'

153

'Well, I'm not a doctor or anything, but her lips were blue. I had to take her dentures out to give her the kiss of life. Her breath smelled of toffee. I think it was the heart massage that saved her. I did a course when I was in the scouts. I say scouts – it was more like a youth medical corps: CPR, field surgery, basic pharmacology, you know. I got an Emergency Revival badge.'

'Look, Jim. I'm in the middle of a transfer. There's a ferry to Piso Aetos in about two hours. Put them on that one and I'll get someone to pick them up over there for a transfer to Vathy.'

'Right.'

'I'll be looking into this when I have more time. You're not off the hook. If you really saved that lady, you might get away with this. I've had a call from your guest Mister Tickell—'

'I'm at a payphone, Donna. My money's about to—'

He hung up.

Thank you, Hitler!

He turned back to his tourists and saw that their cluster had changed shape. They were now grouped around a figure lying on the ground. A toppled walking frame glinted in the sun.

Lord Jesus – please let it be her.

He ran over and saw with soaring joy that it was indeed the old woman.

'What happened?' he said, concern playing about his features.

'She just fell,' said one.

'Must be the heat and the waiting,' said Straw Boater.

'She needs her heart pills,' said Fungus Hat.

'Stand back,' said Jim. 'I've got an Emergency Revival badge.'

He put his ear to her mouth. She was still breathing. She seemed to be whispering: 'My pills. My pills.'

'Well, everything seems to be fine here,' he said.

'You didn't even touch her!' said a man who looked like a geography teacher.

154

'I practice non-contact diagnostics. Listen – there's a ferry in two hours. Everyone go to that café there and wait in the shade. I'll go and get this lady's heart pills.'

'Should we just leave her lying in the car park in the meantime?' said Geography Teacher.

'She seems comfortable enough. Perhaps you can drag her into the shade of that kiosk.'

Jim sauntered back towards the café where the handbag might be found. Should he wait with them until the ferry came? That'd be two hours out of his planned afternoon off. Better just to leave them and get the bus back to Exogi. If they were stupid enough to miss the second ferry, they deserved to spend the night homeless in Sami. In fact, his presence there was more likely to complicate matters. As long as he was around, they'd wait on his every instruction like a kindergarten class. What if he didn't tell them to get on the ferry in clear enough terms? What if there was no signal to get on, to walk, to breathe?

On the other hand, he'd almost certainly get a written warning if the old woman died. Say goodbye to Istanbul and Cairo. Say goodbye to a host of life-defining experiences. He quickened his step. Surely this day couldn't get worse.

Noon, Main Set, near Sami

Grace watched the next shot being set up: a father-son confrontation between Crag and Chet in which they would use their mandolins literally as weapons, swinging at each other until the instruments were destroyed. It was meant to be symbolic.

Some props and FX guys were checking the dummy balsa-wood mandolins one by one to ensure that they'd come apart as required. Of course, the stunt co-ordinator had made his point about splinters and eye-damage, but Crag and Chet

155

had been adamant about performing their own stunts. It was a scene of rage and passion – they wanted their faces in shot rather than the back of a stuntman's head or a masking edit.

'Are ten mandolins going to be enough?' she said.

'Once they're broke, there ain't no fixin' 'em,' said an FX guy with a shrug.

She tried to imagine the finished scene on a big screen. Choppy edit, urgent score, a lot of close-ups. It was going to take all day to shoot this. Perhaps two days if the fight choreography was off.

'Grace?'

It was Granger, waving from across the set.

'Grace – could you come to Tony's trailer for a minute?'

Tony Brass. The director. Had something gone wrong with Crag?

She made her way through technicians, hoping to ask Granger about it before they met Brass. But Granger was already stepping into the trailer as she caught up.

Inside, a small group was sitting around a table. Chet and Crag were in costume for the scene, their clothing bulging slightly with the impact pads they'd need in the fight. Brass was looking through a print-out and marking it with a pencil. An elderly peasant was sitting beside Chet. Granger stood to one side. There was a distinct smell of movie politics in the air.

'Grace. Some things have come up,' said Granger. 'Crag has asked that you be present.'

Grace looked to Crag, who winked and beckoned her to sit beside him.

'I'll do the introductions and then I have to leave to finish up the shot,' said Granger. 'Grace – I know you've seen each other around but let's make it formal. Tony – this is Grace Willetts: Crag's production assistant.'

Brass nodded, barely registering her.

'You know Chet, of course. The gentleman next to him is Eleftheros, Chet's character advisor. Eleftheros speaks no English.'

156

The old man heard his name and looked up briefly before drifting away again.

'Over to you, Tony.' Granger touched Grace's shoulder on the way out.

Brass exhaled slowly. 'Right. Now we're *all* here.' His British accent made him sound like an evil school principal. 'The studio and the backers have been viewing the dailies and they're not happy. They've got a lot of money riding on this blah, blah, blah – you know the script. They want to see some . . . well, some changes.'

'What changes?' said Chet. 'Hell, let's make them.'

A great weariness seemed to weigh on Brass. 'It seems mandolins aren't that cool. There's been some research done by a test-marketing agency. Apparently, only oboes are less cool.'

'This is a *mandolin movie*,' said Crag. '*Captain Cornetto's Mandolin School.*'

'Yeah, that's another thing,' said Brass. 'Unilever own the rights to "Cornetto" – they've been in touch via their lawyers. We've got to pay them a giant wad or drop the brand name. The shooting title is now *Captain Cornolli . . .* '

'Jesus, Tony!' said Crag. 'How am I supposed to get a feel for the part if I don't even know what I'm called? Why not just call it *Captain Corn on the Cob* or *Captain*-fucking-*Cornflakes*?'

'I think "Cornflakes" might be a Kelloggs trademark,' said Grace, half raising her hand.

Brass scowled at her. He sighed. 'I know, Crag. Don't you think I don't know?'

'What about everything we've already shot?' said Chet. 'I spent months learning how to play.'

'Relax, guys,' said Brass. 'It's still about mandolins. Only, from now on, it has to be electric mandolins. The Jimi-fucking-Hendrix of mandolin playing. The electric guitar is officially the coolest instrument according to this bloody study.'

157

'Look, Tony,' said Chet. 'I've done my research. I know that electric mandolins don't exist. They certainly didn't exist in the period we're shooting the movie.'

'Doesn't matter. Corelli . . . I mean Cornolli is supposed to be some genius player, right? Let him invent an electric mandolin. We'll change the script.'

'Who's going to do that?' said Chet.

'Not Scott LaBrava,' said Brass. 'Have you seen the headlines? Auto-asphyxiation. They say animals were involved. He's alive but they say he'll never speak, have kids or be allowed to keep a domestic animal again. Besides, we need to get on this right now. Do you know how much this location is costing daily?'

'Grace is a writer,' said Crag.

Brass looked at her properly for the first time. He didn't seem convinced. 'Are you accredited and paid up?' he said.

'Yes, with WGAW, but . . . '

'What have you written, Grace?'

'Just a script for my summer-school course . . . '

'Grace can do it,' said Crag. 'She's smart.'

'With all due respect, Crag – do you really want to hand this movie to a kid straight out of film school with a summer school screenwriting certificate?'

'What other choice have you got, Tony? Wait for the studio to argue over their favourite candidate for a month while the budget runs out or they replace you? That'd be great for your resume. We've got to fix this here and now.'

Brass squirmed. 'We could work something out between us.'

'Like Forster and Craig did on *Quantum of Solace* during the writer's strike?' said Crag. 'Look how that turned out. We need someone who understands the craft. Grace – have you ever been to any of Bob McKee's lectures?'

'Uh-huh.'

'That's good enough for me.'

'I don't know . . . ' said Brass.

'What else do you want?' said Crag. 'Grace is young. She knows what's cool. She probably knows more about the contemporary market than I do. She's seen last year's Best Foreign Film. Have you?'

'That underwater thing from China . . . ?'

'Yeah, exactly.'

'OK, look, look. Work up some pages and I'll read them. We'll all read them. But do it quickly. We'll shoot the fight scene today and tomorrow. After that, we need more cool, more action. We need the art department to make us some convincing electric mandolins. And amps – big Marshall amps like Led-fucking-Zeppelin. Grace – are you up to this?'

'I . . . I don't think—'

'Great. If you need anything – software, paper, whatever – ask Granger.'

'Tony . . . ' prompted Chet. 'Didn't you say something earlier about . . . ?'

'Shit. Yes. The studio is sending someone out to keep an eye on their investment.' Brass looked through the print-outs. 'Guy called Test Weedle. Anyone know him?'

'Weedle?' said Crag. 'He's a tool.'

'Mel Weitz calls him "The Hitman",' nodded Grace.

'Well that's something else to look forward to,' said Brass. 'Right – you two get yourselves into make-up. And Chet – can you persuade your spiritual advisor or whatever he is to get a wash? He smells like his pockets are full of chopped onions and dirty underwear.'

Eleftheros sat staring out of the window, oblivious.

Crag took her arm as they left the trailer. 'Don't sweat it, Grace. I know you can do this. I have faith in you. You wanted experience, and look what you've got!'

'Yeah, I know, but . . . '

He was searching his pockets. 'Have you seen my crystal?'

159

The crystal he'd told her about: the crystal he'd had in his pocket for every shot of every film since *Hangman's Noose*. His lucky crystal, given to him when he was nine by a Native American seer.

'It's by my bed at the villa,' he said. 'I remember seeing it there this morning.'

'I'll send someone—'

'No, Grace. Only I can touch it.'

'I could slip it into an envelope without touching it. I can call Lomu—'

'No. I'll just borrow a car from transport and drive myself. It'll be twenty minutes, max.'

'Are you sure? I mean, the shot . . . '

'They'll wait. Tell them whatever you have to. Twenty minutes max, OK?'

And he was gone.

12:30, Private House, Allomeros

Professor Stratigakis adjusted the glasses on her nose and squinted at the laptop screen. These days, it was easier to copy and paste the text into a Word document and print it magnified, but this American university had somehow blocked her ability to do that and so she'd been forced to spend ages hunched over the machine.

The piece was entitled "Gynaekomorphism and Gynaekotheism in Early Greek Mythology" – not exactly mainstream reading matter, admittedly, but a fascinating article for those with a special interest. Of course, there were instances in Homer of female gods taking mortal form in battle or to pass intelligence to their favoured mortals, but the precedents were certainly fewer than male gods doing the same for seduction. Might bounteous Aphrodite deign to visit them, here on Kefalonia, in human form?

160

The doorbell drew her from her thoughts and she went to the answer it.

'Niki! I thought you were doing the movie in Sami this week.'

'I am, I am . . . but they didn't need the extras this afternoon, and . . . '

'What is it? You seem . . . Come in, come in. Do you want coffee?'

Niki entered. 'I've done something bad, but . . . I think it might be good for us . . . I just don't know . . . '

'OK, calm down. Sit. I don't think coffee is the right thing. I'll make you some mountain tea for your nerves. Take it slowly. Start from the beginning.'

'Well, you know we were talking about a possible visitation from Her?'

'An embodiment – a metamorphic representation. Yes, I was just reading about it.'

'Well, you know, I was a bit cynical. I know I should be more open, but I was on set yesterday and they were doing a scene with Hannah Caro.'

'The girl from the newspaper? The young star?'

'Right. And I was watching her, and the more I watched her, I couldn't take my eyes off her. I've never seen such sensuality, you know? Her body seems to radiate something. It's more than beauty. And she caught my eye and she stared at me and I felt like . . . like . . . it sounds stupid now . . . but I felt like she *knew* me . . . and I thought . . . '

'The Goddess.'

'Yes! Could She have come to us in the form of Hannah Caro? Would there be a more perfect mortal vessel?'

'Interesting. It would certainly make sense: a high-profile, young and beautiful woman from another country . . . but you said you'd done something bad.'

'Yes . . . I went in her trailer.'

'Oh, Niki . . . '

'She wasn't there! She was shooting. I thought if I could borrow something personal of hers, we might be able to . . . I don't know, *test* it or something. I

161

took a dress, some shoes and a hairbrush. Nothing expensive. But Sergeant Nikos from Exogi was there today. He went to see Hannah in her trailer.'

'I hope you didn't leave any clues.'

'People are saying that some guy did it, you know – to have something of hers. Did I do the wrong thing?'

'It was impetuous, but you've always been that. The Goddess would probably approve. Where have you hidden the things?'

'I have them here in my bag. Do you want to look?'

'I . . . OK, let me see.'

Niki took them from the bag and laid them out on the table: a folded white dress, a strappy pair of heels, and the hairbrush with long strands of that long, dark hair.

'Should we feel something?' said Niki. 'How would we know?'

The professor teased a hair from the brush and wound it round a finger. She held one of the light shoes by the heel and studied it. 'We might have to take them to the shrine . . . '

The doorbell rang.

They looked at each other.

'I'm not expecting anyone,' said the professor. She got up and started to walk to the door, glimpsing a uniform cap and navy trousers through the glass. 'It's Sergeant Petras. Hide those things. Quickly.'

Niki grabbed the items and stuffed them back into her bag, which she threw to the corner of the sofa before resting a cushion on it.

'Professor Stratigakis – good morning,' said the policeman.

'Sergeant Petras. Are you well?'

'Very. I was hoping that you might be able to help me with . . . well, not an investigation, exactly. Let's call it a mystery. It pertains to things of a historical nature.'

'How intriguing! Come in, come in. Will you have a coffee?'

'*Frappe, sketo.*'

162

'Of course. You know Niki, I think.'

'Naturally.' He nodded a greeting and flashed a flirtatious eyebrow before sitting opposite her.

The professor stood in the kitchen and made the coffee. 'So what's your mystery, Sergeant?'

'I've had reports – foolish reports, I'm sure – of certain so-called pagan practices in this area and I was wondering if you might advise me.'

Niki held her smile until it hurt.

'Really?' said the professor. 'How odd. What would you like to know?'

'This oil burner was found at the ancient site here.' He took it from his pocket and placed it on the table. 'It looks quite old and has a strange smell. Do you know anything about pagan practices?'

'It depends what you mean by "pagan", sergeant. That tends to be a word used by Christians to disparage every other religion.'

He smiled. 'Let's say the old religions – the ones celebrated in Greece, on this island, before Christianity.'

She came over and put the coffee before him. She took the oil burner, looked at it and sniffed it. 'Well, it looks like it might be Roman, perhaps first century. The smell is frankincense.'

He sipped the coffee and nodded an acknowledgement of its quality. 'How might something like that be used?'

'A lamp like this would typically have been used for light. Just like a candle.'

'And the incense?'

'Incense is more often used in supplications to a deity.'

'Really? How does that work?'

'The flame burns as prayers are said to the god or goddess in question. When the prayers are finished, the flame is blown out and the prayers ascend with the smoke. The incense sweetens it for the god's enjoyment.'

'Interesting. Interesting. The shrine in Allomeros was to a goddess, is that right?'

163

'Aphrodite. Yes.'

'Would a rabbit be used for any reason in these rites? In the past, I mean.'

Niki's gave an exaggeratedly dismissive laugh and blushed instantly.

'Sacrifices were made in many ancient ceremonies, Sergeant,' said the professor. 'Larger animals were generally used: sheep, cows, goats. But I suppose a rabbit might have been used if the worshippers were poor.'

'And today?' he said.

'What about today?'

'Are such things still practised today?'

'Perhaps you have heard of Hellenismos, Sergeant. There are many people in Greece today who still worship the old gods: the Twelve Olympians. The Orthodox Church would prefer modern Greeks to think that it's illegal to believe such things. As it is, the only illegality is to practise without a licence – a licence that must be granted by the same church which forbids other religious practices.'

'This is very interesting, Professor. Myself, I don't care what people believe as long as they don't cause trouble for each other. In a village like this, small matters become big matters. I'm sure you know what I mean.'

'I certainly do.'

'Discretion is better in all things, wouldn't you agree? We can do whatever we like as long as other people don't find out.'

The professor smiled. 'I think I understand you very well, Sergeant.'

He nodded and sipped the coffee, gilding the ends of his moustache with froth.

Niki maintained her smile.

'Well. That was a fine *frappe*,' he said, 'but I must leave you now and make a call on Diogenes.'

'Is it about his naked walks?' said Niki.

'He's doing that again? No, no – it's something else. I'll see myself out.'

The door closed. The professor smiled. Niki fell back into the sofa with a huge sigh. She removed the cushion from over her bag and gasped.

164

'What is it?' said the professor.

'The hairbrush was half out of the bag this whole time? Do you think he saw it? He didn't say anything, did he?'

'He doesn't work like that.'

'What should we do?'

'I think the sergeant's visit must be a sign. You should probably return the things you took.'

'Yes.' said Niki. 'Perhaps that's best.' She studied the hairbrush, stroking the silky strands with her fingers.

1.00 p.m. Exogi-Sami road

Bakery bags and sweet wrappers swirled in a blizzard around the interior of the Marbella as Jim sped along the Sami road. He beat out a rhythm on the steering wheel with one hand and groped around in the glove box for the half *loukanikopita* he'd left there that morning. It should still be edible. Certainly, it would be warm.

Freedom! The open road! The Ithaca tourists were gone and so was his uniform. Time to get a greasy *pita* in Sami and then pop to Myrtos beach for a swim. Work up an appetite for Apicius or Maria's grill in Exogi. Today, he'd saved a life. Someone might write a letter of praise. There might even be a bonus in it. Now where was that *loukanikopita* hiding . . . ?

He bent to peer inside the glove box: nothing but old rooming lists and passenger manifests. Had the pie dropped to the floor when he'd opened the glove box? He dug around in the litter with his foot.

That's when it happened.

A thump.

A groan.

A flash of colour at the corner of his eye.

The clatter of the remaining wing-mirror hitting the road.

An inert body glimpsed in the rear-view.

He hit the brakes. The Marbella left two long black marks in the road surface and sheared off into the scrub. Airborne litter rained into the front of the car.

Hang-gliding Christ!

He got out. There was a smell of burned rubber. The road was silent. The body wasn't moving. An apparently empty car was parked up a path partly concealed by olive trees.

'Are you OK?' shouted Jim.

The body didn't move.

Just drive away. Nobody saw. Just drive away now while the road's still empty.

He got back into the car. His legs were shaking. If his was the only car coming along this way – the only Seat Marbella on the island – they'd soon figure out it must have been him. Or at least that he'd seen it.

He got out again. The body still wasn't moving. He walked towards the body, fearful of seeing blood against the asphalt. Fearful of attack if the guy was just shamming and waiting to leap up and beat the crap out of whoever had hit him.

'Are you OK?'

Jim nudged a shoulder with his foot. The guy was lying face down. There was a dark stain of what smelled like urine at the road's edge. So that was it: the guy had pulled his car in for a piss and Jim had clipped him while coming round the corner. He was lying in the centre of the lane.

Should he move the body? What if there was a spinal injury? Jim bent and took hold of an arm to turn the body.

The face was unmistakable.

James Craggan.

Christ on a Space Hopper! James Craggan. *Cocaine Train. Hangman's Noose, Kung Fu Tyrant.* Run over by Iliad Holidays rep Jim on the Sami road.

He felt himself turn pale. This was *really* going to ruin the summer.

He put an arm under each of Craggan's armpits and dragged the Hollywood star to the side of the road, fighting the persistent thought that it looked exactly like Craggan, even in death. Looked like Craggan – *was* Craggan.

Still no cars. What to do? Put the still-breathing body in the car parked in the bushes there? Let them think he'd passed out or had a crash? No – the star was too heavy, and it'd look suspicious if someone came by while he was doing it. His gaze caught a dusty plastic sheet wrapped round the base of an olive tree. He snatched it, shook it to gauge its size and looked down at Craggan lying unconscious at his feet.

Nothing was going to ruin this summer.

1.30 p.m, The Church, Exogi

Kyriakos rested the motorbike on its stand and stood looking at the church. There was nobody around. The place seemed to be closed. Perhaps this wasn't such a good idea after all.

But then nothing else seemed to be going right. The graffiti was being painted over as quick as they could spray it. The bars in Exogi had actually asked for more of the doctored alcohol. Apparently, the English couldn't get enough of the stuff. Hallucinations, involuntary defecation and unconsciousness was obviously their idea of a good night out. Someone had said that the health centre at Sami was full of them: sun-burned, injured, dehydrated, reeking.

He hadn't been inside the church for years. A christening, a baptism, the occasional family wedding. The only good bit was the party afterwards. But there was the *Filiki Eteria* action plan to think about. Maybe Achilleus was happy to draw up lists and make big speeches, but Zorbas was a man of action, not a talker. This had to be done.

The door was open and the interior had that familiar church smell of incense and polished wood – the smell of Orthodoxy. It was a nationalist smell, whatever the others said. He took off his sunglasses and let his eyes adjust to the dimness. A garish *pantokrator* Christ looked down on him from the interior of the fibreglass dome. Hadn't He, too, been something of a freedom fighter, expelling the bankers from the temple and challenging the occupying authorities?

A shadow moved: Xenomachos kneeling before the iconstasis. He seemed to be polishing the wood and muttering to himself.

Kyriakos coughed.

'Eh? Who's that?' said the priest, turning. 'Kyriakos? Is that you? What are you doing here?'

'I . . . I was hoping to give a confession, *pappas*.'

'Really?' Xenomachos stood. 'What is that shirt you're wearing?'

Kyriakos remembered, too late, that he was still wearing the pagan-metal t-shirt featuring a pneumatic blonde writhing tortured on an inverted cross. 'Nothing, *pappas*. Just a band.'

'Is it blasphemous?'

'No, *pappas*. Blasphemous is a Norwegian group. This is God Rape: a Swedish band.'

'What? What was the name?'

'Nothing. It's not important. Are you able to hear a confession?'

'Yes, yes, I suppose so. I will have to stop polishing, of course. Come and sit over here.'

Xenomachos scraped a chair across the stone floor and sat at the end of a pew. Kyriakos came to sit beside him, glancing sideways at the great beard and noticing evidence of whatever the priest had recently had to eat. Something white. A smear of tomato sauce. *Moussaka?*

'I'm not sure what the proper thing is, *pappas*. What do I need to say?'

168

'We must first make certain that you do not stand in any mortal sin, boy. Have you been guilty recently of denying Christ, of apostasy, idolatry, mutilation, sacrilege (including sorcery or witchcraft), murder, paedophilia, bestiality, incest, extramarital intercourse, theft, greed, necrophilia, drug abuse, disrespect, or wilful acts of schism?'

'I wasn't planning to talk about—'

'Your soul is at risk. You must answer.'

'OK, OK. The schism thing.'

Xenomachos looked up. 'Are you sure?'

'My teacher at school, Miss Niki. I think about her and I . . . ' Kyriakos mimed his sin. 'You know . . . *taka-taka-taka*.'

'I think you are confusing schism with something else, boy.'

'Look, *pappas*, what I really want to tell you about is the nationalist cell we've set up – me and two friends. We're pledged to evict the tourists, international investors, and industry from Greece so we can return to the glorious, pure nation that was born in 1832 – the nation won through blood and faith.'

Xenomachos blinked.

'And also the Jews,' added Kyriakos, 'because they run Europe through the German banks.'

'This is not particularly . . . What you are telling me is very serious.'

'I know. But you can't tell anyone or you go to hell, right?'

'That is correct. There is a sanctity to confession. But why are you telling me these things? I am not sure they are sins.'

'We want to know if you'll join us. You hate the tourists, too. You think that Europe is meddling with the power of Orthodoxy. Perhaps you also know about the Jews. In fact, I bet you know more about it than we do – secret Church gossip and conspiracies and all that.'

'This is very serious . . . Where do you stand on the matter of pagans?'

'If they're against our aims, we're against them.'

169

'What do you expect me to do, boy? I am a figure of authority and respect in this community. I am no terrorist.'

'Neither are we, *pappas*! It's a secret society. We need a revolution on Kefalonia to get rid of the tourists and the foreign investors and the industry. Have you heard of Philotheos?'

'The holy brother at Athos – of course.'

'I've been reading his blog online. I mean, I know he doesn't write it himself because Satan invented the Internet and all that, but they're his words and he seems to believe the same things we do. If he came to the island, we might have our revolution. Couldn't you contact him somehow? Isn't there, like, a priest network – a Churchbook site or something where you all talk to each other?'

'It is not how you imagine, but your ideas are certainly . . . I myself have been thinking about Philotheos in recent days.'

'Great. We can make you a member of the cell. You could have a secret name. Something religious. Moses. Noah. Belshazzar.'

'Isaiah.'

'Whatever. Does this mean you're going to join us?'

'These are serious matters. I must think and pray . . . ' Xenomachos stroked his beard. An idea seemed to come to him. 'In the meantime, while I pray, perhaps you will do something for me – something similarly secret that will help your own aims.'

'What is it?'

'You know the ancient site in Allomeros?'

'I suppose so.'

'For many years, we have believed that the bones of a sainted Christian martyr are buried there, but I think it is being used to enact sacrilegious pagan practices. It is even possible that the teacher you mentioned is involved – she and other women whose behaviour is suspicious. But I have no proof. I need somebody to watch that site after dark and report back to me. I need proof of their paganism.'

'Miss Niki? Pagan sacrifice? Like, naked stuff?'

'I have no idea what they do. I need to know.'

'I'll do it!'

'And remember, boy – not a word to anyone. The confession is a holy pact of silence. Eternal damnation awaits he who disrespects it.'

'Yeah. Cool. Thanks, *pappas*! And look, I'll try to go easier on the acts of schism now I'm working for you.'

'Working . . . ? Wait!'

But Kyriakos was virtually out of the door. Miss Niki! Pagan sacrifice! He'd be schisming so much he'd need a wheelchair.

3.00 p.m. Main Set, near Sami

'Tell me again. Exactly. What. He. Said.'

Penelope hadn't blinked for about five minutes. Her stare radiated a fearful intensity – prosthetic glass rather than human eyes. Granger stood beside her. Others loitered close, hoping to hear, but Penelope lashed them with a vitreous glare and they moved away.

Grace felt her face burning. 'He just said he was going back to get his crystal. Twenty minutes max, he said. I told him I'd call Lomu, but he said he'd borrow someone's car.'

'Well, that's what he did,' said Penelope. 'He took one of the rental cars we've been using. But there's absolutely no sign of it between here and the villa.'

'I don't understand,' said Grace. 'He said—'

'And you believed him?' said Penelope. 'You're supposed to be looking after him. He's played you. He's an *actor*, remember? I bet there was a whole

171

speech, wasn't there? How his old granddaddy gave him the crystal on his death bed, or how a passing eagle dropped it into his palm when he was a boy. Something like that?'

'A Native American seer.'

'There you go.'

'But he's had it in his pocket for every shot since *Hangman's Noose*.'

'Has he? *Really*? Think about it Grace – since when were the Native Americans into crystals? Maybe he couldn't fit a feathered dream-catcher or woven rug in his pocket, so they gave him a crystal instead. What? *What*? Sulking because he played you? He's an *addict*, Grace. The reason we can't find his car is because he's driven somewhere on the island to snort a kilo of blow or honk crack until he meets the eternal soul of Geronimo. I just knew this was going to happen.'

'It might be something else,' said Grace. 'It could be anything. Maybe he wanted to buy a gift for someone and took a detour. It's only been four hours. He told me he was clean and I really believe him. We all do. Talk to Lomu or Chen or . . . Honee. We've been living with him.'

'Do you realise what it'll cost this production if he's relapsed?'

'A lot, I guess.'

'A lot? Yes, a lot. You know that Test Weedle is on his way, don't you?'

'Uh-huh.'

'Hey, look,' said Granger. 'Let's stay focused. We can shoot around the fight scene until Crag turns up. I'm sure Grace is right. There'll be a good reason for this. Grace – why don't you call Lomu and head back to the villa? Crag might make his way back there and he'll be glad to see you. Don't worry about this. It's not your fault. You couldn't have stopped him.'

Penelope snorted her disgust. 'Nobody says a word about this, is that understood? Not. A. Word. If it gets out that he's missing, we're dead. *You're* dead. The story if anyone asks is that he's got heat exposure . . . no, that's basically a euphemism for relapse. OK, right – he's got dysentery. Don't make it

172

that explicit, though. Something embarrassing to do with his bowels. I know it's not very "rock 'n' roll" but, frankly, he deserves it. Maybe I'll get the caterers fired just to lend it some credibility. Not a word, right?'

Penelope stalked off to the dining area and Granger shrugged. This is how it goes.

'I believed him,' said Grace.

'You're probably right. Just go back to the villa and we'll see if he turns up tonight.'

A production assistant came over and looked plaintively at Granger.

'What is it, Jo?'

'Chet's started speaking only Greek again. We need the translator.'

Granger nodded, touched Grace on the shoulder and walked off with the PA.

7.00 p.m. Main Street, Exogi

Jim rattled the ice in his third ouzo and held up the glass to the passing waitress. He picked the last chip from the plastic plate and used it to scrape a smear of *tzatziki*. And he listened. His ears sought, combed, sieved the conversations around him for the words "Craggan", "dead", and "Seat Marbella" used together in the fateful accusatory sentence that would see him locked away forever. Perhaps in a Greek prison. The food would be good, but he'd be the least hairy guy in there: the bride with unlimited grooms.

He was sunburned. After dealing with the body, he'd backtracked to one of the tiny coves and spread his towel there. Let someone else find the body – he'd look innocent. What, me? I've been on this beach all afternoon. No, I didn't drive past that place. James who?

173

A few cars and the odd motorbike, had gone that way, but there'd been no sirens, no fuss. Nothing. Had the body even been found? *Somebody* had to be missing him! It was hardly the kind of thing he could bring up himself. So what about that James Craggan then? Anyone found him dead on the Sami road today?

'What yer lookin' so depressed about? 'Ad another run in wi' Mister Trellos?'

Kelly breasts were like jostling bald dwarves ready to erupt from a spangly top.

'Want to join me?' he said.

'Aye, go on then. 'Ow's it goin'? I 'eard about yer guy 'oo got run ovver.'

'*What*? What are people saying?'

'On the transfer this mornin'. Feller under the coach.'

'Oh. Mister Tickell. No, he was just making a protest. We didn't run him over.'

'Protest, eh? Another one of yer guests caused a fuss at the airport – a lass covered in puke? Been 'ad by everyone in the village?'

'Ms Grockle. Did she get her wheelchair in the end?'

'Aye. But they didn't let her on the plane cos she downed half a bottle of duty-free voddy and went mental like that girl in the devil film.'

'*The Exorcist*?'

'Summat like that. So what's up wi' yer, yer maungy git? Not enjoyin' summer in Exogi?'

'It'd be a great job without the tourists.'

'Yer need a shag, that's what it is. Get yer oats and yer'll be fine.'

'That's very kind, Kelly, but . . . '

'Not wi' me, yer cheeky bastard! Yer couldn't 'andle *me*!'

'Literally.'

'Eh?'

'Never mind. Listen – what do you know about Tripa?'

174

'"Ave they given yer the property in Tripa?'

'Yeah. Donna says I've got to drive over there and do a visit three times a week.'

'*Shiiit.* It's right over near Lixouri, in't it? I went past it with Yiannis on the bike once. Someone said they used to test chemicals there after the war. Yer know, like, for killing insects and that. There's only one 'otel and nothin' for miles around. Feller threw 'imself off the roof a couple of years ago, he was so bored. There was a load of oil on the beach last winter.'

'Wonderful.'

'Well, there's nowt yer can do about it. Just fill out the forms.'

'Yeah. I've been told I've got to do a Greek night, too.'

'Oh, that's cool! I've done 'em before – loadsa fun!'

'I don't know where to start.'

'Talk to Anthi, Mister Trellos' granddaughter. 'Er boyfriend plays keyboards and 'is mate's got a bazooka. Any of these places'd 'ost it. In fact . . . 'ow about me and Philippa sell tickets for it, too? Bit of a money spinner!'

He waved a hand, encompassing the street. 'But it'd be so depressing watching these people pretending to be Zorba and shouting *opa*! The t*zatziki*, the Greek salad, the *mousaka* – it's all such a tired, predictable parody.'

'Yer snobby bastard. Just do it or yer'll defo get fired. Listen – d'yer want some really juicy gossip?'

'How juicy?' Let it be about Philippa's sexual proclivities.

'Philippa told me the secret tourist is on the way 'ere.'

'Secret tourist? Like a secret shopper?'

'Yeah. Golden, Smithson and Iliad – they all use the same company in the Ionian. Nobody knows what the person looks like. They just appear on the roomin' lists under false names.'

'So it's someone travelling alone?'

'Might be. Or they might double up, I s'pose. Just to trick yer.'

'And what? They observe your welcome meeting, go on excursions – all that?'

'I s'pose. I got checked in Corfu last year. I think I know 'oo it was, but I can't be sure. Anyway, I was fine. *Yer'll* be in deep shit if they check yer, though.'

'Do you think so?'

'Yer the worst rep ever, Jimbo. I've got money on yer getting fired before the end of July.'

'Cheers, Kelly. How does Philippa know, anyway?'

'She's got connections. Admit it – yer fancy 'er a bit, don't yer?'

'Has she said something?'

'Yeah – that yer 'aven't got an 'ope in 'ell.'

'That's a lot of dropped aitches.'

'Eh?'

'Who was that guy she was with at Apicius the other night? Her boyfriend?'

'It were just a mate of Yianni's. Visitin' from Patras. Yer jealous?'

'No. I'd hate to be a perfect physical specimen like him. I'd rather eat cheese pies than do sit-ups.'

'It shows. 'Er boyfriend is Christos: the guy who works at the ferry office in Sami.'

'The one who looks like a classical statue of an Olympian?'

'That's 'im. Look, Jimbo – I've got to go. I'm meeting Yiannis in a minute. He says he knows where Hannah Caro is stayin' and we're gonna try to see her. Maybe get a picture. Try and cheer up. Why not 'ang around No Name about two this mornin'? There'll be some slappers falling down drunk 'oo'll 'elp yer out.'

'Romance isn't dead in Exogi.'

'You're a weirdo, Jimbo, but I kinda like yer. Yer like the retarded brother I never 'ad.'

'Beautiful sentiment. Someone should print that in a card.'

She snorted and was off: a prehistoric fertility figure moulded in clay by men and transplanted to the twenty-first century by a deity who knew the Greeks would like her. Gap-toothed, fleshily abundant and with only a nugatory education, certainly, but she was also some kind of ally here in the kingdom of the common. He was just a traveller in her polyester-uniformed world – the opera-goer at the vaudeville show.

The fourth ouzo arrived. Probably best to order another *pita* parcel of greasy *giros* meat to absorb the alcohol. Here, at least, was some pleasure in his exile among the damned. If he could just keep the image of lifeless Craggan out of his mind . . .

He stirred the drink with a straw and leaned back to watch the pageant unfold: the raucous groups, the mottled limbs, the primary colours, the moped *kamakia*, the conflicted scents of after-sun and duty-free perfume. And here – a silken shadow – came the village priest: ecclesiastically bearded against the swilling sin of Exogi.

Xenomachos scowled, frowned, grimaced and looked askance as he strolled. Immorality was everywhere. Semi-nudity, drunkenness, godlessness – and his own congregation was at the core of it, encouraging it, stoking the embers of sin to coax the precious euro flames. Their savings might be increasing, but their righteousness was running ever deeper into debt.

Perhaps a pre-fabricated church was all these people deserved. It had been different in the previous century, and in the centuries before that, when all had stood against the Turk and marched to freedom under the sign of the cross. Those Greeks *deserved* their beautiful frescoes and gilded icons. Such things were revered then not only as holy objects, but as *national* symbols.

His thoughts again returned to the Athonite monk Philotheos – a brother of the old order, an anchorite living wild among the rocky wastes of the Holy Mountain itself: almost a legend even among his own kind. The stories about him were legion, each more remarkable than the last. A late-season pilgrim is lost on the peak and encounters Philotheos – dripping, ragged, spectral – in the fog. 'Good day, Sotiris,' says the monk, having never met the man before. 'Go that way and you will be safe. Pray to Saint John and your sister's aggravated boil will be healed.' And it was so. Or, a fellow brother becomes mad with loneliness and doubt. He plots to fling himself into the sea from great height and sneaks from his cell before dawn to commit the act. But Philotheos is waiting at the suicide spot and says he will leap too if the other insists upon proceeding. A seabird lands between them and drops a scrap of scripture forbidding self-murder. The young monk repents and goes on to a career of esteemed scriptural analysis.

But how to contact the man? The website was apparently handled by an acolyte in Thessaloniki, but there was no address listed on it. Indeed, Philotheos was himself quite adamant in his rejection of the Internet. As everyone must surely know, the sixth letter of the Hebrew alphabet is "waw", whose nearest approximation is "W". Therefore, any email address beginning "www" translated directly as 666: the Number of the Beast. Nor was it possible to phone around some of the monasteries at the edge of the Holy Mountain and pass on a message, because Philotheos had spoken at length about the dangers of a misdial that might, again, conjure the apocalyptic digits.

So, what? Send a letter addressed to "Philotheos, somewhere on Mount Athos"? There seemed little other choice. And if the cause was worthy, surely the prescient monk already knew of it, just as he had known the climber's name and the intentions of the lonely brother. What could be a worthier cause than the creeping threat of paganism, heathen sacrifice and the lapping flood of sin?

Philotheos would help. Yes. He would come with the sword of truth and smite these sinners. A church would be built – not bought and delivered – in honour of the crusade and become a shrine overseen by him, Xenomachos, as the keeper of its eternal flame. Not for his own pride or magnification, no – but as a turning point in Orthodoxy itself.

His wife waved to him from the Kyanni Akti café. Six of their eleven children were sitting with her, not notably delighted at his arrival. They, too,

178

were sinners. Especially the older girl Andriana, whose long, slender legs had the boys of the village chasing her round like dogs on heat. Thank the Lord that there was a fine convent on the island. It might not be the birthday present Andriana was hoping for, but the path of true faith was hard, and seldom involved Lycra.

11.00 p.m., Diogenes' Bar, Allomeros

'Life is like a flower. It grows from a fertilised seed, develops into a thing of beauty in its youth, but quickly degenerates through decay. Its scent turns to sweet death and its petals curl, drying, and fall to leave only a withered, naked head. The stem wilts, trodden underfoot.'

Diogenes stood in a declamatory pose, one arm outthrust, the other holding a square bottle of whisky instead of Yorick's skull. Tonight, he was dressed in an old green tuxedo and an embroidered black sombrero.

'Thanks,' said Grace. 'That really puts everything into perspective.'

They were the only ones in the bar. Some kind of muted Greek jazz played. Cannabis smoke curled into the twin ceiling fans from Diogenes' colossal joint.

'Do you think I could be in the movies?' said Diogenes, showing her his profile.

'Anybody can be. You just have to want it more than anything else – more than love or dignity or family. Stardom consumes stars. Look at Demi. Look at Winona.'

'A Faustian pact.'

'I suppose. But let's not talk about movies. I'm not sure I have much of a future there. Have you seen that British guy around – the one I was talking to the other night?'

'The holiday company fellow? He hasn't been in since then. He lives somewhere here in the village, I think.'

'I'd like to talk to him again. He seemed relatively normal . . . for round here, I mean.'

Diogenes bowed. 'I take that as a compliment.'

'Do you think if I drink all of this bourbon I'll be able to sleep through tomorrow?'

'"Tomorrow is another day" – who said that?'

'Nostradamus?'

'Vivien Leigh. *Gone with the Wind*.'

'Right. That picture almost brought the studio down, you know.'

'Art must have its casualties.'

'And I'm one of them. You should see the shit I've been writing for this movie.'

'You're a writer?'

'No – that's the point. I just did a course once. They want it to be "cooler".'

'I'm cool. I could give you some ideas.'

She smiled. 'You're on a whole different planet of cool. I need commercial cool, not individual cool. There are lists now that tell you what's cool. It's not oboes.'

'You should have . . . what's his name, the hero?'

'Captain Cornolli.'

Diogenes did a brief double-take. 'You should have Cornolli riding a Harley and smoking a big cigar. Sunglasses. He should have a line he repeats. Like Schwarzenegger. "I'll be strumming", eh?'

'You think you're joking, but it might come to that. I've been trying to write cool electric mandolin scenes for Chet Braddock.'

'Set it on fire, like Jimi. Play it with a violin, like in *Spinal Tap*.'

'Yeah, right. Only, he's dressed as a peasant fisherman. Wearing a plastic finger.'

180

Diogenes took a prolonged hit on the joint and exhaled thoughtfully. 'The secrets of Hollywood. I read somewhere that Bing Crosby was molested by aliens.'

She looked at him. His pug face was sweating under the sombrero. Meeting him would be at least one positive experience she could take home from all of this.

'I'm drunk,' she said.

'Bravo!'

She didn't want to go back to the villa. Honee wouldn't stop crying. Lomu was out driving all over the island in search of Crag. Chen had no one to cook for. None of them seemed willing to talk to her. She, the new girl – the spectral daughter – was somehow to blame.

Diogenes topped up her already ridiculous measure of bourbon. 'Let's go out and look at the stars. Come on – bring your glass. I'll tell you which one I'm from.'

Police Office, Exogi

Two dark-suited security men entered the office. Nikos leaned back in his chair and smirked as they unsmilingly looked around to verify that he was alone.

'I think I have seen this movie,' he said. 'Now you flash a light in my eyes and I forget everything, yes?'

They didn't smile. One of them mumbled into a tiny microphone on his lapel and a woman's heels sounded on the stairwell below. Nikos sat up straight – was it Hannah Caro, come in person to enquire about her missing property?

Penelope appeared framed in the doorway. She seemed even tenser than the previous day.

'Ah, it is you,' said Nikos. 'I have been asking questions about the robbery from Ms Caro's—'

'Forget that, Sergeant. The things have been returned. Something else has come up. Something much more serious.'

'Yes?'

'Are you taking this seriously, Sergeant? Do I have to contact your superiors?'

'That depends. Is this more serious than a missing brush?'

She glared. He grinned.

'What I'm going to tell you must remain absolutely confidential. You mustn't even tell your colleagues. Is that agreed?'

'I have no colleagues.'

'Good. James Craggan has disappeared. We need your help finding him as soon as possible.'

Nikos leaned forward, his elbows resting on the desk top. 'Disappeared?'

'He left the set in a rental car yesterday, heading for his villa. He hasn't come back. Someone was sent to look for him but found no trace of the car. Now we've found the car on the road to Exogi, but not the man.'

'The car is still in the same place where you found it?'

'Yes. Unmoved. About halfway between here and Sami. Someone is watching it until you can investigate.'

'You have looked in all the usual places?'

'The villa, local bars, the other trailers on set – yes. He hasn't spoken to his girlfriend or any of his staff. It seems he hasn't left on any ferries. His passport is still at the villa.'

'He has enemies?'

'He has *fans*. Perhaps some deranged middle-aged woman who has a shrine to him. Did you get that movie *Misery* in Greece? Caan. Bates. He was a writer; she broke his ankles—'

'With a big hammer. I have the DVD.'

182

'Right. So something like that.'

'Or maybe he just jumped in the sea, yes?'

'He's rich, famous and screwing a woman with plastic tits who's half his age. He's on his way back. Would *you* kill *your*self?'

'Every man is a mystery.'

'Jesus! Is everyone a philosopher in this country? Are you going to find him or do I have to go over your head?'

'And flash the light in my eyes to make me forget?'

'What are you talking about?'

'Of course, I will be happy to help find your missing star.'

'Tell nobody. If this gets out, you'll be policing goats on the border with Albania, I swear to God. *My* people know how to keep quiet. This is a multi-million dollar production that could bring your little island unbelievable wealth.'

'I understand. I saw the last mandolin film.'

She scowled. 'Just make sure it's done quickly. You need anything, call me – cars, boats, helicopters, divers . . . whatever. And be discreet. I can't have my own people doing this or the paparazzi will shit. I'll be calling you hourly for updates. OK?'

He nodded and leaned back in the chair. 'Is that all?'

'No. If you have time, I'd also be grateful if you could look into some thefts we've been experiencing from sets around the area. A couple of electric mandolins have been taken during lunch breaks. They're quite useless as instruments – just hollow props. But it's the principle. It may be tourists – souvenir hunters.'

'I have heard that such things appear on an Internet site called Ebay.'

'Please – just look into it. But Craggan is the priority.' She offered a final glare and was gone, her heels clacking down the stairs. The two security guys followed without glance or comment.

Nikos took out his mobile and turned it off. He stroked his moustache. In any other summer, this disappearance would look just like a typical tourist misadventure. But it was turning out to be not like any other summer.

Was there the slightest possibility – absurd, ridiculous – that there was something to this *Filiki Eteria* nationalist cell business after all? There was the graffiti. And Diogenes had told him that the toxic weed traces found in the illegal alcohol grew abundantly across the local hills. True, it could have found its way accidentally into the still . . . or it could have been put in there on purpose to poison the tourists.

He thought briefly of Maria, who hadn't called since the letter from her husband. Neither had Aliki. These nationalists and the movie people were disrupting his leisure time in a very unwelcome manner. The sooner they were gone, the better. He took his cap and rattled the car keys on his trouser pocket.

Location Shoot, near Exogi

The descending sun coloured the few clouds ochre-purple and bathed the rock-and-tussock edge of the precipice in a fleeting violet light. A low mist drifted at knee height. A figure strolled beside the void: a local peasant boy – a fisherman, perhaps – wearing sunglasses and a cap tilted at an angle. He carried an instrument that shone cherry-red with varnish and glittered with silver strings – an electric mandolin, whose pickups flashed as he twirled it into playing position.

And there, far above the great sweep of sand framed beautifully below, he postured and posed in the rapture of a prolonged solo: eyes closed, knees bent, pelvis thrusting at the back of the instrument as he exorcised stretched notes and blurred arpeggios from it. The left hand worked the frets like a lover. The fingers danced lithe and limber at the strings, faster and impossibly faster until bone and sinew melded with woven steel to wring tears from Orpheus himself.

But there was no sound. That would be added later from a studio session. Instead, there was only the muted tinkle of the unamplified strumming and the whirring fingers, so indicative of talent – closer, closer until the frame was filled with them in all their virtuosic dexterity.

Then one finger – the little finger on the right hand – seemed to bend unnaturally and droop. It dangled pendulously. It dropped and fell to the ground at the player's feet.

'Cut!'

'Godammit, Chet!' said the assistant director. 'I told you this would happen. If you can't keep the prosthetic on, we're going to use a double.'

'No – no doubles. People have to know it's me – I mean, Efthimios – playing.'

'Well, we've lost the light now. We'll have to shoot it tomorrow. That's a wrap for today.'

Technicians entered the frame and began to remove lighting rigs, reflectors, diffusion filters. Someone from props took the electric mandolin. Granger spoke to the camera operator.

'Can I see the playback?' said Chet, walking over to the AD's monitor.

The screen flickered and there he was, framed beautifully against beach and sunset.

'Looks cool,' said Chet.

Granger's mobile rang and she walked away to take it. She nodded, spoke briefly and returned. 'That was Tony. Test Weedle is on the island and wants to talk. He's at the main set. We should get down there.'

Main Set, near Sami

'Sure, they invented triangles and sodomy, but where's the friggin' air-con round here! Is this the Third World or what? It must be a hundred degrees in here. And can I get a *cold* water? Evian or Perrier – in a *glass* bottle. Come *on*, guys! France, Greece . . . it's all virtually the same country anyway. Ya could fit the whole of Europe into California. They got fifteen different kinds of water in my local deli, including one from Fiji. And let me tell ya – the friggin moon's closer to Fiji than that deli is.'

Test Weedle: Lustre Productions trouble-shooter, numbers man, target-range buddy of Mel Weitz, and notorious intercessor between producers and director when films started to drift off budget or into less commercial marketing demographics. Some said he'd started out as Don Simpson's pool boy. Others said he was in tight with both the Kabbalah crew *and* the Scientologists – the kind of guy who always got the best table, the first special-edition hybrid car, the complimentary courtside seats. If you lived and worked in Hollywood, you knew the name even if you didn't know what he did.

He looked just like a blond Ken doll: the same shaped eyebrows, the orthodontic glare, the ultramarine eyes, the tanned, plastic face without a single impairing pore or wrinkle. And he was doll-sized – about five feet tall in his built-up Cuban heels. A violet cashmere jumper was slung with aesthetic insouciance over slender polo-shirted shoulders and his uncreased slacks ended in a pair of butter-coloured loafers made from the ultra-soft hide of some animal embryo.

'How many shots you used that Aquila for?' asked Test, pointing to one of the camera cranes. 'I know how much they cost to hire. Someone make me a list so I can do a cost-benefit analysis. And what's with all those extras I saw earlier? Haven't you guys heard of CGI? Just use six of them and we'll pixellate their asses in post-production – do a *Gandhi* with PhotoShop or whatever they're using these days.'

186

Tony Brass nodded and maintained the sycophantic smile with increasing effort. 'What do you think of the newer rushes, Test?'

'Better. Yeah, better. The electric mandolins – good. Remind me, is there a battle scene? An air strike?'

'There's the mandolin fight between Cornolli and his son. There's the showdown with the neo-Nazis at the end.'

'Yeah, right. Right. Explosions. We need explosions. I want to see some action every eleven minutes in the final edit. There was study: they did a test screening with heart monitors and sweat probes – all that stuff – and they found that people can only take eleven minutes of story at a time. You have to chop it up with action. Car chases. Jeopardy. Shark attack. Meteor strike. Time-bomb wired into to a public service vehicle. Got it?'

'Sure, Test. But this is a mandolin movie . . . '

'Right, right. I know you'll use your creative vision. Chet's a fisherman, right? There are sharks in the Mediterranean – I know it. Shepherds – rabid goats. Village life – satanic incest. Germans – pornography. I'm just spitballin' here. Whatever fits with the script – but every eleven minutes. Ya got a scriptwriter on it, right? Poor Scott LaBrava – ya know he's being sued by the ASPCA? Poor bastard's in hospital, never gonna speak again, and they're chasing him for what he did to the dog. It was *his* dog, man. The dog's fine. You believe this shit?'

'It's crazy. Yes, we have a writer – one of Crag's people. She's accredited. She wrote the electric mandolin stuff.'

'The spectral daughter girl?'

'Yes. Her name's Grace. She should be here for the meeting.'

'He banging her? I heard she's legal and I know he's been into some far-out stuff . . . '

'No. He has another assistant: Honee.'

'Honee D'Angelo? Yeah, I've seen her. Pretty much all of her. She used to be a dancer at—'

187

Tony stood. Granger and the AD had finally arrived, apparently having met Grace and Penelope somewhere en route from the unit shoot.

'How did it go?' said Tony.

'It fell off,' said the AD.

'Right. Let me introduce you all to Test Weedle. Test – this is our AD Mike Kendall, his assistant Granger, and this is Grace Willets: Crag's production assistant. You know Penelope, of course.'

They shook hands.

'OK,' said Test. 'Let's go somewhere private. We got big things to discuss. How about we use Crag's trailer? I guess it's free.'

Granger led the way. Grace hurried to walk beside her.

'Am I in trouble?'

'As long as there's a chance of Crag coming back, you should be safe,' said Granger. 'Just keep this guy happy. He's the one calling the shots right now. There's too much riding on the movie now to let it all crash.'

'Do you believe what they're saying? That Crag's fallen off the wagon?'

'I don't think so, but I've been proved wrong before.'

They entered the Winnebago and sat. There was much exchanging of glances.

'OK. Right,' said Test. 'First off: James Craggan. What the frig?'

'I've got the local policeman on it,' said Penelope. 'He knows every inch of this island and most of the people on it. I think it's better for him to do it than having security running all over the place.'

'Good. Agreed. But what's the deal – is Crag juicing again? Smoking? Shooting up? What are we looking at here? If he does turn up, can we just give him a cup of coffee, or will he need his blood changed?'

Granger signalled that Grace should answer.

'I'm sure he's clean. I've been living with him. All he drank was orange juice and mineral water. All he ate was wholegrain rice and organic pulses. No alcohol in the house. No tobacco. He looked good. The whites of his eyes were bright.

188

He was happy, motivated. Whatever's happened to him, it must have been an accident.'

'For what it's worth, I agree,' said Brass. 'He was on time, knew his lines. He was sharp.'

Test nodded. 'Yeah. Maybe. Or maybe he had you all fooled and he was pushing stuff up his ass. He wouldn't be the first. I could tell ya stories, but let's go with your version. The fact is, we can't shut down just 'cause he's gone AWOL. You're already over budget and the Qataris are asking questions. They're not in this for the art, right? For them, it's about names on screen and getting blown, Allah willing.'

'It's not like we can shoot around him,' said Brass. 'He *is* Captain Cornolli. He's in most of the scenes.'

'Then get creative – that's ya job. Find a reason for his face not being in shot. Use a body double. Ya got a writer here – a writer who knows the man. Look at Brandon Lee in *The Crow*, Oli Reed in *Gladiator*. Being dead didn't stop *them* from featuring. Think of a storyline. He's so ashamed of being the world's best mandolinist he has to wear a bag over his head. I don't know. OK, not that. I'm not a writer.'

'Can you do that, Grace?' said Granger.

'I . . . I guess.'

'Now we're making movies!' said Test. 'I've already spoken to Tony about pace so I won't go over that again here. In fact, I'll come straight to the point: we need more sex. Ya think any young guy's coming to this picture 'cause they wanna see Hannah Caro play a friggin mandolin? No. Ya think we booked Caro for her character acting? No. She's in it for the tits and ass – excuse me ladies, but it's true. The girl's dynamite with chilli sauce and she doesn't mind going nude. I checked her contract personally.'

'There is a love scene with Chet's character,' said Brass.

'Love shmuv! I want humping. I want scenes so hot the MPAA threatens not to release the movie unless we cut five minutes of beaver shots. And that five minutes'll be our unofficial marketing, right?'

Test winked at Penelope, who smiled indulgently.

'Remember *Sliver*? Remember *Postman*. Remember *Don't Look Now*? I want people for the next ten years to be wondering whether Chet Braddock really slipped it to Caro in that scene. Hell, tell them to do it. I know *he* would if it meant bringing the character alive. She'd probably do it for a pair of shoes or a stick of gum, God love her. It doesn't have to be vulgar. Just write it in. And can we get her something tighter or shorter to wear? She's dressed like a nun in the rushes. I want every guy who sees this movie to imagine it's his schlong she's playing – sorry ladies, but you know what I mean.'

'More sex,' nodded Grace, the writer.

'I do have one quite serious concern,' said Brass.

'Shoot,' said Test.

'*Captain Cornolli's Mandolin School*? It sounds like a bad porn knock-off, like *Shaving Ryan's Privates*.'

'I hear ya, Tony. We're working on it. We're going back to this Bernie guy. Whatever he wants: a horse, a condo, an animatronic sex doll – no limits. But if he still says no, don't sweat it. Look at *Battlestar Galactica* – a knock-off *Star Wars*. Look at *Piranha* – a knock-off *Jaws*. People don't care what it's called as long as the product's good.'

'It's not really the same—'

'Tony, Tony, Tony – let me worry about this stuff. You're the artist; I'm just the bean-counter. The main thing is that everyone's straight with the plan. Is everyone straight?'

They nodded.

'Right. So let me see those new pages when they're ready, and let's make this movie!'

'Are you sticking around, Test?' said Brass.

'Why not? No harm in a little vacation. It can't be work work work all the time.'

'I suppose not.'

Grace stared at her shoes. Robert McKee had never said anything about this kind of screenwriting.

Stone Hut, near Sami

The three motorbikes came to a stop in a swirl of dust. Each rider wore his helmet hanging from an elbow in case Sergeant Petras decided to enforce the law that day.

'This had better be good,' said Andreas. 'Nekros Bar in Sami is having a *Metallica* day today. Someone said Lars Ulrich might turn up.'

'Yeah,' said Achilleus. 'Perhaps he'll come on a bus with the guys from *Anthrax* and *Slayer*. You know how all those millionaire superstars can't resist Sami.'

'*Malakas.*'

'Hey!' said Kyriakos. 'Trust me, this is massive. This is going to make *us* stars in *Filiki Eteria*. This is going to take us back to 1832 quicker than you can say "time machine".'

'I hope you haven't done anything stupid without us,' said Achilleus.

'Come on. I'll show you.'

They went inside.

'Jesus!' said Andreas.

'Christ!' said Achilleus.

A mature man had been blindfolded and cable-tied to a chair, which now lay on its back on the floor. The man's legs were in the air. A pair of headphones had been secured over his ears with duct tape that ran under his chin and around the top of his head. The long cable ran to a laptop. He wasn't moving.

'He must have tried to escape,' said Kyriakos. 'He was sitting when I left him. Don't worry – he can't hear us. There are five-thousand songs on the hard drive.'

'Is it . . . is it James Craggan?' said Andreas.

Kyriakos nodded, grinning.

'Did you get his autograph?' said Andreas.

'What the *fuck* have you done?' said Achilleus. 'He's an American citizen! Do you understand what trouble we're in? You can't just kidnap people. The CIA are probably surrounding us with snipers right now. Forget going to university – we're all going to Guantanamo Bay for the rest of our lives. I hope you like orange jumpsuits. There'll be no goodbyes – just immediate rendition.'

'Relax!' said Kyriakos. 'We've got the power now. The graffiti, the alcohol – it was all a waste of time. Now we've got a star.'

'And what are you going to do with him?' said Achilleus, his voice rising higher and higher.

'Make a video, like Al-Qaeda.'

'Yeah!' said Andreas. 'I'll do a bitchin' soundtrack! We can mix it on the MacBook.'

'What kind of video? We talked about this! All the tourists and industry and Jews aren't going to leave Kefalonia because you've kidnapped James Craggan. They're just going to arrest us and put us in a cargo container and blast heavy rock at us for the next twenty years.'

'Cool!' said Andreas.

'I didn't kidnap him,' said Kyriakos. 'I saved him. He owes us.'

'What?'

'If you just let me tell the story . . . '

'Go on, then. But it'd better be good.'

'I was coming back from the church—'

192

'*The church?*'

'Wait a minute! I was coming back and I stopped for a piss just round the bend after Exogi – you know, where nobody can see. Well, there was a car hidden in the bushes and an old plastic sheet laid out. I looked under it and there was Craggan. It looked like he was dead, but I could kind of see him breathing. I knew straight away what I had.'

'So, what? You hung him over the back of your bike and drove him here for all the world to see?' said Achilleus.

'No, *malakas*. I left the bike and took his car to bring him here. Then I returned the car and came back on the bike.'

'Fingerprints?'

'I wiped the wheel, the door handle and the controls. Anyway, Petras isn't CSI is he? You think he's got DNA analysis in his office at Exogi? He's still using faxes and landlines.'

'Is Craggan still alive?' said Andreas. 'I've not seen him move yet.'

'Maybe he's sleeping,' said Kyriakos.

'With five-thousand mp3s of thrash metal piped directly into his head?' said Achilleus. 'I doubt it.'

'He might be meditating,' said Andreas.

'Look – we need some sort of script,' said Kyrialos. 'What are our demands? It doesn't have to be high tech. We can use the camera on the laptop.'

'No, I've got a proper camera and tripod at home,' said Andreas. 'And we need to film it somewhere where they can't guess the location. Like bin Laden did. A cave or something.'

'Are you two crazy?' said Achilleus.

'There's only one question as far as I'm concerned,' said Kyriakos. 'How committed are you to the cause? Do you want to reclaim Greece, or are you afraid of the Jewish foreign investors? Ask yourself, what would Achilles have done if the Greeks had captured Hector at Troy? Apologise and send him back?'

'Yeah!' said Andreas.

193

'If you're unsure,' said Kyriakos, 'why don't you write to *Filiki Eteria* HQ in Athens and ask what the procedure is.'

'I might do that,' said Achilleus.

They looked at the figure tied to the chair.

'I've seen *Kung Fu Tyrant* about eighteen times,' said Achilleus.

'"Now you've got lead poisoning!"' said Andreas, emulating Craggan's snarl.

'Why were you at the church anyway?' said Achilleus.

'Let me tell you about that. I've got a secret mission. How would you like to see Miss Niki in a naked pagan sacrifice?'

Friktos Hotel, Tripa

Jim drove past it twice before he realised it was there. Only God knew why anyone would have chosen to build anything in that unearthly landscape of reeds and dunes. The place looked like a prehistoric swamp that had withered to sand over the millennia and ended up as this incandescent glare of infesting flies and airborne quartz. The wind off the sea was relentless. Heat seemed to pool in the hollow where the hotel squatted. It would have made an excellent penal colony.

Penal colony. Jail. Hard labour. Convict marriages. Penile colony. Such thoughts kept springing unbidden to mind. He'd dreamed about Craggan for the last two nights – Craggan visiting him like Banquo's ghost with accusations from beyond the grave. Was this how his freedom would end? Known in perpetuity as the guy who'd killed James Craggan while looking for a sausage pie in the footwell of a Seat Marbella? Such ignominy could surely not be borne. He'd be forced to take his own life.

He left the Marbella parked askew in the empty car park. Bitumen clung stickily to his soles. The hotel seemed closed, but he passed through the plate-glass entrance to discover a marbled reception with a real, live person sitting behind it.

'Hi. I'm Jim. I'm with Iliad. If you don't mind, I'll just sit in reception for an hour in case anyone wants to book an excursion, complain or threaten to sue me.'

The girl – probably the owner's daughter making some summer money – smiled. 'Mister Overy has been asking twice a day when you'd come. He's waiting for you on the seats there.'

Jim turned to see a middle-aged man with a face so red he was either badly sunburned or on the verge of a stroke. Possibly both. A white sun hat was perched on the top of his head and he seemed to be making extensive notes on a sheaf of papers.

'Has he been causing any trouble?'

'He complains a lot,' said the girl. 'More than usual. He takes pieces of food from the restaurant and puts them in little boxes. He says he will have them examined by scientists.'

'What a dick.'

'This is what I said. I feel sorry for his wife.'

Jim nodded his thanks and approached the man. Could this be the Secret Tourist, sent to test him? A superhuman pretence of professionalism might be required.

'Mister Overy! How very nice to see you. Lovely weather we're having. I trust you're enjoying your holiday?'

'No. I am not.'

'Oh dear. Would you like me to register an official complaint?'

'Yes, I certainly would. I've written a full report here, detailing my dissatisfaction on every level. Ten pages. You have no idea how long it's taken me. Hours. Days. I haven't had time to go to the beach or enjoy swimming. I've been in my room drafting and redrafting this document. Here – take it. I've made three copies by hand.'

195

'That's very thorough, Mister Overy, but all complaints must be written on the Iliad Holidays CC-Ex form by me alone. So, you see, I can't take your document. Maybe you can tell me the salient points – just the bullets – and I'll jot them on the form.'

'But I've spent days on this!'

'Yes, yes, I see. It's unfortunate – a grievous waste of your time, I'm afraid. As I say, only I can record the nature of the complaint. Rules are there to help us, Mister Overy.'

'I'm not going to trust you! I want my complaint documented *exactly* as I've written it. I know – I'll read it out and you transcribe it word for word on to your precious form.'

'That's not really the way we—'

But Mr Overy wasn't listening. He sat straight, held his sheaf of papers at optimum reading distance and began to orate:

'On arriving at Kefalonia airport, it was my displeasure to note the surliness of the Greek gentleman of whom I asked the whereabouts of the nearest water closet. My wife has long suffered from a weak bladder, and the delayed plane had left her in a state of some distress, she not wanting to use the facilities on board, whose powerful flush has been known to suck the uterus from some women. Notwithstanding the fact that the gentleman in question was not an employee of the airport or any holiday company known to me, his response was both insulting and flippant, setting the tone for a catalogue of disappointment that would . . . '

Jim caught the first few sentences before tilting the clipboard so that his notes might not be seen. Thereafter, he moved the pen at random, waiting for Mr Overy to reach the end of his multiple clauses with a salient point. And as his mind wandered, he caught a vision of a ponytail and some slender legs at the edge of his vision. Philippa! She must also have clients here at the edge of civilisation. Would she come and rescue him from this?

196

'. . . whereupon I berated the waitress for her temerity in offering us red wine with the fish. One would expect waiting staff to be thoroughly versed in the art of the sommelier if they are required to perform such a role. I should have known from her choice of footwear – sandals revealing painted toenails – that the girl was not at all of the calibre expected . . . '

Jim kept his phantom pen at work and flicked a glance over towards reception, where the perfect peach of Philippa's bottom was exhibited to sublime effect as she leant forwards to rest her elbows on the counter. Perhaps here, away from the office and the *kamakia* of Exogi, she might agree to a coffee and a chat – get to know him and realise that a prematurely balding and out-of-shape man could provide erotic fulfilment that would literally stop her heart.

'. . . roofing tiles that could, in a strong storm, blow down and crack the skull of anyone passing below . . . '

If he could just get rid of Mister Overy, the whole afternoon could be free. A story about a puncture on the mountain road would satisfy Donna. There were numerous stretches of deserted beach where Philippa might consent to a naked ravaging.

'. . . the manager's attempts to make amends only merely served to make matters worse. My wife is allergic to flowers, and though I repeatedly requested that the bouquet be removed from our room, I was ignored. I should note here that the manager himself is quite overweight, with a propensity to excessive perspiration. Somebody of his bulk should change his shirt at least daily . . . Jim? Jim! Are you actually listening to me?'

'Uh? Oh, yes. Very good, Mister Overy. I'll see that all of this gets back to Iliad HQ.'

'Let me see your notes.'

Jim looked at his notes: *Airport, surly . . . uterus . . . notwithstanding . . . psychiatric help . . . inner thighs.* He shook his head. 'I'm afraid that's not allowed. It's confidential once I've written it. You can put in a Freedom of Information request, but I can't show it to you.'

197

'That's preposterous!'

'Bureaucracy gone mad – I agree. But it's the law. Anyway, I must be off now. There may be others who have concerns about the roof tiles and the, er . . . painted toenails.'

'I'm only up to page four!'

'I think we've got enough to be going on with. The hotel may have to be closed down when they see what you've mentioned so far. Also, I have to call on an elderly lady guest who's on a life-support machine. If I don't put another few euros in the meter, it'll be the end for her. I'm sure you wouldn't rest easy with that on your conscience.'

'Don't you think you'll be getting away with this, young man! My wife is sitting crying in our room even as we speak! I've told her she's not going anywhere near the beach until that so-called seaweed has been examined for industrial waste contamination.'

Jim trotted to reception as Mr Overy continued ranting from the seating area.

'Is he happy now?' said the girl.

'I don't think he's ever been happy. Did I see Philippa here? The Smithson rep? Has she got guests here?'

'Yes. But she left. Her tourists don't complain.'

'When did she leave?'

'Just a few minutes ago.'

'OK. Thanks. And don't worry about Mister Overy. Just send some more flowers to their room. We expect our guests to complain anyway. I'll just put these forms in the bin when I get back to the office. I don't suppose Philippa left a message for me?'

'She just said to say "hi". She'll talk to you later.'

'Really?'

His mind raced. If he left now, he might be able to catch her up and—'

The reception phone rang. The girl answered it. '*Xenodocheio Friktos. Pios? Ne, ne – eine etho tora.*' She handed the phone to Jim. 'It's for you.'

'Is it Philippa?'

The girl shook her head.

He took the receiver. 'Hello?'

'Good afternoon. This is Sergeant Petras in Exogi.'

'What? How did you know . . . ?'

Craggan's body found? . . . tyre treads from Jim's car? . . . forensic proof? . . . police currently on the way from Argostoli? . . . hardened criminals being handed photos of Jim in stockings and suspenders?

'The blonde holiday girl in Exogi,' said the sergeant. 'She with the very large—'

'Kelly.'

'Kelly told me you are at Tripa today. There is only one hotel there.'

'Yes. That's right. How can I help you, Sergeant?'

'Will you come to see me in the police office as soon as you get back to Exogi?'

'Of course, of course . . . of course. I have to call on a few . . . It might have to be tomorrow. Although that's my day off . . . Why?'

'It is a sensitive matter. Something to do with the movie. We will discuss it in the office.'

'Sensitive? Is it something to do with James Craggan?'

'Why do you ask about Craggan?'

'Oh, no reason. I'm a fan, you know. "Now you got lead poisoning!" Ha! Yes. A true Hollywood great. Do *you* like him? I suppose men who carry guns have a special affinity with him.'

'Have you been drinking?'

'No. Certainly not.'

'I will see you tomorrow. Drive carefully.'

'I always do. My eyes are *never* off the road.'

199

The line went dead.

Exogi-Sami road

Sergeant Nikos dropped the phone in a pocket and looked again at the story told by the various tyre tracks. The car driven by Craggan had evidently arrived from the direction of Sami, been reversed out towards Exogi and come back again from Sami. Of course, there was little indication of the time period between these events, or who might have been driving the car each time. Very possibly, it could have been a different car each time, only with the same tyres – most of the hire cars on the island were the same. He'd have to make a much closer examination of the treads to figure that one out.

Then there were the other vehicles. A car with very thin tyres had left rubber on the road and treads in the dust just further on from where Craggan's car had been found. Again, it could be any one of the locals taking the corner at Grand Prix speeds, or it could be directly related to the disappearance. Evidence of a swerve *away* from the actor? Or *towards* him with intent to injure? Whoever had been in the second car, they had evidently made some attempt to disguise their footsteps in the dust by dragging their feet and raking over the surface with a freshly broken olive branch. The place on the tree was still sticky with sap. Here was a clear indication of someone aiming to hide their presence, and therefore of crime.

And how about the motorbike? Its knobbly treads had left perfect impressions, but more interesting was the suggestion that it had been run up into the bushes before being taken out later. The pattern of overlaying treads suggested that Craggan's car had been moved after the bike had arrived and that the bike had left after the car had come back. Knobbly tyres. Hadn't the person who'd bought the spray paint also had a bike with knobbly tyres? It wasn't conclusive, but it was highly suggestive.

Nikos sniffed. Urine. Nothing unusual there – the location of the spot made it perfect for impromptu toilet stops. Any sign of moisture had long ago dried in the summer sun, but the fact was again suggestive. Might not Craggan have stopped here to relieve himself? Might his assailant have come across him quite unexpectedly – even accidentally – surprising him, perhaps striking him, as they came round the bend?

A large plastic sheet lay discarded among the bushes. The pattern of dust and plant matter showed that it had been recently disturbed. A receptacle for the body? Nikos reached between branches and tugged it loose, unfolding it and bending close to sniff it. What was that? Some kind of cologne? Certainly something expensive and relatively fresh.

Nikos leaned against the side of his car and lit a Marlboro. Ithaca rose shimmering from a cobalt ocean to the east. The crickets creaked and chirruped in the trees. A hot wind whispered down across the hills, bringing scents of wild thyme, mint and oregano. This was how summers ought to be: just sea and sky, a cool drink, a lazy afternoon's adultery, and freedom from all the troubles of the world. If only there was some way to make all the other irritations disappear. If only it had been Hannah Caro who had gone missing. How sweet her gratitude would be!

A car came screeching round the corner from Exogi. The driver saw the police car, braked urgently and fishtailed across the road surface before continuing. Nikos reached into the car and turned on the blue lights. No need to chase. They knew he'd seen them. They knew he knew who they were. They'd be a little more careful for the next week or so. *This* was the kind of crime-fighting he was used to.

James Craggan's Villa, Allormeros

'What am I going to do?' sobbed Honee. 'How will I live without him?'

Grace leaned back from her laptop and looked at Honee across the kitchen table. 'You really love him, don't you?'

'Uh-huh. I guess.'

'Well, you're taking it really badly. I mean, there's every chance he'll turn up.'

'He's with another woman, I know it.'

'Who? He's always either here or on set. Where would he meet another woman?'

'He's *Crag*, honey. Women come to *him*!'

'But he's chosen *you*, Honee!'

'Yeah, sure. What do I do if he doesn't come back? You know how old I am? Do you? Take a guess.'

'I . . . don't really . . . forty?'

'*Oh God*!' Honee fell forward on to her arms and sobbed harder.

'I mean, you *look* about twenty, but you asked—'

'I *am*, I *am* forty! Take away the Botox and the implants and the nose job and the make-up and I look like Jack fucking Nicholson!'

'You can't handle the truth,' muttered Grace, blanching when she realised she'd said it out loud.

'What?'

'Nothing, nothing. Look – there's no need to get so upset. He'll be back, I'm sure.'

'He'd better be. There aren't many left who'd have me. I've got . . . well, a reputation. Crag doesn't care. He's a maverick. But there are stories about me . . .'

'He'll be back. Why don't you go and see Chen about some tea-infused brown-rice pancakes. I've really got to write this scene.'

'Ha! You think I'm eating? I've already lost three pounds. I'm gonna look outstanding when he comes back!'

'Great. That's great. But I've really got to . . . '

She concentrated hard on the blank screen and wrinkled her brow in concentration. Honee finally seemed to get the message and wandered out to the rear patio, where Lomu was studying a detailed roadmap of the island for places to search. He was spending most of each day out in the BMW.

Grace stared at the screen, willing ideas to come. Sure, they were coming – but each one was dumber than the last. The whole plot was ludicrous and becoming more so with each successive scene. If she was really unlucky, there'd actually be enough material for a screen credit and that'd be the end of her career in Hollywood. She'd be directing dog-food commercials for ad agencies, or straight-to-video flicks.

She sighed and typed:

INT. – CORNOLLI'S HOUSE

The house appears empty, but it seems someone within is playing a mournful mandolin refrain. We move through the rooms in search of the player, noting various international trophies for mandolin playing, a signed photo of the Pope, a picture of Cornolli playing a duet with the Dalai Lama, Cornolli on stage with Led Zeppelin, Cornolli playing to a group of children in an African refugee camp etc.

The house is empty, but we track through an open door to a patio area, where we glimpse legs on the ground, then a torso . . . a figure is lying prostrate on the ground playing a mandolin. A barbecue smokes blackly beside him.

Moving closer, we see that Cornolli's face and part of his hair have been so hideously disfigured by burns that he is literally unrecognisable. A can of lighter fluid and a spilled box of matches lie on the ground beside him. He is the victim of a home grilling accident that has robbed him of his identity.

Cornolli's face is reduced to raw flesh. As he plays the pain away with his beloved mandolin, a sooty tear rolls from the corner of his eye. A siren is heard in the distance . . .

Grace became aware of her own face reflected in the screen. She was gaping incredulously at what she'd written. She looked at the Post-It note Granger had given her, now stuck next to the keyboard. It was the list of new scenes they needed as soon as possible:

Cornolli loses face in credible accident / psychological episode
Chet jams with blues / jazz players
Caro humps / strips / makes love to mandolin
Nazis plot massive explosion
Shark attack?

There had to be someone who could help. Someone with a diseased imagination and some sense of story. What about Jim, the holiday guy? Hadn't he said he'd read Goldman and Eszterhas? He'd seen some good movies. He seemed to have reasonable taste. Hadn't he also said that he'd studied literature? It was a long shot, but what other choice was there? Just go home and forget it all? What happened then to the director's course at UCLA? Or the money that was going to pay off film school? It'd be back to getting Starbucks for Tony Hopkins and pretending not to notice all the sniffing in the ladies' toilets.

Come back, Crag, wherever you are. People need you. Chen's stopped giggling. Honee's becoming unbearable. Lomu's getting edgy and might turn homicidal again without your good example. I'm not your spectral daughter, but I had started to like you. Come back, wherever you are.

204

Stone Hut, near Sami

'Man, these balaclavas are hot!' said Andreas. 'Couldn't we wear masks like the guys in *Korn*?'

'Since when do terrorists wear masks?' said Achilleus. 'Did you ever see a Muslim fundamentalist wearing a clown mask?'

'But we're not Muslims,' said Kyriakos.

'Or terrorists,' said Andreas.

'I know! But the point is, we're *secret*. The balaclava is a symbol of struggle. Look at the IRA. Look at ETA. It's either this or we make him wear the blindfold for the video. But we want him to be recognised, don't we? That's the whole point.'

'Yeah, but they're so hot,' said Andreas, pulling at his balaclava.

'We should use our *Filiki* codenames when we're around him,' said Kyriakos.

'Are you forgetting that mine's the same?' said Achilleus.

'Just change it,' said Andreas.

'Ah, no, but then it won't be official,' said Kyriakos. If someone in Athens sees the video they'll start asking questions. They might think we're a splinter cell – unofficial – and take us out.'

'Take us out?' said Andreas.

'Assassination.'

'That's ridiculous,' said Achilleus.

'What's ridiculous is that they didn't reply to your letter asking for guidance on this,' said Kyriakos. 'Are they amateurs? Don't they realise what we've got here?'

'We'll just not use any names at all, OK?' said Achilleus. 'Let's make it quick. We don't want to start chatting to him or we might get Lima Syndrome.'

'Don't you mean Stockholm Syndrome?' said Kyriakos.

'No, Lima is the opposite of Stockholm: when the hostage starts to convert his captors. He's rich and famous – he might bribe us. We have to be strong.'

'1832 or death!' said Andreas.

'I'd prefer to avoid death,' said Achilleus. 'Speak only Greek unless we're talking directly to him. OK? Right, are we ready? Let's do this!'

They stepped from the cramped hallway into the main room. James Craggan was sitting tied to the chair. Behind him on the stone wall, a bed-sheet with the *Filiki Eteria* emblem had been pinned up as a backdrop to the video. A handheld video camera was positioned on a tripod in front of him. The star himself seemed relatively unconcerned, sucking cola from a bottle via a long PVC tube they'd rigged for him.

'We are *Filiki Eteria*,' said Achilleus in a gruff voice. 'You are our hostage. You will make a video explaining our demands to the world.'

'Is there a script?' said Craggan. 'Or are we improvising?'

'Eh?' said Andreas.

'Well, I don't know your demands, so you've either got to organise some sort of autocue or rehearse the demands with me. It's up to you.'

'We . . . we want the tourists out, the foreign investors out, industry out. We want Greece like it was in 1832 at the birth of our nation,' said Achilleus.

'And the Jews,' muttered Andreas.

'And the Jews out also,' said Achilleus. 'They run Europe through the German banks.'

'Right, right – I get it,' said Craggan. 'It's a kind of extreme anti-modern nationalism, right?'

'Er, yes. That's right,' said Achilleus.

'So, do you want to write something or shall we just go with it? I guess, we need to say what happens if your demands aren't met. Do you send them an ear? A finger?'

Achilleus looked to the other two, his eyes staring madly from the balaclava.

'I'm not cutting anything off him!' said Kyriakos in Greek.

206

'Couldn't we just shave his head and send them the hair?' said Andreas.

'Why not give him a massage and pluck his eyebrows while we're at it?' hissed Achilleus.

'It's cool if you haven't decided yet,' said Craggan. 'We can save that for successive videos. It's best to do these things as a series. Build the tension, grow the narrative organically. It's fine.'

'Eh?' said Andreas.

'Have you got any lights?' said Craggan

Achilleus looked up at the single naked bulb.

'No, that'll look yellow on digital. Daylight would be better, but we'll need to reflect it. If you can position some kind of reflective material at forty-five degrees to that window, it'll catch my profile just right – give me a gaunt look. Emaciated, you know? I suppose you guys don't do make-up? Never mind – we can work with what we've got. What lens are you using on that thing? How tight you going to shoot me?'

'We not shoot you!' said Andreas.

'He didn't mean with a gun!' said Achilleus. 'Just don't speak!'

'How about you shoot a couple of seconds now, like a screen test, and I'll tell you how close you want to get,' said Crag. 'Look, I guess you guys know more about history than film-making, but let me help you out here. I got a lot of experience. You seen those al-Qaeda videos? Shocking! Bad light, bad angles, bad sound. If you're going to do it, you got to do it properly or nobody's going to take you seriously.'

Eyes stared from balaclavas.

'And look – one of you has to hit me', said Craggan.

'What?' said Achilleus.

'Well, if you haven't got make-up, I'll need a bloody nose or a split lip. It'll help me get into character, elicit pity, give weight to the dialogue, you know? It'll increase the threatening sub-text. About halfway into it, I can spit out blood. Trust me, the effect'll be great. OK, let's get going while we still got good light.

Run a couple of seconds and show me the screen of that thing – you need to get your flag framed right in the background. Who's going to run lines with me? Let's rehearse.'

'Eh?' said Andreas.

'OK, I'll just start and you give me notes – tell me if I'm saying the right things.'

The three exchanged glances of increasing bemusement.

Craggan sagged in his chair. One eye drooped and he seemed to lift his head with great effort. He looked into the camera's eye with fearsome intensity. 'My name is James Craggan. I've been taken by a cell of the extreme ultra-nationalist *Filiki Eteria* movement. They've threatened to set fire to me unless their aims are met . . . Mom! Mom! I love you . . . '

He looked up at his captors with a grin. 'Yeah. Yeah. *That's* when you hit me. Are we ready? Come on guys! Somebody sort out the reflector near the window . . . '

They moved numbly, putting his instructions into action – half glad of the professionalism, half aware that this was definitely more Lima than Stockholm syndrome.

Ancient Site, Allomeros

Niki strolled down through the village with a basket in the crook of her arm. The last muddy-red glow of day was vanishing behind the western peaks and the land was starting to exhale. Someone nearby had lit a barbeque. Wild herbs unclenched after the onslaught of the sun. Olive trees shook off their dust and sighed at the touch of the first night breezes. It was an eternal time: primeval Earth following its ceaseless cycle – the same pattern now as three thousand years before, when the Twelve Olympians had reigned.

Why had they slept for so long? Was it because humankind had been beguiled by other, newer faiths – faiths enforced in battle and through the mechanisms of empire? Was it the obsession with science and logic that had rendered faith a form of madness? Or perhaps mankind – yes, and womankind – had simply lost the respect of the gods and become unworthy of their guidance. What need did gods have of mortals, whose generations were as the leaves of trees to the timeless offspring of Chronos?

She paused as the site came into view. There was no sound but crickets and the whisper of leaves. A goat bell clanked and was still. She reached into her basket and took out an old silver box that had belonged to her grandmother. It was tarnished and slightly dented now – almost crushed in the earthquake of '53 – but it had been mined from the earth and the earth would recognise it on return.

Again looking around, she took out a piece of folded tissue into which she'd put the hair from Hannah Caro's brush. She pushed it into the silver box and clicked it shut. The rusting barbed wire of the site was perhaps four metres away. There was till time to turn around and go back.

The professor had been clear: no more visits to the site for a week or so. Heed the sergeant's warning. The Goddess would wait. If She had a sign, She would give it in Her own time. Nothing could stop that – not Xenomachos, nor Petras, nor anything else of human provenance.

But there was just something about Caro. Perhaps she herself didn't know that her fleeting mortal vessel had been possessed. A connection had to be encouraged.

Niki stopped at the wire and scanned the bushes all around. Nothing. She ducked between the sagging strands, crouched, and used a butter knife from home to quickly scrape away the dry soil. She dropped the silver box into the shallow hole, covered it, and whispered: 'Oh, Goddess – receive this portion of her body and tell me: is she your chosen form? Is Hannah Caro your transubstantiated choice?'

209

She stood and pressed her foot over the loose earth. A breeze came down through the valley, susurrating among the branches, and took hold of her clothing, pressing it against her body with Aeolian hands. A sign? A recognition?

A goat bell clanked close by and she slipped back through the wires. The place still seemed deserted. She set off back towards the village, her buttocks closely observed by a young man lying in the bushes. He held a goat bell in one sweaty palm. In the other was something else.

Police Office, Exogi

Jim ascended the steps on leaden legs. Would he be leaving in ankle irons and with a blanket over his face to protect him from the paparazzi? Would the body of Craggan be lying there in the office, still wrapped in its plastic sheet: the evidence laid out to elicit his guilt as surely as Hamlet's play within the play? Had there been a tell-tale fingerprint? The rubber skid marks he'd left in the road?

The sergeant was sitting at his desk smoking. He nodded a greeting and gestured to a seat opposite.

'It's my day off today,' said Jim, sitting. 'Can we get this sorted out quickly? I've got plans.'

'Do you plan to leave the island?'

'No . . . Is there any reason I shouldn't?'

The policeman shrugged. 'You drive between here and Sami very often, yes?'

'Not very often, no. Just on transfer days . . . and occasionally for a *pita*. Why?'

'Did you drive on that road two days ago? In the afternoon?'

'Hmm. Let me think . . . '

'Your car was seen near one of the little bays. An old Seat Marbella, yes?'

210

'Ah yes. That's right. I went for a swim.'

'Did you see anything strange along that road?'

'Strange? No . . . I'm sure there was nothing strange. What do you mean "strange"?'

'Have you stopped your car along that road before? To urinate? Is that the right word?'

'It depends. Is there a law against it?'

'Not really.'

'Then yes, I might occasionally stop. What's all this about anyway? Has there been an accident?'

'I am not sure yet. I am making an investigation'

'OK, so can I go now?'

'No. This is not the reason I asked you to come. One of your tourists is in trouble. He has been robbing from the movie people. He tried to sell an electric mandolin to other tourists at Kyanni Akti. I have him in a room here. He was very drunken last night. It is possible he drank the cheap alcohol.'

'Oh, oh – right. Can't you just leave him in the cell for the rest of his holiday?'

'He asked for you. You work for the holiday company.'

'But this is a matter for the law, not for me.'

'It is not a cell – just a room. I cannot feed him. I have other things to do. Perhaps you can talk to him.'

'I'd rather not.'

'Or perhaps we will go together to look at the tyres of your car. I have found strange—'

'Where is he? I mean, I suppose I should . . . '

The sergeant led Jim to a room down a short corridor and unlatched a wire-reinforced window at head height. Inside, a man with a black eye and a grazed cheek looked up from a wooden bench. He seemed terribly resigned to his

211

situation. Jim recognised him as Mr Twyford. He was staying at the Sunshine Apartments.

'I will leave you,' said the sergeant, walking back down the corridor.

'What's he going to do?' said Mr Twyford.

'He's said you have to stay here until the next court session in Argostoli. That's in October. You'll be charged with theft and sentenced. If you're lucky, you might be able to see out the jail time back in England. You should know that the American production company is pressing for a maximum, punitive, sentence.'

'It wasn't even a real electric mandolin! Just a mock-up!'

Jim shrugged. 'What happened to your face?'

'Free shots.'

'Did you soil yourself or have hallucinations?'

'How did you know? I thought I was being attacked by bees. I jumped off the jetty but the sea wasn't there when I landed. I stink.'

'Well, as I say. There's nothing I can do. It's in the hands of Greek police now.'

Mr Twyford made a gargling, half-strangulated sound that may have been a suppressed sob. His head fell. He shook it woefully. 'I'm going to lose my job.'

Jim shrugged. His day off was slipping away. 'OK, Mister Twyford. I'll come back later and—'

'Don't tell Donna!'

Jim froze where he stood. 'What?'

'Don't tell Donna that "Mr Twyford" is in a cell.'

'How do you know . . . ?'

Again, the gulping attempt not to break down. 'My name isn't Twyford. I'm not a tourist. My name is Kevin Quigley. I'm . . . I'm the secret tourist.'

Jim stood incredulously immobile.

'Look . . . I can help you out, Jim. They said I should dig up a load of dirt on you. The welcome meeting, the transfer, the welcome boards . . . and it's all

212

true what they said: you're the worst rep I've ever seen. You just don't give a shit!'

'At least I'm not in prison.'

'It was just lying there on a beach! Anyone could have left it. How was I to know it was from the film? Look . . . Look, I can help you! I can write glowing reports. I can say you're the best rep in the world. Just get me out of here!'

Jim wrestled the glee from his features. 'I don't know . . . this is a very serious crime.'

'I'll recommend you for the Gold Award for customer service! Look, I suffer from claustrophobia – I can't be in here. It was just a mandolin. My pants are full of crap. I might have a fractured skull. You'll feel guilty if I die in here.'

'Not terribly.'

'Have some pity! The pain! The pain in my head is—'

'OK – here's what I'll do. I'll ask the policeman to give you some writing materials. Why don't you draft some of the things you're going to say about me. If I like them, I'll see what I can do.'

'But I've got to get out of here now! The walls! The walls!'

Jim closed the window and went back down the corridor, stopping halfway for an impromptu tap dance.

The sergeant looked up from his desk. 'Well?'

'Can you keep him just until the end of the day? Give him a pen and some paper. I'll take him after that. But he has to think the charges are still valid.'

'There are no charges.'

'Does he need to know that?'

The sergeant smiled and offered a small salute. The phone on his desk started to ring. He looked at it reprovingly.

'Are you going to get that?' said Jim.

The sergeant stared at it a little longer and snatched the receiver from its cradle: '*Ne? Ti? Ti malakies! Amesos!*'

He grabbed his hat. 'I must go. Out. Out.'

213

Jim descended quickly to the street and watched as the policeman skidded off towards Allomeros. At least now he was free – free and with a golden ticket to shaft Iliad Holidays! He almost skipped along the road to the resort office.

Passing the dust-caked and neglected car, he saw something glint on the driver's seat and reached through the window to take a silvery object between thumb and forefinger. A memory stick. He looked around to see if anyone passing might have dropped it accidentally, but no one seemed to have passed recently. It was still too early for the tourists to be awake.

Somebody's homework? A presentation of some sort, flicked from someone's bag as they passed? A cache of specialist porn? He slipped it into his trouser pocket and went up the alley beside Kyanni Akti. The Iliad laptop would reveal if there were any goodies on the stick.

The office door was open. Kelly printing off some early rooming lists? Philippa trying some newly-purchased lingerie or body butter? She might need help.

'Hey, Jim!'

Grace – the American girl from the movie. The leer fell from his face.

'Are you busy?' she said. 'The other girl – the one from Golden Holidays – said it'd be OK if I waited here . . . '

'It's OK. I wasn't expecting . . . Were you looking for me?'

'Yeah. It's a little weird . . . I wouldn't normally . . . I guess I'd be grateful for your help.'

'Really? Is it urgent? It's just that it's my day off and . . . look, are you free? I mean, you could come with me. I was going to go for a swim, a drive to Fiskardo, a nice lunch somewhere. I can't stay round here or the tourists'll plague me.'

'Er, yeah. I suppose I could. Why not? You leaving right now?'

'Definitely.'

'Let's go!'

Ancient Site, Allomeros

The diesel engine coughed and a plume of smoke billowed from the faded yellow backhoe loader. Xenomachos dipped his fingers into a bowl of holy water and sprinkled the machine in blessing, his words lost to the exhaust roar and his black robes writhing in the breeze. Villagers stood around to capture the incident on their phones. It was not every day one saw the Church actively ripping a protected ancient site from the earth.

The machine revved again and flexed its metal arms. Xenomachos turned to the gathered people:

'Paganism! Heathenism! Hellenismos! This is a site of unholy worship and devilry – a direct channel to Hell itself. It must be uprooted in the name of our Holy Father! I will find the bones of the sainted martyr. I will return this place to Orthodoxy!'

There were some smirks, some nudges, some heads shaken sorrowfully. The site itself meant little to them because it generated no revenue, but this was drama enough to sustain gossip until Christmas. It was a village occurrence, and there were precious few of them in Allomeros.

They parted with a murmur to reveal Professor Stratigakis striding awkwardly towards the site. Now the show would really begin!

'*Pappas! Pappas*! What are you doing?' she shouted.

'Devilry! Pagan worship! This place must be torn from the earth and consecrated in the name of Christ!'

'It's a protected archaeological site! You are breaking the law!'

'As did those others martyred in His name! There is only one law.'

'This is madness! It hasn't been fully excavated. There may be secrets hidden here that—'

'*I* will excavate it!'

Xenomachos signalled to the backhoe operator and stepped back as the machine jerked towards the barbed wire. Smoke belched from the vertical

215

exhaust. The giant shovel rose, pulling a tangle of wire and fence posts from the earth.

'Forward! Forward in the name of Christ!' mouthed Xenomachos.

The shovel descended and dug into dry earth. Dust rose and curled off in the breeze.

A siren was heard over the noise. The audience turned to see Sergeant Petras' car, blue lights flashing, come racing down the hill to the site. Phones swivelled to catch this next part of the story. The policeman was out of the car and striding towards Xenomachos.

'Stop! Stop this now!'

'I have proof!' yelled the priest. 'Someone was seen committing pagan acts here just last night! The law has been broken – no permit has been issued!'

Nikos made a repeated throat-cutting gesture to the backhoe operator and the engine died. Silence returned with a rush. 'What are you talking about? You have no authority to attack a protected site.'

'Pagan acts! Something was buried here. It was witnessed.'

'Burying something isn't against the law, Xenomachos.'

'Look! Look! I have it here – see?'

Xenomachos fumbled among his robes and brandished the silver box. He opened it and pulled out the strands of hair, holding them up so all could see.

Nikos noted the colour and length of the hair but said nothing.

Professor Stratigakis leaned on her stick, evidently troubled by some sudden thought.

'See?' said Xenomachos. 'This place must be destroyed. I will build a church here – a cathedral to the vanquishing of paganism! A cathedral to he whose bones lie undiscovered here!'

'You'll build nothing,' said Nikos. 'Nor will you be destroying anything. If you want to make a complaint to your bishop, I'm sure there are official channels. Certainly, I'll be contacting him about your behaviour.'

216

'Judas! You will be sorry. Philotheos is coming here. I have sent out my prayers to him – and also a letter.'

'Philotheos the mad monk? The "666" man?'

'The *visionary* Philotheos! He comes now on winged retribution, heralding a new crusade against paganism.'

'Does he get air miles for winged retribution?' shouted someone from the audience.

'Laugh now!' shrieked Xenomachos, turning on the crowd. 'Yes – all of you – laugh now, but the smiles will drop from your faces when he comes with the fragrance of grace and the sanctity of the Holy Spirit to cleanse us in the fires of purity.'

'Well, until then, stay away from this site, *pappas,*' said Nikos. 'I'll have to arrest you if there's any more of this nonsense.'

'You may cook me on a griddle or pierce my flesh with arrows. I am not afraid.'

'That won't be necessary. Go back to your church.'

The sergeant went to speak to the driver of the backhoe and it reversed out of the site, dragging wire and fence posts with it. Some of the villagers began to leave. The show was over.

Professor Stratigakis, however, had noticed something: a hollow exposed by the tearing shovel of the earthmover – a dark hollow that suggested a cavity . . . a cavity that suggested a pocket of history unseen for more than two-thousand years. She waved to get the sergeant's attention.

'Sergeant! Sergeant Petras! I'm the guardian of this site. I should organise a new fence and document any damage done. The machine may have made the ground unstable. Nobody should enter.'

'Yes, yes, of course. Do whatever you must. I will speak to you later about this. I think we have things to discuss.' He maintained eye contact and she nodded, trying not to bite her lip. 'In the meantime, I'll take Xenomachos back to Exogi, away from temptation.'

217

She nodded, feigning contrition and trying to keep the excitement from her face.

Fiskardo

'James Craggan? Missing?' said Jim.

'Shh! I'm not supposed to tell anyone,' said Grace. 'It's absolutely confidential. They're shooting without him. That's why I've got to do the rewrites.'

'Does anyone know what could have happened to him?'

'They think he's back on the booze, but I don't believe it. It's probably an accident.'

'Why do you say that?'

'What else could it be?'

'Yeah, I suppose. Do you know if the police have any leads?'

'No, I'm not responsible for any of that . . . Anyway, my point is that I have all these rewrites to do and it's . . . it's just not working. It all seems so absurd.'

'It does sound pretty absurd.'

'Yeah, but they're just filming whatever I write. I'm pretty sure Tony Brass is close to quitting. He just keeps getting overruled by Test. The atmosphere on set when we were shooting the grilling accident scene . . . it was nasty.'

They sat in a café at the little harbour, each drinking a *frappe*. Jim was wearing one of his own white polo shirts (the one with the least amount of food on it) and Grace was wearing a pair of denim cut-offs with her CBGB t-shirt. Her legs were tanned and freshly shaved or waxed. Jim wondered idly why he hadn't noticed before how attractive they were.

'What happens if Craggan *does* come back?' he said. 'You've already de-faced him.'

'Exactly! That's one of the scenes I'm supposed to write in case he reappears – some kind of miraculous dermatological procedure.'

'Can't they just scrap the film? It's become a total joke, hasn't it?'

'Are you kidding? Have you heard of *Heaven's Gate*?'

'I have actually. It was the biggest flop in Hollywood history.'

'Wrong! That's what everyone thinks. Sure, it bombed. It brought down the studio and destroyed Cimino's career, but it wasn't the biggest disaster by a long shot. *Cutthroat Island* lost almost a hundred mil.'

'Geena Davis as a pirate, right? I enjoyed that one.'

'Yeah, and she's had such a great TV career ever since. Then there was *Sahara*. That lost about a hundred and twenty mil.'

'McConaughey didn't take his shirt off enough. Cruz wasn't speaking Spanish.'

'Ha! And did you know it was the second adaptation of a Clive Cussler book to bomb? *Raise the Titanic* was the other. The point is: there are loads of bigger bombs than *Heaven's Gate*. There's a bunch more. Dozens. Goldman was right: "Nobody knows anything". They just keep on blindly making these movies, no matter how bad. They don't seem to know how bad they are until they see the box office returns or the opening weekend. I don't know – call it blind hope or delusion. Maybe the whole Cornolli thing's some kind of tax dodge or money-laundering package. It's mostly funded by Qatar.'

'I'm no film history expert, but it seems to me that this film failed as soon as it became *Captain Cornolli*. Can you imagine a film called *Spidleman? Ghostblusters? Hatman?*

'Totally. But I still have to write these scenes. I need ideas. I'll list you as a co-writer if you can help me. For example, how about this dermatology thing – the miraculous cure scene if Crag comes back.'

'"Crag"?'

'Don't ask.'

'Well, you said it yourself: how about an actual miracle? Cornolli goes to the local church with his mandolin . . . let me think . . . Yes – he plays the mandolin in the church – a nice atmospheric scene, very visual – and prays for a cure. He's Italian – I suppose he's Catholic, right? It's virtually the same as Orthodoxy. Anyway, there's a flash. He's unconscious. When he wakes up, he stumbles over to the baptismal pool or the font, whatever, and sees his face: cured, even more youthful. His mandolin is cradled in the arms of a statue of the Virgin, her alabaster fingers miraculously playing a chord.'

'I've never heard such bullshit in my life.'

'Maybe not, but you've certainly seen worse on the silver screen.'

'Let me write it down. The mandolin, the church, the visuals . . . yeah, Mario would go for that . . . '

She typed it into her iPad and Jim gazed out over the fishing boats. Grace was cool. Grace was easy to talk to. Should he tell her? Should he tell her about Craggan? Would it spoil his chances? Wait . . . *What* chances? When did chances come into it with Grace? Her legs were very nice, true. It occurred to him, out of nowhere, that he'd like to lick them from the back of the knee to—

'Jim. Jim? Are you listening?'

'Yes, er, no. Are you hungry? There's a really nice place along the coast.'

Stone Hut, near Sami

'And then she took off her clothes. She wasn't wearing any underwear.'

'Was it the sacrifice? Did she do a sacrifice?'

'She stood, totally nude, and did some sort of, you know, religious aerobics. It was hot and she started to sweat. Her body was shining, man. It was like a lap dance.'

'I would have come in my pants. Did you get pictures?'

'I couldn't, could I? I was so close she would have heard the camera clicking.'

'Can't you turn the clicker off on your camera?'

'That's not the point. It's all in my head now. I'll always have it.'

'So did you go and tell it all to Xenomachos?'

'Yeah. Well, I left out the bit about the aerobics. I didn't want to shock him.'

'What kind of aerobics were they exactly?'

'You know – gyrating, bending over.'

'And did Xenomachos say he's going to join us?'

'He said he was too busy to discuss it. He had someone coming to clean the icons. But he said he was going to contact Philotheos. You know – the Athonite monk who talks about Jews.'

Achilleus sighed. It seemed he'd been listening to "Zorbas" and "Kolokotronis" for hours, though it couldn't have been more than five minutes. They were all smoking outside the hut, their hostage James Craggan still occupying the only room within.

'"Religious aerobics"?' he said, finally. 'You talk such shit, *malakas*.'

'I was there, *re*. I saw it. Thanks to me, Xenomachos says that Philotheos is coming to get rid of the pagans. While he's here, he can do the Jews and the foreign investment.'

'We'll see. We might all be in prison by then. You didn't tell him about Craggan, did you?'

'No.'

'Good. Don't. Andreas – are you sure you put the memory stick in the right car?'

'A Seat Marbella. It had an upside-down sticker in the window.'

'Yeah, that's it.'

'I saw him take it. I was hiding behind a palm tree. He went into his office and came out with the American girl from the movie.'

'Right, so he must have given it to her. Now we just wait.'

'What about Craggan?' said Kyriakos.

'What about him?' said Achilleus. 'We keep him until the demands are met.'

'What if they haven't met the demands by the time school starts again?' said Andreas.

Achilleus snorted. 'Just the sort of question Kolokotronis himself would have asked.'

'Kolokotronis wasn't at school when he was fighting the infidel occupiers,' said Kyriakos. 'And he didn't have to babysit a Hollywood star. I mean, can't we just gag him again? I just can't listen to him any more.'

'We could blindfold him again and leave him by the road where you found him,' said Andreas. 'He's never seen our faces. He doesn't know where the hut is. We could just forget it ever happened and do something different for the action plan.'

'It's too late,' said Achilleus. 'The English guy has the memory stick, remember? Do you want to make another film with Craggan, this one saying the last one was just a joke?'

'Could we?'

'We've come this far,' said Achilleus. 'We're committed. Now let's go inside. Balaclavas on.'

They trod their cigarettes, pulled the wool over their faces and went in. James Craggan was sitting at a table making notes, his hands having been released but his legs bound ever more elaborately to the chair with cable ties.

'Hey, guys!' said Craggan. 'Listen, I've been planning something cool. Your whole crusade is about national purity, right? Greece untainted by foreign influence, right?'

They nodded warily, half-guessing what was coming.

222

'So I was thinking: how would you show that in a movie? A montage – right? We'd need some cinematic shots of beaches, mountains, faces – all the symbols of nationhood. Dawn and dusk – the best times for dramatic light. You'd edit that together on your MacBook and then you'd put a voiceover over that. I guess it'd be too much to get a professional. I mean, I could do it, but it should really be in Greek. Some Greek music would be good, too. It'd be like a campaign film. I've made a kind of rough storyboard here to give you some ideas about angles and framing, but you'd have to do the words yourself.'

'Er, thanks, Crag,' said Kyriakos.

'Any news on the other film? Have they seen it yet?'

'We've indirectly put it in their hands,' said Achilleus.

'Test Weedle – he's the guy who needs to see it. Forget the rest. Just get it in front of Test. Hey – have you got any more of that mince and macaroni stuff you gave me?'

'The *pastitsio*?' said Kyriakos. 'My mum's making it again today.'

'That's some great cooking. I'd like to meet her and thank her.'

'She'd like to meet you, too,' said Kyriakos. 'Maybe you could just write her a note.'

'Sure. Who's it to?'

Achilleus coughed and glared. Kyriakos backed away from the table.

'What kind of music?' said Andreas.

All turned to look at him.

'In the montage, I mean. What kind of music would be best?' said Andreas.

Achilleus rolled his eyes.

Kyriakos seethed beneath the itchy balaclava. This was going nowhere. Maybe it was time to pay Xenomachos another visit and see how the other part of the revolution was proceeding.

Myrtos Beach

Grace lay back on the pebbles and felt herself melting into them. Her vision was filled with limitless, cloudless blue through Ray Ban lenses. She pictured the day as a series of scenes: the coffee at Fiskardo, the fantastic lunch and the mess Jim made of his shirt, the beginner's Greek lesson he'd tried to give her, and the stories he'd told about his experiences in the north of the country. In fact, it'd probably work better as a montage. There'd be more scope for capturing the variety. The subtext would be brought out in the edit.

He groaned and fell dripping to the pebbles beside her. 'You should go in.'

'I'm not going to ruin my clothes with salt, thanks.'

'Suit yourself. A bit of salt would enhance the vintage look.'

'Yeah, and I'd have to sit in wet clothes all the way back.'

'The car seat'll absorb most of it.'

She turned to him and lifted her sunglasses. 'Jim – you're just looking for an excuse to see me strip.'

'I wasn't! . . . I was just . . . It's just that the water's so nice and . . . '

'I would if it was just the two of us, but there are too many others.'

Jim looked at the rows of sun beds and umbrellas. 'Another reason to hate the tourist.'

She smiled. 'I was thinking about the sex scene.'

'What? What about all the other people?'

'In the *script* – Chet and Hannah.'

'Oh, right. Didn't you say there was already a love scene?'

'It's too romantic. They play a mandolin duet. The music represents their love; they touch each other only with notes. It's titillating, but it's too figurative. There's no actual nudity in LaBrava's script.'

'Strange, considering . . . '

'Yeah, exactly. Test said he wants "humping", but this isn't a porno. It needs to fit the rest of the story. It's got to be sexually charged, but not vulgar. I think it's got to turn men and women on. Is that possible, do you think – to excite both with the same stuff? I mean, what movies have turned *you* on?'

'I've enjoyed certain parts of *Showgirls* repeatedly.'

'Oh, Jim . . . '

'Not the story – just the nudity! I suppose my point is that men don't watch a film to get turned on these days. There's porn for that. You watch Jessica Alba in *Into the Blue*, but then you go online for something hotter. She's just an erotic hors d'œurve. An amuse-bouche.'

'An erotic hors d'œurve??'

'Not me personally . . . necessarily. I'm speaking generally. I knew a girl once who was very taken with the scene in *Dead Calm* where Billy Zane does Nicole Kidman. Or is it vice versa?'

'A girl you knew once? A girlfriend?'

'Something like that. I think the difference is that men just want immediate gratification – the dessert before the main course. Women reward themselves with dessert. That *Dead Calm* scene has a lot of psychological subtext – power games, risk, manipulation. Same with the voyeurism element of *Sliver*, or Mickey Rourke's wealth and importance in *Wild Orchid*. Both shit films, obviously, but quite popular with women, apparently.'

'Everything's about eating with you, isn't it? You always hungry?'

'You have no idea.'

She raised her sunglasses again to show him her eyes. He looked starving.

'So, what?' she said. 'What do we do with Chet and Hannah? Something to please everyone.'

'Well, she has to strip. That's a given. And there has to be a tease . . . I've got it – they *do* play their mandolins, but as a duel rather than a duet.'

'Go on.'

''Something like the banjo thing in *Deliverance*. They challenge each other to play a difficult series of notes. Whoever hits a wrong note has to take a garment off until they're both naked with only their instruments to cover their genitalia.

It's still like the original, but more erotic. You could . . . I don't know the right term, cross-fade? . . . between the hands on the instruments and the hands on each other. That preserves the metaphor while getting some flesh on screen.'

'You know, Jim – that's pretty good. Hold on . . . '

She took the iPad out of her bag and began tapping at it, aware that he was watching her.

'Has that thing got a USB port?' he said.

'Nope, but I've got an adaptor. Why?'

'I just wanted to check something on a memory stick. It's for work. Just take a second.'

'OK, let me save this. Here, take it. I'll go and get us a drink. Water OK?'

'Fine, thanks.'

Jim plugged in the white cable and attached the memory stick to the port. He was only vaguely acquainted with the software and tapped a few wrong places before figuring out how to open the single mp4 file entitled *Filiki Eteria*.

He tapped the full-screen option and tilted the device to avoid the fierce glare. There was a flash of hand over the lens, some kind of Greek design on a bed sheet, a jerky glimpse of feet and then blackness. He was about to check the battery when the picture flashed back on to reveal Banquo's ghost staring gauntly into the camera's eye.

'My name is James Craggan. I am the prisoner of a Greek ultra-nationalist cell called *Filiki Eteria* . . . '

Christ in a call centre!

Grace crunched over the pebbles towards him with a bottle in each hand.

'Jim? Are you OK? You look like you're going to throw up.'

Diogenes' Bar, Allomeros

'You sure this is the place?' said Test Weedle. 'They said it was a bar. This looks like somebody's house.'

Lomu nodded. His sunglasses gave little away but a reflection of the setting sun.

'Don't talk much do ya?' said Test. 'But I guess Crag didn't employ you for your conversation, did he? Just between us – you really clip that guy in New York?'

Lomu gripped the wheel.

'Well, I guess I wouldn't tell anyone if I'd done it, either. Wait for me, man. I'll be out in a second.'

Test opened the door of the air-conditioned BMW and stepped out into the furnace. Today, he was wearing salmon-pink linen trousers and a Ralph Lauren shirt. His sandals had been made for him by Moses, a guy in Little Israel who was the current sandal-maker du jour. He'd also shod Spielberg, the Weinsteins, Tom Hanks, Pierce Brosnan and Halle Berry. Kosher, too, if that was a requirement.

He knocked on the window. 'Hey! Anyone in there? Anyone home?'

He looked back at Lomu. The driver sat impassive in the driver's seat and showed no interest.

'Can I help you?'

Test jerked round and saw a bug-eyed, leering face at the window. 'Oh Jesus!

'Not Jesus, no. I'm Diogenes.'

'Are you open? I mean, is this a bar?'

Diogenes opened the door. 'I'm always open. Can I get you a drink?'

'I'm twelve-stepping. Three years clean and clear. I was in a bad place. I drowned a Great Dane at Lake Mead near Vegas . . . it's long story. But I heard you got some killer weed. Are ya gonna invite me in?'

227

Diogenes looked with new interest at the flawless complexion, the linen and the sandals.

'Ya know . . . ?' prompted Test. 'Mary-J, wacky baccy? Pot? Grass?' He mimed taking a hit.

The door opened and Test slipped inside.

'I don't normally sell,' said Diogenes, sipping a tall glass of Johnny Black. 'My bar is a place to enjoy conversation and relax. If people want to smoke, they do.'

'That's cool, yeah. But I haven't got time. I'm running this movie and it's all cutting loose. I need to be mobile. I need perspective, ya know? Need to open up the portals and chill. Can't drink, but I can smoke. What ya got? Is it home-grown? Organic – no pesticides?'

'Only the finest quality,' smiled Diogenes.

'Great. Gimme five – no, make it ten – ready-rolled.'

'I would have to prepare them for you. Can you return—?'

'I'm a busy man. Can't ya give me some of your stash? I'll pay premium.' Test pulled a wad of euros from his trouser pocket.

'I smoke something a little stronger than the usual. I fear that you—'

'Strong's good. Strong's what I need.'

Diogenes seemed amused. He made a little bow and went behind the bar to fetch a metal cash box in which a dozen joints lay fragrant and ready to smoke. 'I must warn you – they are a very special blend that—'

'Yeah, cool. How much? Here take a hundred.'

Diogenes emptied the joints into a napkin and folded it.

'That's cool,' said Test, sniffing the package. 'Be seeing you, man!'

Diogenes watched him go. The ice machine groaned and clattered some fresh cubes into the stainless steel tray. He took one and looked into its frozen core. Marilyn Monroe was there, dancing naked for his entertainment. She waved and he winked back. He had a feeling that the film was about to start getting a lot more interesting.

Jim's Apartment, Allomeros

Jim turned off the engine and sighed. What a great end to his day off. Grace's reaction to the video had been predictably dramatic. Then the headlong rush back to the main set near Sami. The panic. At least he'd managed to evade mentioning that it was he who'd run Craggan over, somehow casting him into the arms of the terrorists. God alone knew how that had happened.

Was that half-bottle of ouzo still in the kitchen, or was he going to have to go up to Diogenes and risk a lethal measure of whisky? He sighed again, slammed the car door and crunched over the gravel to the stairs.

There was someone sitting in the shadows at his door. He stopped. The figure was slumped against the glass as if sleeping. A girl? He could make out bare legs, a high-heeled shoe, dark hair . . .

'Jim? I've been waiting for so long.'

'Philippa?'

'Where've you *been*!' Her voice was slurred. She moved heavily.

He went up the stairs, triggering the infra-red beam and illuminating the stairs in brutal white light. She was wearing a halter-top mini dress – *those legs!* – and some strappy black heels. Her mascara had seeped down over her cheeks, her hair was all over her face and her lipstick was swiped up the side of her cheek on one side. With her legs positioned the way they were, he couldn't help noticing she also wore some lacy white underwear. Just couldn't help it.

'Philippa – what are you doing here?'

'Christos . . . the cheating *malakas*! He . . . I saw him . . . some whorish tourist *slapper*!'

'I'm guessing Christos is your boyfriend?'

'Not any more!'

'I'm a little confused. I mean, I'm happy to see you, of course, but . . . why did you come here? How did you even know where—?'

229

'I went to Diogenes ... he said you lived nearby ... You're a nice guy, Jim. *Nice.* You're not like . . . I can't go home. He'll only bang on the door all night, that *malakas*!'

A light came on in the landlord's apartment below.

'Look – how about a nice cup of coffee?' said Jim. 'Come on, let me help you up.'

She stood uneasily, wobbling on her heels, and fell against him so that he had to put an arm round her waist. Warm waist. Soft waist. Perfume rising from her hot skin. Holding her, he fiddled with the key and reached around to turn on the lights.

'Bright!' she said, covering her eyes.

He staggered with her over to the bed and manoeuvred her on to it, whereupon she toppled back and lay there with her skirt hitched high on her thighs and her arms outspread.

Jim went to the kitchen area and set the kettle going. There was only Nescafe, but she probably didn't care too much about good-quality coffee anyway. He looked at her lying there and felt the old elemental stirring. The legs, the glimpse of underwear, the depilated armpits, the long hair spread across his pillow – he willed himself to remember every aspect of the sight. Certainly, she'd never be on his bed again after tonight.

His hands shook slightly as he poured the water and stirred. Sugar? He turned to her.

'I'm afraid I haven't got—'

She was naked except for the tiny pants. She must have sloughed off the dress in a single, sinuous movement as he'd made the coffee. Now she writhed on his bed: long, lean, generously-breasted. She had no tan lines; all was delicious café au lait skin.

He slopped coffee over the brim and on to his hand. It didn't burn.

'*You* wouldn't cheat on me, would you, Jim?'

'I . . . I . . . no.'

230

'Come here. Sit here.'

He went. He sat beside her head. She turned over on her front. The pants didn't cover much of her.

'You like my bottom, don't you?'

'Uh-huh.' It was more guttural grunt than human speech.

Her red-nailed hand started to slide up his thigh into the leg of his shorts. Her eyes were wet with intoxication, intensified somehow by the mascara bat wings around them. 'You're a nice boy, aren't you Jim?'

'Ur ugh.'

'Ooh! But not *too* nice. What's this?'

Her hand palpated what she'd found. His eyes drank in her body.

'I should really thank you . . . I mean, for taking me in,' she said, removing her hand and using it to unzip his shorts.

'Huuuuhg.'

'Tell me if you like it,' she said, shifting herself up the bed and taking his burning tip into a mouth of impossible softness and dexterity.

'Hnnng!'

Her hair tickling his thighs. Her beautiful bottom. The smell of her perfume. Those long, long legs, wantonly parted. Her tongue. Her tongue. Her tongue. The blood pounded in his ears. He hadn't blinked for about five minutes. The timpani in his head was threatening to explode in a crescendo elsewhere: pounding, beating, reverberating as Philippa worked with intuitive tempo in his lap.

But the noise wasn't only in his head.

The door opened.

'Hey! Can't you hear me banging out here? I just really wanted to say thanks for today and to apologise for—'

Grace's eyes goggled.

Philippa began to raise her head clear.

Jim's mouth opened. His eyes closed. White light pulsed behind his eyelids and the cataclysmic eruption burst forth.

Philippa reapplied herself with vigorous expertise.

'*Huuuuurrrrrrgh a-a-a-a urrrrrg!*'

He was caught in the strobing maelstrom between ecstasy's pinnacle and humiliation's depths.

'*Aaaaaaaaah uh ah urrrrr!*'

It went on and on: an elemental, pulsing release from some inexhaustible animal core.

'*Uuuuuunnng.*'

When he opened his eyes, there was only the open door.

'Oops!' said Philippa, wiping her eyelid with a finger. 'You were ready for that, weren't you?'

Jim looked down at her heavenly-sinful mouth: her smudged lipstick, her swollen lips. He took in her mascara massacre, her burning, drunken eyes. In another twelve hours, she'd have passed it off on the alcohol and the break-up. She'd have chosen to forget it.

But Jim wouldn't forget. And neither would Grace.

Ancient Site, Allomeros

Professor Stratigakis waved to the receding tail-lights and listened as its rattling engine faded off into the valley. The dust settled and she looked again at the new fence posts and barbed wire erected round the site. It had taken long enough, but the carpenter had also put in a small gate with a hasp and a padlock, to which only she – as site guardian – was permitted a key. It would hardly prevent any determined attempts at access, but at least in future she wouldn't have to duck under the wire.

It was now quite dark, but a full moon silvered the bald mountains and the olive trees – a full moon signalling the end of the ancient Athenian month. Thargelion was ending; Skirophorion would begin at midnight: a propitious time – a time of transition and transformation. Perhaps even a time of transubstantiation.

She tried the key in the padlock and swung the gate open on its oiled hinge. She took a torch from her pocket and shone it at the place she'd seen the hollow revealed by the earth-moving machine. Yes – there it was: an empty black eye socket into the ground. A chamber? A burial cache? Or just an old animal burrow?

The sensible thing would have been to formally document it with photographs and properly recorded grid measurements, but that would take time and bureaucracy. It certainly wouldn't happen over the summer. Another slight seismic tremor or an unseasonable downpour and the cavity might close up or be contaminated by the elements.

She made her way carefully over the uneven ground, leaning on her stick to avoid toppling into the trench or the backhoe's tyre tracks. The beam of the torch showed pottery fragments in the loose earth where the hole had emerged and she knelt to examine them: pale clay with no markings. They were consistent with other finds on the site. She aimed the torch into the hole and saw that it was lined with stone. Not just a random cavity in the earth, but an intentional receptacle for something.

Eschewing all caution now, she lay on the still-hot ground and reached into the space. It had a small diameter – a storage space rather than a burial plot. A font of some description? A hollow for storing oil used in the ancient rites? She felt around inside, half fearing a snake bite, half hoping to discover something magnificent. There was dried grass, loose stones, empty snail shells . . . and a smooth, rounded surface.

Her hand followed its contours: a small pot something like a globular aryballos that might once have been used to store perfume or oil. It felt whole.

233

There was some sort of stopper or bung in its top. Her heart thudded. Could it be? An intact contemporaneous container with its contents still inside?

She closed her hand around it and began to lift. There was definitely something inside. She withdrew it with infinite care through the aperture and greedily shone the torch upon it.

'Oh my!'

Here, surely, was the key to a lifetime's research into the idea of a proto-Aphroditic cult. The detail! The colours! The symbolism! She felt her eyes hot with tears.

And then she froze. Somebody was coming. The heavy, dragging steps announced a stealthless, oblivious presence. It didn't sound like Diogenes on another stoned ramble.

The professor struggled to her feet while attempting to keep the aryballos safe. She flashed the torch around the olive trees and down the road.

'Who's there?'

She made her way back to the gate and closed it, leaning against it to catch her breath. The footsteps were coming closer. She aimed the torch down the road and saw a figure in white. A white dress. Long, dark hair. It was someone she had seen before in a magazine that Niki had shown her.

It was Hannah Caro.

The professor watched amazed as the young star staggered towards the site. She seemed to be talking to herself:

'This isn't the way . . . no . . . so hot! . . . Don't mix with vodka next time . . . so hot! . . . this is the way.'

She seemed not to notice the professor at all, but kept on walking towards the gate, pulling at her dress and muttering, 'So hot! . . . It's just so . . . '

Finally, she managed to work her arms out of the straps and let the dress drop to the ground, revealing a figure that was a perfect statue in the moonlight. She continued nakedly, past the amazed professor and through the unlocked gate, where she tripped and fell to the ground.

234

'Are you OK?' said the professor? 'Do you know where you are?'

'Uh? Uh? I'm home. Isn't this home?' said Caro before drooping into unconsciousness.

The professor looked at the beautiful naked girl at her feet, at the remarkable find in her hand and at the benevolent face of Selene, the moon. Perhaps Niki had been right all along. Here was the Goddess made flesh.

Main Set, Sami (next day)

Granger pulled down the blinds in Craggan's Winnebago. Grace connected a laptop to the big plasma screen in the seating area. Test Weedle paced before the select audience of Tony Brass, Penelope, cinematographer Mario Cacciatore, assistant director Mike Kendall, Sergeant Petras and Chet Braddock, accompanied by his Greek character advisor Eleftheros.

'Chet – does he *have* to be here?' said Brass. 'He smells like old fish wrapped in dirty laundry.'

'He has to see what I see, Tony. It's essential to what I bring to the role.'

'Right.'

Test clapped his hands. 'We ready yet? Where's the remote?'

Grace nodded and handed him the remote. There was nowhere to sit, so she perched on the arm of the seat that Chet was in.

'Right, listen up,' said Test. 'Some of us have already seen this. We all know what it's about. But I think everyone has to see it. Where's Hannah?'

'Late,' said Granger. 'I've got someone waiting to bring her as soon as she arrives.'

'OK. Right. Recap: Craggan's been kidnapped by terrorists. They've sent this film on a memory stick they dropped into the car of some British holiday guy. No idea why it was his car instead of someone else's. We'll look into that. Grace – you know this guy, right? What's his story?'

'He's a douche.'

'Right. Typical stiff-assed Brit.' Test glanced sidelong at Brass. 'No offence. Well, let's watch it and then compare notes.'

The screen jerked with the initial flash of hand and foot. Craggan's face appeared framed against the backdrop of the *Filiki Eteria* symbol on the bed sheet. He looked gaunt and world-weary. There was a trickle of dried blood on his chin from a cut lip. The audio was tinny.

> *My name is James Craggan. I am the prisoner of a Greek ultra-nationalist cell called* Filiki Eteria. *They've taken me hostage and won't release me until their demands are met. If they don't receive notification of your agreement to their demands, they say they're going to start sending you bits of my body. If their demands are not acted on by the end of summer, they say they're going to burn me alive . . .*

Grace looked at the now familiar face. Was he acting? The cut on his lip certainly looked real, but even as she felt her compassion being elicited, she couldn't quite feel it responding. Just another charming liar? Another one she'd thought she might be able to trust.

> *They demand that all tourists leave Greece, never to return. The remaining tourist infrastructure will be retained only for the use of native-born Greeks. All foreigners must also leave, whether poorly-paid migrant workers or millionaire foreign investors. When Greece has returned to an agrarian state, there'll be no need for a cash economy. The Jews who control the EU through the German banks must also withdraw any and all claims over the free state of Greece, which will return to the glorious origins of 1832 . . .*

Just why *had* Jim been the one whose car had been chosen? Why not one of the film crew? Why not just post it to the production company? Was it actually possible that Jim was connected in some way? Whatever. It was his problem now. Let the police talk to him.

. . . and a new character will be inserted into the script of the Cornolli movie – someone who champions the goals of Filiki Eteria *and promotes them to the world. Failure to do this will result in boycotts of the movie in Greece and possibly further action . . . Mom! Mom! I don't want to die as a human torch! I've done so much bad in my life! I was only starting to put it right. Oh God, give me more time on this earth. Let me keep all my fingers and ears! Give these people what they want . . .*

The image turned black. Test turned off the TV and signalled for Granger to lift the blinds.

'So guys – what do we think?'

Each one looked stunned, apart from Eleftheros, who picked his nose and examined the find with interest.

'Is this some kind of a joke?' said Brass.

'No joke, Tony. They've really got him,' said Test.

'And they want us to return Greece to the nineteenth century by the end of the summer?'

'Uh huh,' said Test.

'Does that strike you as something we might be able to do?'

'Probably not. But I don't think that's the main issue here, people.'

'You don't believe they'll actually cut him or set fire to him?' said Chet, his own digitally-deficient hand held up in illustration.

'No, you're missing the point. Look what we've got here. Can't ya see it? This is friggin art! *This* is what we need in our movie!'

They stared. Eleftheros went for another highly-involved delve.

237

'Mario. Mario,' said Test. 'Look at that lighting. Look at that framing. Tell me it's not good stuff.'

Mario shrugged. 'Under the circumstances – guerrilla style – I guess they did a pretty good job. It's tight. The tonal feel is good. It has a basic visual narrative. Of course, I might change—'

'Yeah, yeah. Chet – you're an actor. Tell me, is he acting?'

Chet sat up straight. 'It's really hard to say. I think he kinda is, but he's drawing on such deep personal reserves that it comes over as genuine. Pure method. He's channelling the victim in himself. I'd suggest a few rewrites on the phrasing, but I guess the terrorists aren't professional writers.'

'No shit,' said Test.

'What do you mean when you say "we need this in our movie"?' said Brass.

'The passion,' said Test. 'The art. The vision. Craggan on fire – not literally. Not yet. And do ya know what the best thing is? He was in costume when he was taken. It means we can cut this footage into the film and he'll be Cornolli! All we need to do is re-jig the script.'

'Even more?' said Brass.

'Can ya do it?' Test asked Grace.

'Would it occur before or after the grilling accident we already shot?' she said.

'Does it matter? Whatever works.'

'So you're giving in to their demands about publicising their aims?' said Brass.

'Shit, the movie won't be out for another year. They'll all be in prison by then and this'll just be fiction. Isn't that right, Nikos?'

Sergeant Petras nodded absently.

Brass cast a glance at Mike. Grace looked to Granger for guidance and got nothing.

'Nobody says a word about this,' said Penelope.

'Shit, no!' said Test. 'This is going out as a teaser trailer right now!'

238

'What?' said Brass.

'Stop the press, Tony! James Craggan's been kidnapped by ultra-friggin-nationalists. He might be burned alive. This film is getting made whether he comes back or not. It'll be a hit just because of the publicity around it. Look at *Mr and Mrs Smith* – mediocre movie, but something else entirely when ya know Pitt was porking Jolie.'

'Test . . . are you sure?' said Penelope. 'Do you understand the kind of media heat you're going to bring down with that kind of gesture?'

'Bring it on! We're not exactly making the right kind of headlines right now with all this "Cornolli" shit. If it wasn't for darling Hannah screwing everything that moves, the paparazzi wouldn't even bother being here.'

Chet folded his arms but said nothing.

'Yeah, bring it on,' said Test. 'Just release the whole thing for now. No . . . wait. Let's pretend we've lost it and we'll let them find it. Then they can try to figure out if it's part of the film or not. We'll cut it into a teaser later. Someone get a rough cut to me by the end of the week.'

'Isn't this going to hamper the police investigation?' said Brass, looking to Sergeant Petras.

'Hell, no! said Test. 'It'll make it easier if everyone's looking for Craggan. I wouldn't be surprised if the *National Enquirer* finds him.'

'On the moon with Elvis,' muttered Grace.

'This movie needs publicity like . . . like Scott LaBrava needs some good advice on his choice of leisure activities. Just make it happen. Who knew Craggan had this kind of talent? I mean, it's obviously him behind the film, not those kebab-jockeys.' He looked at the sergeant. 'No offence.'

Grace raised a hand.

'Yeah, shoot.' said Test, still pacing.

'Has anyone considered what happens if they really kill Crag?'

'We're insured against his accidental death or suicide,' said Penelope. 'The kidnapping could be considered as either for legal purposes.'

'We'd probably make back his fee,' said Test, nodding.

Grace looked at Granger for support. 'No – I mean, Crag would be dead.'

'I got ya,' said Test. 'Worried what happens to the movie. Don't sweat it – we go with the burger-face thread. The Brandon Lee scenario.'

'I . . . I'm not sure I'm making myself clear,' said Grace. 'Crag would be dead.'

'Yeah,' said Test. 'Like Elvis. Did ya know he's sold more records since he died than he ever did living?'

Granger shook her head slowly. Don't pursue it any further.

'OK!' said Test. 'That's enough time wasted. We need to be shooting shooting shooting. Time is money, people! What's next, Tony? What are you shooting today?'

'The sex scene: Chet and Hannah.'

'Right. Right. Is it hot? Closed set, right? Ya been taking ya vitamins, Chet?'

Chet shrugged.

'Where is she anyway?' said Test. 'Where's the golden girl?'

The Church, Exogi

Xenomachos jabbed the mouse pad and squinted at the screen of the laptop he'd recently confiscated from his sons. The filth they'd been watching was not only obscene, but also blasphemous – which was clearly worse. Unfortunately, he had little experience using such machines and he'd had to call a few people to figure out how the net connection worked. Only now, accidentally, did he realise that the prefabricated church came with a 'Wi-Fi router' as standard. Certainly, it explained what all those people were doing with their phones during services.

240

Philotheos' administered website was encyclopaedic in its gathering of news about the great man and articles supposedly written by him. Of course, he was most famous in the heathenish national newspapers for his pronouncements on the Number of the Beast, a subject area that seemed to offer limitless scope.

Brothers and sisters beware of Satan in your shopping! The barcode is on almost everything we buy now: a series of lines telling machines how much things cost. But did you know that each line is allocated a number, and that every bar code is divided into three by two thin lines at its beginning, middle and end? The number of this slender pair is six and together, in triplicate, they spell "666" on everything you buy! Satan, be gone! Amen.

And do you, brothers and sisters, shop with a credit card? Then consider this: "VI" in the Roman system stands for six; "S" in our own language represents 6"; "A" in the ancient Babylonian tongue stood for "6". What does it spell? VISA! And do not think you can change to MasterCard, for "Master" is another name taken by the Beast! Satan, be gone! Amen.

Xenomachos stroked his beard. The Athonite certainly made a good case for cash transactions. No wonder he was so wary of using modern technology. The only way to contact him was, apparently, to pray earnestly. And to send a postcard – just in case – to the Evangelistrios monastery: the one closest to the mountain wastes where Philotheos roamed.

The church door opened and a figure stood silhouetted indistinctly in the bar of white light.

'Brother Philotheos!' said Xenomachos, dropping to his knees. 'You have come!'

'No, *pappas*. It's me: Kyriakos.'

'Oh, oh. Yes. Come in, boy. Would you like to confess?'

'Kind of.'

241

'I must thank you for your vigilance the other evening at the site. Because of you, I have the silver box with the pagan offering. I have proof to show Philotheos when he comes. Sergeant Petras may not take it seriously but the matter will soon be out of his hands. He will be sorry.'

'He's coming here? To Exogi? Philotheos is coming?'

'I have sent out the prayers. And the postcard. I believe he will come.'

'And he'll support our cause? The nationalist cause for 1832?'

'Perhaps, perhaps. I believe that paganism is his primary interest.'

'Wait a minute, *pappas*. I didn't lie in the dirt all night to prevent paganism. I want to get the tourists out, and the foreign investors and the Jews. Don't you want that, too?'

'The Jews, certainly, are a problem. And the tourists, yes. They are blasphemous.'

'OK, look. Are we in confession mode right now?'

'What do you mean?'

'I mean do we go to hell if one of us talks?'

'Oh, yes. Yes – you may tell me your sins.'

'Right. Well, we've kidnapped the Hollywood film star James Craggan and we've got him tied to a chair. We've forced him to make a film, which we've released to the world. He hit himself in the face and cried about his mother. Now he's pushing us to make a montage set to music and he's eating so much that our mothers are becoming suspicious. I had to tell mine we found a dog in some bushes and we've been feeding it because all its legs are broken.'

Xenomachos looked. He blinked. 'You have not been abusing yourself further?'

'Didn't you just hear what I said?'

'Yes ... yes, but I'm not sure any actual sins have been committed. Kidnapping is probably against the law, but I do not believe it is mentioned in the Bible.'

'Neither is computer hacking or using your mobile as a vibrator, but I suppose they're sins.'

'The phone one, certainly. Have you done that?'

'No! Why does it always have to be about sins? We're in trouble, *pappas*! We've got a Hollywood star who won't stop eating or giving us filmmaking advice.'

'Yes, yes, I can see the difficulties.'

'And you're involved, *pappas*. You're one of us. We're in this together. I helped you with the pagan thing and you're helping me with the revolution. That was the deal.'

'I . . . nothing was really signed. Not officially.'

'What?'

'Do not raise your voice in God's house!'

'More like God's garage! No wonder there are "No Smoking" signs everywhere. This place would melt if there was a fire!'

'Do not insult my church!'

'Look. Look. We're in this together, *pappas*. If we go down, you go down. What should we do with Craggan?'

'I . . . I . . . Do not do anything. Do not tell anyone about it for now. Philotheos will know what to do. He knows all. He will advise on this matter.'

'Is he definitely coming?'

'We must believe in the power of prayer, boy.'

'Yeah, and the mail.'

Police Office, Exogi

It had been less than three hours since the meeting with the movie people and already the world seemed to know about Craggan. According to Penelope, a

243

copy of the kidnappers' memory stick had been dropped strategically just outside the main set and picked up by a hungry paparazzo not thirty seconds later. Forty-five minutes later, it was on an entertainment blog as an 'unconfirmed' story. An hour later, it was confirmed (with stills images) on Fox News. The internet had then lit up like a Christmas tree, with James Craggan trending on Twitter and Google as if he'd remade *Kung Fu Tyrant* co-starring with whatever 14-year-old popstrel was hot at the time. It would become even more frenzied when the full film (slightly edited) was released later that day.

What it meant for Nikos was his landline and his mobile ringing non-stop. Of course, he'd incapacitated both of them, and the fax machine, but he was stunned when the owner of Kyanni Akti walked up the stairs to the office and handed him *his* mobile.

'It's for you, Sergeant.'

'What? Who is it?'

A shrug. The phone made tinny noises as somebody shouted on the other end. Nikos took it.

'Hello?'

'Petras! What are you doing with your phone turned off? What's happening with the fax? Have you seen what's happening with this Craggan man? The whole world is watching!'

'Captain Bastounis. Good morning.'

'Is it the nationalists? Is it *Filiki Eteria*? Didn't I warn you about them? How many men do you need? I can give you twenty. Guns? Do we need more guns? Do I need to call the anti-terrorist squad?'

'Send nobody, Captain. Everything is under control.'

'*Under control*? An international star has been kidnapped in your area! By terrorists!'

'Take a breath, Captain. They aren't terrorists. They're not dangerous. I am pursuing my investigation, as I have been all along. I have leads. I know my people and my villages. A load of unknown policeman could create panic and force the captors into hasty actions. Trust me.'

'Trust you?'

'I believe I'm close.'

'Petras – if this Craggan isn't returned safely by the end of the week, I'm coming up there personally. I'll have you directing traffic in Tripa.'

'Yes, Captain.'

He handed the phone back to the café owner. The captain was still ranting at the other end.

'Problem?' said the owner.

'No problem. But if he calls again, tell him I'm out.'

'Out where?'

'Out investigating where you and the other bars buy that awful illegally-produced alcohol.'

'Yes, Sergeant.' The owner descended the stairs rapidly.

Nikos sighed and turned his attention back to the dusty police-issue laptop on his desk. Penelope had assured him he'd be able to scrutinise the original film by simply plugging the stick into a socket, and so he now turned the machine about, studying which port might be the one.

When finally he managed to get it to play, he watched the jerky opening frames over and over. A hand. A shoe. A flash of stone wall. The sheet with the symbol. He watched James Craggan addressing the camera and studied the light, the sounds, and the suggestion of other sounds outside the building. A passing car? A goat bell?

He clicked the mouse: pause, rewind. Re-play, pause. There had to be a clue somewhere here.

Resort Office, Exogi

'What are you smirking at, Kelly? Have you been talking to Philippa? She told you, didn't she?'

Jim felt his face beginning to warm.

'It's secret,' said Kelly with a wink. 'Girl talk. Can't tell yer.' She put the end of her pen in her mouth and began to lick it suggestively.

'Jesus!' said Jim. 'Is nothing sacred? *I* haven't told anyone.'

'Yeah, right. So yer've not sent any emails about it? Yer've been tappity-tappin' all mornin'.'

'That's different.'

'Sure.'

'Look, what did she tell you? I mean, did it mean anything at all to her or . . . no, why are you laughing? Or was it just a drunken lunge. Come on, Kelly! You know I fancy her a little bit.'

'A *little* bit?'

'OK, quite a lot. What did she say? Help me out here.'

'She said yer've got a small cock.'

'Well, that's . . . that's just wonderful.'

'But, yer know, Christos is supposed to be 'ung like a dinosaur, so yer shouldn't feel too bad.'

'No, no . . . I'm over the moon.'

'Aw! Poor Jim! Don't sulk. Look – she'd 'ad a big argument with Christos. She were upset. She saw yer as someone she could go to. She'd 'ad a bit to drink and it makes 'er frisky. Look on the bright side: at least yer got a blowie from a girl yer fancy. Think of it as a "thank-you". It won't 'appen again.'

'No?'

'Not a chance. Different league, Jimbo. Forget it. Yer think yer could keep 'er 'appy with yer little chipolata?'

'A lovely point, delicately made, as always.'

246

'Yer welcome. Listen – 'ave you 'eard about James Craggan being kidnapped?'

'I may have heard something . . . '

'Yeah. Taken by terrorists. They reckon he's still on the island somewhere. They're talkin' about 'ouse to 'ouse searches. Can yer imagine if they cut bits off 'im?'

'They should have taken Chet Braddock. He would have appreciated it more.'

'Sarcastic git. Look, I've got to go and do me visitin' hours. Don't go moonin' over Philippa.'

'Yeah, thanks.'

He watched the equine arse jiggle out the door and turned lugubriously to the letters of praise drafted by Mr Twyford, the secret tourist.

Seldom have a seen such a knowledgeable rep as Jim. His passion for the island, its attractions and its excursions is quite remarkable and his solicitude towards guests is astounding to behold. I look forward to the Greek Night he has organised, which I'm sure will be the highlight of my holiday so far . . .

A little over-egged, perhaps, but a few judicious edits would make it more credible. Mr Twyford had also been compelled to persuade some of the genuine tourists – at least, those who didn't actively and vocally despise Jim – to write or email Iliad HQ with positive comments. The evangelistic fervour was quite impressive to behold, although there was no guarantee of it continuing beyond Mr Twyford's escape from Greece's justice system.

Such thoughts were soon interrupted, as were all his thoughts these days, by what might happen if James Craggan was released from captivity to relate how his plight had been initiated by a collision with a irresponsibly-driven Seat Marbella. Had the star turned slightly before the impact? Had he really glimpsed the car before losing consciousness? Was that why the nationalists had put the

247

memory stick in *his* car rather than anyone else's? A message? A threat? Or just a wild coincidence?

And now the whole world was watching. His job at Iliad Holidays would almost certainly be in jeopardy if it became clear he was indirectly responsible for the abduction, torture and death of a Hollywood star. Bad publicity. Not the kind of thing you'd want on your CV. It might even affect future relationships. Would there *be* any future relationships?

It was Grace's face he remembered: her smile turning to shock, disgust and disappointment before the climax crashed down upon him. She wasn't answering her phone. She must be busy with all the Craggan chaos.

The desk phone rang and he snatched it from its cradle. 'Grace?'

'What? It's Donna. You know that's not the right way to answer the phone, Jim.'

'Iliad Holi-days! My name's Jim – how can I help?'

'With less sarcasm, please.'

'Sorry, Donna.'

'OK, look – we've got a bit of an emergency. The girl who leads the excursions, Charlene, has ended up in hospital with an infected tattoo. We've got a coach of people on their way to the Melissani Cave but no guide. You're only about twenty minutes away by car. Get over there and make sure they enjoy their excursion. Am I making myself clear? Any questions?'

'Do we know what Charlene's tattoo was?'

'Jim . . . '

'No. No questions.'

'You know all the information about the cave, don't you?'

'More or less.'

'Right. By the way – you've got a tourist called Twyford, haven't you?'

'Yep. A lovely chap. Holidaying alone. He's a movie fan. We're like best mates. Why?'

248

'Nothing. I just wasn't sure which resort he'd gone to in the end. Forget it. Get yourself over to the cave. Now.'

Donna hung up.

White-water-rafting Christ! Could the day get any worse? Excursions were torture – like kindergarten for halfwits. Still, if he could get rid of the cave dwellers – the troglodytes, ha! – in rapid order, there'd be time to drop by the main set and ask after Grace. If she'd still talk to him. He grabbed his car keys.

Location shoot, near Fiskardo

Grace sat in the shade at the edge of the shingle beach and looked over the script pages on her iPad. She'd read the same line three times without seeing it. Maybe it would be a good thing if the whole production *was* called off. Go back to LA, pay off some of the school fees, do more PA work and save up for the Masters. It wouldn't take more than a couple of decades.

Granger came over and squatted beside her. 'Hey. How are you doing?'

'I've been better.'

'I'm sure Crag'll be found. The terrorist's demands are just ridiculous. They have to be amateurs.'

'Yeah, I suppose. But I keep thinking about Gaddaffi or Kim Jong Il – *they* were insane and they became national rulers. They were still dangerous, no matter how absurd.'

Granger nodded. 'Concentrate on the work. How's the script going?'

Grace shrugged and puffed out a breath.

'Don't worry about it. The editors'll make it what it is. You know *The Godfather* was created in the edit, don't you?'

'Yeah.'

'Look, I'm not supposed to tell anyone, but it's starting to look like Hannah's disappeared, too. She wasn't just late like we thought. There's no trace of her. Nothing. You've seen the press, right?'

Grace looked up to the taped-off perimeter, where security was holding back dozens of people. Most of them seemed to be photographers.

'Penelope's got that look,' said Granger.

'The "glass eyes" thing?'

'Uh huh.'

'Is it the terrorists again? With Hannah, I mean.'

'We have no idea. They've told the police guy, Sergeant Petras. I think Tony might be close to quitting. Test has been smoking some extra-strong skunk or something. He's not making a lot of sense at the moment. It might be best to keep away from him for a while.'

'So we're still shooting today?'

'Yeah. The lion and his trainer cost a lot of money. The stats show that audiences like a movie with a dangerous animal in it, even just a cameo. That's why LaBrava put it in.'

'Right. Of course – he's an animal lover. Listen . . . thanks, Granger. For everything.'

Granger touched Grace's shoulder and winked. She strode towards the truck with the barred enclosure on the back and fired up her walkie-talkie.

Granger was cool. Granger was attractive in her efficient, androgynous way. Someone who could be trusted. Someone reliable. But were women any better in the end? Not if you believed *the L-Word*.

Focus! *The scene.* Flashback: Cornolli is looking for his son Efthimios, who has gone to spend the day at the beach but not returned for lunch as arranged. He finds him cowering before a wild mountain lion, lured down from the peaks by the promise of human flesh. Cornolli is carrying his mandolin as always and uses it to beguile the beast with Orphic enchantment so that Efthimios can escape.

She watched as Granger briefed the lion trainer, Chet and Crag's stand-in (his face a swirl of masking latex) for the master shot in which Cornolli would come upon the scene and see the lion trapping Efthimios against the rocks. The lion itself appeared to be asleep. Drugged? The ASPCA representative stood by making notes. If he wasn't satisfied, there'd be nothing on the end-credits about "No animals were harmed . . . " The production might be sued.

'OK, everyone,' shouted AD Mike Kendall. 'Positions!'

Chet and the stand-in took their places. The trainer brought the animal from its cage and led it to where it would growl and threaten. It seemed very lethargic and uninterested, but would react, apparently, on cue.

'Action!'

The stand-in paused mid-step (the close-up would come later). He raised the mandolin and began to play a dissonant twang (the music would be added later).

The lion stood and turned towards the stand-in. The trainer shouted commands. The lion turned towards Chet and growled half-heartedly.

'More threat!' shouted Mike.

The trainer took a whistle from his pocket and began to blow a series of shrill commands. The lion took a few steps towards Chet and growled with not much more enthusiasm.

'I got it!' said Chet. 'Keep rolling!' He bent to pick up a pebble from the beach, hefted it experimentally, and tossed it at the lion.

'No!' shouted the trainer.

The pebble arced with inconceivable slowness towards the lion, which raised its shaggy head and watched the missile falling, falling, falling to strike it between the eyes with a muffled thunk.

It shook its head. It looked towards Chet and roared with terrible ferocity, swatting the air with a colossal paw.

'Great!' muttered Mike. '*That's* what we need. Did we get that roar on the boom mic?'

251

But the lion was now running towards Chet with silent and lethal intent.

The trainer blew his whistle madly, ineffectually.

The beast reared up and descended upon Chet, who let forth a strangulated scream.

'The tranq gun!' screamed Granger. 'Shoot it! Shoot it!'

The trainer ran to his truck and grabbed the rifle, raising it to his shoulder. There was a crack. Then another. The trainer looked at the rifle in his hands and seemed to reel back from it.

'It's down. The lion is down!' said Granger. 'Medic! Medic!'

The ASPCA representative was walking over to the trainer, who was fumbling urgently in the back of his truck.

Grace ran towards the lion's body. 'Chet! Chet! Are you hurt?'

He was lying in a foetal position beneath the beast, cradling his arm and whimpering.

'Chet? Are you bleeding? Can you hear me?

Granger arrived beside her, followed rapidly by Mike and others rattling across the pebbles.

Chet held up his hand. There was blood. There was something missing.

'It took my goddamn thumb!' he sobbed. 'Bastard took my thumb! Cut the lion open! Get it back!'

Grace wondered about the provision for microsurgery at Sami's health centre. Granger looked doubtfully at the inert creature.

'Is it breathing?' said Mike.

The ASPCA representative crunched towards them holding two similar-looking rifles. 'I'm afraid you have a problem. *This* is the tranq gun. This other one isn't. Guess which one he used to shoot the animal?'

The secured perimeter crackled with chatter and the clicking of thousand photos being taken.

'Penelope's gonna shit molten lava,' muttered a sound technician.

252

'*Where's the medic?*' shouted Chet. 'Get a vet! Get a butcher! Just get my thumb back!'

A siren was heard warbling intermittently on the hot breeze.

'Thank God!' whimpered Chet.

But the siren wasn't for him. It would soon become apparent that something quite terrible had occurred nearby at the Melissani Cave.

Private House, Allomeros

'Is she sleeping, or is she in a coma?' said Magda.

'It's more than sleep,' said Niki. 'She was totally lifeless when I dressed her.'

'Is it part of the transformation, do you think?' said Magda. 'How do you recognise a goddess when she walks among mortals?'

'The gods decide if they are perceived or not,' said Professor Stratigakis. 'They come in the form of animals, as rainfall and mist, and also in the guise of humans. In Homer, they generally reveal their divinity to strangers only as they depart.'

'But how should we know?' said Niki. 'I mean, I prayed for it. I buried the hair at the site and she came, didn't she? From the way you described it, she seemed drawn to the place. She thought she was home.'

'Yes, yes . . . ' said the professor.

Hannah Caro lay on the bed. She had been dressed in a white classical *peplos*, fastened at one shoulder with an ancient pin and cinched at the waist with a golden cord. Her hair had been combed and her skin lightly coated with virgin olive oil. A tanned thigh showed through a slit in the garment.

'She's so beautiful,' said Magda. 'She's perfect.'

'Not perfect,' said Niki. 'She has a small scar on her wrist there, just where it joins the palm. I saw it when I was preparing her.'

253

'I know what you're thinking,' said the professor. 'According to Homer, the Goddess was injured in exactly the same place while fighting in the Trojan War. Diomedes struck her and she bled ichor before fleeing the battle.'

'You have to admit it's a coincidence,' said Niki.

'Isn't there some test?' said Magda. 'If the gods bleed ichor, could we prick her finger and check? What colour is ichor?'

'Golden, like nectar,' said the professor. 'But it might be dangerous to wake her if she's undergoing her transformation now.'

'Does it normally take so long?' said Magda.

'We have no idea,' said the professor. 'The gods haven't visited for two millennia.'

'People will be looking for Hannah Caro,' said Niki. 'Especially now James Craggan has been kidnapped. There are journalists everywhere. Should we tell someone she's safe?'

Professor Stratigakis looked at the figure on the bed. Surely only a goddess could be this beautiful. Why had she come to the site? Why had she come at the exact time of that other remarkable discovery in the earth? Why had she come following Niki's burial of the hair? Such things seemed absolutely absurd when measured against the facts and rigorous reasoning of academic study. And yet an entire civilisation had put their faith in this world of deities walking among them.

'Wait a moment,' said the professor. 'I have to show you something.'

She went to the small cabinet beside the bed and took out an abject wrapped in a pillow case. The reverence of her movements had Niki and Magda exchanging curious glances.

'Xenomachos' insanity had one positive effect,' said the professor. 'His machine opened a cavity at the site. I looked inside it last night. I found this.'

She unfolded the corners of the pillow case and revealed the small aryballos pot.

They came closer. The clay was pale ochre and the painting ferric red: a detailed, delicate set of miniatures that went around it like a frieze.

254

'It's beautiful!' said Magda.

'How old is it?' said Niki.

'My guess is Late Helladic – say, just over a thousand years before Christ. It's almost certainly from Mycenae. Definitely from the Argolid region. It's proof that the Linear B tablet I found wasn't accidental. This is the piece of evidence that will finally prove a pre-classical Aphroditic cult was exported across Greece from Mycenae.'

'Is it Her in the painting?' said Niki.

'I think it has to be,' said the professor. 'See how she's naked here, her female attributes greatly exaggerated: large breasts, wide hips, long hair, the pubic region shown hairless. Very rare. She's larger than the other figures, her priestesses. But look – see how they apply the oil to her body and how she becomes mortal in dimension. She walks among them in disguise here and here.'

Niki and Magda stared as the professor turned the pot.

'Is it the original stopper?' said Niki.

The professor nodded. Tears came to her eyes.

'What? What is it, Danae?' said Magda.

The professor wiped her eyes with a sleeve. 'This is a perfume container. The original oil-based scent is still inside. It was hermetically sealed with some kind of gummy resin across the millennia. Here, smell it.'

She took out the stopper and held it for them to smell. It was a heavy perfume that evoked frankincense, wild rose, myrrh, sandalwood and clove – substances that would have come from the limits of the known world to be combined in ancient Greece.

'Is this . . . do you think that this is the same pot shown on the vase?' said Niki. 'The oil the priestesses rubbed on Her body to make the transformation?'

'I don't know. I just don't know . . . '

'There's only one way to tell,' said Niki.

'I'll draw fresh water from the well,' said Magda. 'Niki – you get the oil-burners.'

Iliad Holidays HQ, Argostoli

Donna stared unblinkingly at the mobile phone lying on her desk. She'd been fielding calls from guests for the last five hours, but the one she was expecting – the Armageddon call – had not yet come. It would. With the certainty of death, it would come.

The mobile's screen remained dark. Donna unlocked her desk drawer and took out the emergency miniature bottle of ouzo. No ice. No water. It would burn. She tore the top off and chugged it down, coughing briefly after the last of it scorched down her throat. Please let it start working before . . .

The screen lit up: Morag Cleaver calling.

'Morag – h-hello.'

'The Melissani Cave, Donna. Talk to me. What. The. *Shit.* Is going on?'

'The usual excursion girl Charlene had to go to the health centre—'

'The short version.'

'And Jim was the nearest—'

'Jesus!'

'So I told him to get down there and lead the excursion.'

'How many dead?'

'Nobody actually died, Morag. It seems there was a SCUBA club practising there at the same time. They saved the child.'

'Child? I heard something about a woman . . . '

'Yes, yes. It seems one lady had a panic attack in the boat.'

'What, she didn't know she was afraid of boats? Wasn't the excursion explained to her?'

'No, it wasn't that. It appears Jim may have said something . . . something ill-advised.'

'Go on.'

256

'I'm still piecing it together myself, Morag . . . It might have been a comment – a joke, really – about mutated piranhas. That's apparently what set the woman off.'

'Piranhas?'

'It was a joke – a very bad and unprofessional joke, certainly. He couldn't have known she had a severe phobia about it.'

'What about the others: the other injured people? What happened?'

'The phobia woman was obese. She capsized the boat. The other guests' injuries were sustained then. Just minor cuts and bruises. One concussion. The child couldn't swim. He sank like a stone, but as I say—'

'The SCUBA club.'

'Yes. Is anyone suing?'

'Not yet. We'll see. If they do, it's all on Jim. Did you know I've got the final report from "Mr Twyford"?'

'Really? Jim did say they'd met. What was the conclusion?'

'It's very suspicious, Donna. *Very* suspicious. That's what it is. He says Jim is the best rep he's ever seen: intelligent, helpful, witty, well-liked among the locals, and a font of information about the island. Does that sound like the Jim you know? The same Jim we've had twenty-seven complaints about so far this season?'

'It does sound a little odd, Morag. Although, it's true that the locals do seem to quite like him . . . '

'He's the worst rep ever and you know it, Donna. You saw his application.'

'He's . . . well, he's . . . has *anybody* written a letter of praise?'

'That's the thing. There *have* been a few. One woman wrote a kind of love letter about him. Some weird menopausal shit. She said he'd woken up her womb or something. Wait, I have it here . . . yes, she said he'd "provoked a uterine renaissance" in her. Does that sound like one of our guests?'

'Not really.'

'No.'

257

'You think he's writing his own letters of praise?'

'I wouldn't put it past him. But I've no idea how he got round Twyford.'

'Are we firing him? The thing is, I've got nobody else to take his place and he does cover a lot of ground.'

'Yes, Donna – he covers it with the wounded bodies of our guests. But don't do anything yet. I have an idea. Give him a written warning if you like . . . just to see what he does next.'

'Are you coming up to do an inspection tour?'

'That's for me to know, Donna. Make sure you visit those Melissani victims personally. Try to dissuade them from suing. Give them all vouchers and pens, right?'

'Vouchers and pens. Right.'

'Are you drinking again, Donna? It seems to me I can smell ouzo down the line.'

'What? No, Morag! I stopped drinking last—'

'Whatever. Just keep an eye on him. I don't trust him.'

'Yes, Mor—'

The line was dead. Donna breathed into her hand and sniffed. She looked doubtfully at the phone.

Exogi-Sami Road

Nikos drew his gun and thumbed the safety off. He aimed at the lock and fired three shots at close range, blasting metal from wood. He strode forwards and kicked the door, ripping the remains of the lock away from the jamb in a shower of splinters.

Two masked terrorists stood frozen: amazed at this unexpected intrusion. He aimed without hesitation and took both of them down with double taps to the chest. The room was clear. Gunsmoke hung blue and acrid in the sultry air.

He waited, alert. Footsteps came running and he braced his shooting hand ready for the kill shot. The third terrorist came skidding into the frame of a doorway. He was holding a shotgun. But he was too slow. Nikos let off three shots: two to the chest, one to the forehead. The terrorist dropped.

A muffled cry came from the adjoining room. Nikos stepped, gun extended, to discover a dim room in which Hannah Caro was tethered naked and glistening with perspiration to a steel-framed bed. A fourth masked terrorist stood over her. His pistol was pointed at her head.

'Drop your gun!' screamed the terrorist.

Nikos bent slowly as if to lay his weapon on the ground. But in a flash, he snatched a dagger from his boot and flung it at the criminal.

The slender blade went arrow-true through the gunman's eye, piercing his brain and killing him instantly.

'Fear not. You are safe now,' said Nikos to Hannah. He cut her bonds with the dagger and his senses filled with her animal scent.

'Turn your weapon on me!' she moaned, pulling him down upon her and seeking his mouth with a hungry tongue that . . .

A can horn snapped Nikos from his daydream and he saw that ash had fallen from the cigarette on to his uniform trousers. He brushed it off, cursing. Was there nowhere he could find peace? His phones had become his enemies. The police office in Exogi was under assault from foreign and domestic journalists at every hour of the day or night. Even the *kafenio* had proved to be no sanctuary. And now his occasional speed trap on the coast road had let him down also.

He stubbed out the cigarette with excessive force. It was not good for a man to be without sex for more than a week. It had been proven scientifically. The build-up of essential fluids would turn one insane in less than a year of

259

abstention. Blame Maria's jealous husband. Blame the paparazzi who followed him everywhere hoping for a lead. How was one to maintain an adulterous lifestyle with the world's media trailing one everywhere? It was certainly the worst summer he could remember as a policeman.

Another fax had arrived just as he had fled the office:

CONFIDENTIAL
POLITICAL AFFAIRS DIVISION BRIEFING NOTE
ATTENTION: KEFALONIA REGION

Following clues provided by intelligence data, our Specialist Weapons Unit has recently raided the Athens offices of the outlawed right-wing nationalist group *Filiki Eteria*. The organisers had fled, but left a great stock of promotional literature and correspondence. This is being processed, but initial inspection has revealed a letter from the Kefalonian cell, whose members are apparently codenamed "Zorbas", "Kolokotronis" and "Achilleus". The letter is postmarked Sami and requests guidance on how to proceed with the kidnapping of Hollywood actor James Craggan. We have no evidence as to whether a response was sent.

Captain Bastounis had scribbled his usual addendum:

Three more days – then it's out of your hands.

Nikos sighed a plume of Marlboro smoke. Thank God Bastounis didn't yet know the nationalists had probably taken Hannah, too. The Sami postmark meant nothing. If the nationalists had any intelligence at all, they would have driven there from anywhere on the island to post it. Fortunately, there was little evidence of their being intelligent. A quick call round some of the other regional

260

police offices had revealed that none of them had suffered similar graffiti attacks earlier in the season. Nor had any others experienced the hallucinogenic alcohol, whose toxic ingredient was also local. The Kefalonian cell was clearly close at hand. And one of them very likely rode a motorbike with knobbly tyres. How long would it take to make a search of outlying buildings near Sami? More than three days?

Nikos started the car and pulled out of the lay-by. He turned on the radio and flicked it to the classic *rembetika* pre-set, tapping the wheel as he rounded the corner where Craggan's car had originally been left.

He stamped on the brakes.

A white object was lying in the dirt. It seemed to be a bed sheet wrapped around something. The "something" seemed to be a tall person. Whatever it was, it was wriggling.

Nikos got out of the car and approached the wrapped body. Boots were sticking out of one end. He pulled at the folds at the other end and heard muffled shouts from inside. A head emerged: square-jawed, ruggedly handsome, instantly recognisable. James Craggan.

Nikos untied the gag and Craggan worked his jaw. 'Thanks, man.'

'Are you injured?' said Nikos. 'Did they cut anything from you?'

'I'm fine. No damage.'

Good. Good. I am happy to find you. Are you hungry? Thirsty?'

'I need to be with my people. They'll have missed me.'

'Of course. I will take you wherever you want to go. Just one question for now.'

'You got it, man.'

'Do you know where Hannah Caro is?'

261

Maria's *Psistaria*, Exogi

'It was like *Moby Dick*, mate. You should have seen it!'

'So, what – she just went over the side and capsized the boat?'

'Nah – she kind of stood and fell on the kid. He screamed. His mother screamed. Then they all started screaming, maybe 'cause they thought the piranha thing was true.'

'What about the rep? What did *he* do?'

'Well, at first, he kind of carried on with the tour even though everyone was in the water. Like nothing had happened – treading water and saying something like: "The remarkable blueness of the cave is due to the freshwater source . . . " But nobody was listening. They were all thrashing about. It ruined my photos. I've asked Golden Holidays for another ticket.'

'Of course.'

Jim listened to the conversation behind him and swallowed the rest of the ouzo. Was this the longest day of the rep job so far? He'd wanted to cancel the Greek night "out of respect" for the victims of the Melissani incident, but Donna had vetoed that. Apparently a good Greek night was just what everyone needed to raise their spirits.

Yeah, right.

The tables at Maria's were laid with the Greek-vase-style plates that languish in souvenir shops for decades without being sold. The paper tablecloths featured key-pattern borders. *Tzatziki*, Greek salad, *taramasalata* and miniature *moussakas* had been set out on a meagre buffet trestle, and each ticket holder had been given a mildewed fisherman's cap on loan (and freshly priced) from the mini-market. Mr Trellos' granddaughter's boyfriend Michaelis was setting up his electronic keyboard in a corner.

Jim wandered over. 'Evening, Michaelis. Is the *bouzouki* guy coming?'

'Nah, he's got a gig in Argostoli. Proper money.'

'Right.'

262

Jim looked at the keyboard. It looked more like a toy than a musical instrument: gaudy colours, pre-set beat and tempo buttons, notes marked on the keys. A number of Post-It notes seemed to list pre-programmed elements.

'So what will you be playing?'

'The usual: "Zorba the Greek", "Never on a Sunday", the "Chariots on Fire" thing. Mostly just those on a loop.'

'The eternal classics. Isn't the Vangelis thing quite difficult to play?'

'Nah – it's a pre-set. It came with the keyboard. I just press that button.'

'Mozart would be proud.'

'Eh?'

'Nothing. Have you got the plates?'

Michaelis gestured to a block of shrink-wrapped paper plates. 'Can't use real ones anymore. Health and safety.'

'It doesn't have quite the same effect when you can't break them.'

'You can tear them.'

Jim brooded. The place seemed pretty full. Maria's *psistaria* was a mass of red faces and variegated legs in shorts and skirts. The smell of alcohol and cigarette smoke competed with the scents of shampoo and after-sun. Clearly, Philippa and Kelly had sold more tickets than he had, although neither of them had deigned to turn up. Too awkward? They were probably at Diogenes' place comparing Jim's Lilliputian genitals to the monstrous Jurassic members of their boyfriends. Oh well – might as well start the nightmare. He nodded to Michaelis.

A tinny Bossa Nova beat burbled from the speakers and Michaelis went into his shtick.

'*Kali spera*, everybody!'

'*Kali spera*!' they all blindly chorused, unmindful that this was the same herd mentality behind the Nuremberg rallies and, ultimately, the Holocaust.

'Is there anyone in from Wigan?' called Michaelis.

An uneasy Bossa Nova stillness followed.

'OK! Is there anyone in from Stockton-on-Tees?'

A woman yelped, apparently in response to an enormous beetle that had flown into her hair.

'All right!' shouted Michaelis through feedback. 'Let's hear it for Vangelis and his "Chariots on Fire"!'

He jabbed the pre-set button and retired to a bar stool for a cigarette break.

Jim sat further along the bar and wondered what circle of hell Dante had reserved for people who organised tourist Greek nights. Probably the same one reserved for PR consultants and marketing copywriters. It occurred to him, briefly, that the food on the trestle had been sitting there uncovered and attracting flies since mid-afternoon. It may have become unsafe to eat, but it was probably too late to raise the issue now. People had already started to mime running in slow motion. He signalled for another ouzo and ice. The fourth?

'Drowning your sorrows?'

He turned. 'Grace . . . I . . . I was planning to come to the set but . . . things got out of hand.'

'I heard. Piranhas?'

He nodded. 'I got a written warning. There are five spelling mistakes in it.'

'Are you going to frame it?'

'Look, Grace . . . about the other night. It wasn't planned . . . It just . . . '

'Jim – you're free and single. I've been thinking and I realised I've got no right to . . . There was never any . . . I was just surprised. At least now I know where we stand.'

'I'm glad *you* do. If I embarrassed you . . . I mean, I certainly embarrassed myself.'

'And that other girl. What's her name?'

'It doesn't matter. Can I get you a drink? I don't have to pay in any of these places so choose whatever you like. If . . . I mean, if you can actually stand to look at me.'

'I'll have a Jack on the rocks.' She sat beside him. 'So – this is a "Greek Night", is it?'

264

'It's an abomination. But look at them: they're enjoying themselves. Like monkeys playing with their own shit. How are the rewrites going?'

'As good as you'd expect. Today was a tough one.'

'Yeah?'

'Chet got in a fight with a lion. He threw a rock at it.'

'Was the lion OK?'

'The trainer shot it dead.'

'I thought you used tranquiliser darts these days.'

'We do. We'll probably get sued.'

'Welcome to my life.'

'Cheer up, Jim. I've got some good news, too. I guess that's why I came into town. To celebrate.'

'Yeah? Have they got the go-ahead to use the Corelli name?'

'No. Not that. Crag has been returned safely.'

'What? *Really?*'

'Yeah. It's amazing. They left him in exactly the same place he went missing from. He was wrapped in the same sheet we saw in the background of that video.'

'But what about the ransom – all that stuff about Jews and foreign investment?'

'We don't know. It seems they gave him an evening meal and he woke up at the side of the road. They obviously slipped him something.'

'So they gave him back? Just like that?'

'It looks like it.'

'It doesn't make any sense.'

Grace shrugged. 'It's good to have him back. He's different – more energised. Like the experience has made him realise his mortality more than ever. It's great for the movie. Of course, Hannah's gone missing now.'

'*What?*'

'Yeah. Top secret. The last anyone saw of her, she was doing an extra on the road between Exogi and Allomeros. She was on pills and vodka. Probably fell down a hill.'

'Has he . . . has Craggan said anything about how he was first taken? By the terrorists, I mean?'

'He's been speaking to the police, but . . . I don't know. Jim? What's worrying you?'

'You're close to him, aren't you?'

'I wouldn't call us close, but we talk, yeah. He tells me things.'

Jim swallowed his ouzo at a gulp. 'Look, Grace. I've got something on my mind. Well, on my conscience, really. You've told me secrets; can I tell *you* one? In strictest confidence? You'll probably, well . . . '

'Is it something I'd want to know? You're making me a little nervous.'

'The day Craggan went missing . . . I hit him with my car and left him by the side of the road under a plastic sheet.'

Grace stared.

'He wasn't dead! There was a pulse. I checked. But it was my day off and . . . '

Grace stared.

'I have no idea how the terrorists got hold of him. I mean, it's really not my fault about that.'

Grace shook her head in disbelief. 'Unbelievable! I . . . it's just unbelievable.'

'He's safe *now*,' said Jim.

She stood and walked out of the place without a further word or backwards glance.

'Grace! *Grace*! He was having a piss! Don't tell the police! It could have happened to anyone!'

To anyone? Really? Or only to Jim?

Her Jack-and-ice was still on the bar. He downed it.

266

'Anyone here from Heckmondwike?' shouted Michaelis over the dying strains of "Zorba the Greek".

Sami Harbour

The news of Philotheos' imminent arrival had come to Xenomachos in a dream. The charismatic anchorite had appeared at the prow of an inbound ferry, his soiled robes flapping and the seabirds crying his name. A quick check of his website did, admittedly, also reveal a brief note about the monk's intentions to visit the island on an anti-pagan crusade, but the dream had definitely come first.

Evidently, Xenomachos was not the only one who had been looking at the website. About two-dozen other people were waiting at Sami port clutching branded bags from Kefalonia's various *zacharoplasteia*: cakes and biscuits and bon-bons of such quantity and sweetness that to eat them would surely bring on immediate diabetes. When would congregations learn that syrup-soaked pastries were not the most longed-for gifts of holy men? They prized practical things: a solid pair of shoes, a firm walking staff, a clasp-knife for eating hunks of cheese and bread in their frigid hermitages. Or a couple of billion euro's worth of prime real estate in Thessalonika, if one was talking about the richer monasteries of Athos. But Philotheos wasn't like them. No – Philotheos was truly a man of faith.

'Shouldn't you be at work?' said Xenomachos to a notable local council member.

'Eh, Philotheos is coming and, you know, my sister has that withered leg,' said the man. 'I've brought him some honey cake.'

'One does not pay for miracles with honey cake,' said Xenomachos.

'That's OK. I've got an envelope full of cash as well. Just in case. If he's truly righteous, he'll just take the cake.'

267

'What about you?' said Xenomachos, addressing a group of elderly women from Exogi. 'Don't you normally have your morning swim about this time?'

'Arthritis,' said one, clutching an elbow.

'My bowels,' said the next, touching her abdomen.

'My son wants to have a tattoo removed,' said the third, 'but can't afford the doctor's bills.'

'You're going to ask Phileotheos to pray a tattoo away?' said Xenomachos.

'Or change it to something better,' said the woman. 'He wants a Chinese dragon.'

'What will *you* ask him for, *Pappas*?' said the woman with the problematic bowels. 'Is it about your eldest daughter? The one with Satan in her knickers?'

'What? No! Philotheos is coming specifically in response to my personal request. We are, as you know, plagued by pagans on this island.'

'Not the pagans again!' said somebody.

Xenomachos turned sharply but didn't see who had spoken. He spoke louder, sensing that there was the makings of a congregation here. 'Yes – the pagans! They will quake when Philotheos walks this earth! He is going to bless the ancient site at Allomeros and exorcise the heathen gods. All are welcome. Tell your friends.'

Muttering animated the growing crowd. That might be even better entertainment than the earth-moving incident.

'It's coming!' cried the councilman.

All looked to the south and saw the ferry entering the Ithaca strait. And all began to move very gradually – almost imperceptibly – forward, following an ancient instinct to manipulate their way to the front of any queue or crowd. Xenomachos watched them shuffling with half-steps and faux-accidental gambits, like dropping a coin and stepping forwards to pick it up. This was the calibre of his flock: resolute in fighting off the Turkish occupier, but still more committed to cheating their government and each other – not necessarily to their own advantage, but always wilfully in aid of a neighbour's disadvantage. By the

268

time the ferry docked, some of them would be teetering right on the edge of the quay.

Xenomachos sighed. He strode forward to the place where the ferry would dock, not unduly surprised when a few people engaged him in conversation purely in order to walk by his side and get ahead of the others. The ferry was now clearly on its final approach and preparing to turn its stern on the quay.

Nor were the faithful the only ones to have noted this celebrated arrival. The swarms of press and paparazzi that had arrived following James Craggan's disappearance had become almost cannibalistic in their news hunger. This growing crowd was a carcass that drew them buzzing from across the north of the island in search of a story.

'I can see him!' said Bowels-woman. 'There, at the stern!'

Xenomachos squinted. It was just as the dream had been: the black robes billowing, the grey beard twisting in the offshore breeze. The monk held his hand up in blessing, seemingly ignoring the dozens fawning around him. Even from this distance, his charisma was clear. He had the look of a true hermit, a true holy man.

The crowd at the dock pressed still further towards the water as the ferry reversed in. People began to realise that they might not receive the personal miraculous attention they sought and began to shout over the ferry's engines.

'*Pappas* Philotheos! Bless my brother's lung cancer!'

'*Pappas! Pappas!* My daughter can't conceive . . . '

'Holy Philotheos – if you can't remove the tattoo, could he have a Chinese dragon instead?'

Xenomachos elbowed his way through, trying to signal the dockworkers who were waiting to receive the ropes. One of them saw and beckoned for him to stand beside them the rusting bollard. But there was little altruism in the act.

'*Pappas*. Will you have a quick word with the monk? My wife has an . . . intimate infection.'

'Yes, yes – I will tell him to pray for her health.'

269

'No. Tell him to pray that she doesn't find out about the affair.'

Xenomachos frowned and gave a noncommittal nod. The great hawser ropes were thrown and the ferry doors started to descend. A man further along the quay toppled – or was pushed – into the sea, his bag of cakes bobbing on the surface beside him. Nobody helped. His place was taken instantly.

And here came Philotheos: the first passenger to emerge. He had changed into an embroidered mantle, which, as he strode forth on the hot breath of diesel exhaust, revealed its subject to be a score of grisly martyrdoms hand-sewn by the monk himself as he sat in his cave on the Holy Mountain. The black robes beneath the mantle were dusty and soiled. His feet were bare, brown and rough with knobbled calluses. His hair and beard were as coarse and greasy as a sheep ready to be shorn. His corporeal scent, however, was more akin to a goat: gamey, feral, musky, and with a faintly faecal undertone.

Many on the quay dropped to their knees, murmuring prayers. Xenomachos bowed his head as Philotheos approached him.

'You!' said the monk. 'You are the one who called me in prayer to this place. I sense it.'

'Yes! That's right!' said Xenomachos, taking the extended (grubby and claw-like) hand and feinting a kiss.

'Your island is visited by a plague of amphibians!' proclaimed Philotheos. 'I come to rid you of these Satanic frogs!'

Xenomachos blinked. 'Ah . . . it was . . . the prayer was rather concerning an issue with pagans.'

'Pagans! Yes, that's right. I was confusing yours with another prayer I received at around the same time. Pagans – heathen theomancers in your midst, calling on false gods and making human sacrifices.'

'It . . . it was actually a rabbit.'

'We are all God's creatures, even the frogs. I come here today to lead a crusade against the pagans. Hear me, Christians! Hear me, Greece! I call on all – every monk and nun across our land – to descend upon this island in a wave of

270

righteousness. Together, we will wash a tide of Christ over this pagan corruption.'

'A crusade?' said Xenomachos. 'Truly? A crusade?'

'Come all!' said Philotheos. 'Come all to Exogi!'

The other dock worker approached. 'Excuse me, gentlemen, but could you move to the side and take these people with you? We need to unload the ferry and you're blocking—'

'Away!' called Philotheos, striding towards the shops and cafes of Sami town.

'A crusade!' said Xenomachos, trotting to keep up. 'Wait! I have a car parked over there.'

But Philotheos was unstoppable. 'No! First we eat pizza: pepperoni and capers. Anchovies if they have them.'

Main Set, near Sami

'Grace!'

Granger was calling from inside the security cordon.

'Grace! Crag wants you with him in the press conference. Come through.'

Journalists and photographers turned to look at Grace. Was she someone important? Craggan's woman? Surely not – even a man his age could do better. Probably some sort of assistant.

Grace blushed at the attention and moved quickly towards Granger, flashing her pass at security as she went.

Penelope was waiting to brief her. 'OK, look. Don't answer any questions – not even if they ask you. In fact, don't speak. You're only here because Crag asked for you. Got it?'

'Yes, Penelope.'

'Just so you know, the story about Hannah is that she's got heatstroke and has to stay indoors for a few days. In case anyone asks you. Which they won't.'

'Right. Got it.'

Penelope stared doubtfully and jerked her head towards the town-square set. 'Come on.'

The space was almost full of journalists and photographers, who jabbered and jostled for position. A dais had been constructed and was already occupied by Crag, Tony Brass, Test Weedle, an uncomfortable-looking Sergeant Petras, and Chet Braddock (bandaged) with his reeking Greek mentor. Grace took her place by Crag and blushed again as he reached for her hand in a gesture that set the cameras clicking like a field of crickets.

Penelope turned on a microphone and coughed for quiet. Grace thought of the scene in *Jaws* where Quint scratches his nails down the blackboard at the town meeting. *You all know who I am . . .*

'My name is Penelope McMurdoch. I'm the publicity for this movie. I ask you to remember that Mr Craggan has had a traumatic experience. He's consented to this brief press conference only to reassure his fans of his safety and good health.'

Test Weedle attempted to conceal a gleeful grin.

'OK. First question.'

Hands shot up. The first three rows of reporters bellowed questions simultaneously. Penelope pointed at a woman at the front

'Katerina Papageorgiou, *Kathimerini*. Mr Craggan – how do you feel after your kidnapping?'

'I'm relieved and happy to be alive. My captors treated me well and I never really felt in danger, but . . . but I believe I faced the real prospect of death at certain moments. It made me think a lot about my life – what I've done, what I've never done, what I owe. It was an experience I'm thankful for. I believe I can use it in my performance. I thank all my fans for their prayers and good wishes while I was gone.'

272

Penelope pointed again.

'Derek Balls, *Daily Mail*. Do you know who kidnapped you, Mr Craggan? Could you identify the members of *Filiki Eteria*?'

'I wish I could, Derek, but they were masked all the time. I was unconscious when they took me and when they returned me, so I have no idea where I was held. I've told everything I know to the police.'

Penelope gestured for Sergeant Petras to take the microphone and say something.

He cleared his throat. 'Er, *Filiki Eterias* is an, er, outlawed ultra-nationalist group based in Athens. Their base was raided some days ago by the Greek police and their leaders are running. We have no idea why Mr Craggan's captors let him free, but it could be connected to this fact. I am investigating locally.'

Penelope pointed.

'Briony Plemnik, *CineWorld*. Tony Brass – can you tell us what drew you to this project? It seems a little . . . anomalous on your CV so far.'

Tony took the mic. 'I was eager to work with this fine cast. Hannah Caro, Chet Braddock, the legendary James Craggan, and, of course the wonderful Greek actress Eleni Skouras . . . '

'But Scott LaBrava's screenplay?' said Ms Plemnik.

Penelope glared.

'LaBrava wrote a good foundational script,' said Tony. 'We've been, ah, modifying it. This might not be the movie some people are expecting.'

'People are saying it'll make *Cutthroat Island* look like *Star Wars*,' shouted a voice too quick for Penelope to silence.

'That kind of comment is unhelpful . . . ' began Tony.

'Next question!' said Penelope, pointing.

'Florence Bagley, *Natural World* . . . '

'Not you,' said Penelope.

'What can you tell us about the male lion that was heartlessly killed yesterday at the location shoot?' shouted Ms Bagley.

Test beckoned Penelope over and took the mic. 'Thanks for your question, Ms Bagley. I'm a subscriber to *Nature World* myself—'

'*Natural World*,' corrected Ms Bagley.

'Yeah, and I can assure ya that the lion isn't dead. He was only injured. If he appeared to be dead, it was because he was in shock. As we speak, he is under the care of a skilled vet.'

'Who? Where?' said Ms Bagley.

'The best lion guy in the world. Somewhere the press can't bother him with questions,' said Test, who had in fact ordered the animal frozen and sent back to LA so that he could have a novelty barbeque when he returned.

Penelope threw a lethal glare at Ms Bagley and pointed to someone else. 'Last question.'

'DeAnne Brine, *Celebrity Magazine*. Can you confirm or deny that Hannah Caro is not in fact ill with sunstroke but has also been kidnapped by the ultra-nationalists?'

The crowd erupted.

Penelope looked like lasers were about to beam from her eyes.

Test grinned. 'Anyone who repeats that in print will be hearing from our lawyers. Hannah's resting. She'll be back on set in a couple of days. In the meantime, perhaps someone'll ask Chet about his thumb, which he lost bravely in the name of art.'

Penelope pointed to a man in a wheelchair.

'Hiram Curricle, *Prosthetics News*. Mr Braddock – you've famously gone without a prosthetic for your pinky finger. Will you be choosing an articulated or servo-aided mechanical thumb to replace the living digit?'

Chet cradled the mass of bandages. 'It's too soon to tell, Hiram. I've got a micro-surgeon flying out from LA to assess the damage. All I know is that my next project might be in jeopardy.'

Ms Plemnik of *CineWorld* raised a hand. 'Are you referring to *The Olivetti Diaries*?'

'That's right,' said Chet. 'The story of the world's fastest typist. I'd got my speed up to 200 words per minute, but now . . . I just don't know. I'm not even sure about next year.'

'You mean *Master Po?*' said Briony. 'The story of the Japanese finger-puppet genius.'

Chet nodded. He seemed to wipe a tear away with the bandaged hand. Cameras clicked.

'OK, that's enough about other films,' said Briony. 'We're taking about *Captain Cornolli's Mandolin School,* which is going ahead and will be the smash hit of next summer. Write *that* down. We're done – thank you for your time.'

The press pack erupted again, but Penelope led her people out of the town-square set as security moved in to clear it.

'Let's go to Crag's trailer for a minute,' said Test. 'There's some things we gotta discuss offline. You, too, policeman.'

They followed and took their places. Grace took bottles of water from the fridge and handed them out. Crag patted the place beside him on the sofa and she took it.

'What's on your mind, Test?' said Tony.

'I think we got some issues,' said Test.

'No shit,' said Tony.

'You heard what the girl said about ya CV, Tony. How'd ya feel about that?'

'What can I tell you, Test? Sometimes good directors make shit films. Look at Coppola.'

'Yeah, but I don't want this to be a shit film, Tony.'

Tony shrugged and spread his hands.

'That's why you're fired,' said Test.

'*What?* Who else is going to direct it. You? I know Mike will walk if I walk.'

'Crag's gonna direct it.'

'*What?*'

'You saw that hostage video. He's got talent. I sent it back to LA and they loved it. Mel Weitz virtually shat himself. They're loving the new dailies – the cool mandolins, the cleavage, even the melted-face storyline. Crag's got experience. More than that – he's got heart. He believes in this movie. He *is* Cornolli. He's suffered. More importantly, this whole terrorist thing has got the world looking at him. This is a James Craggan picture now – not a Tony Brass picture. You go and direct something for your CV. Some Wilhelm Shakespeare or Charlie Dickens. Stick to period costume.'

'Fuck you, Test! You're a total philistine.'

'I'm not Jewish, Tony, so save your insults. Crag – what do you think? Do you want it?'

'Hey, I don't want to insult Tony,' said Crag, 'but it's an open secret I've been wanting to direct. I think I'm ready, yeah. I've got some ideas. I've got a writer I trust.'

He patted Grace's leg. She blushed again.

Tony stood, shaking his head incredulously. He slammed the Winnie door as he left.

'Strike one,' said Test. 'OK – Chet. Don't sweat the stump. We'll write it in. We might have to use a stand-in for the strumming shots, but it'll add something when you triumph over the injury. This is a movie where reality meets fiction.'

Chet stroked the bandages, noncommittal.

'I was thinking,' said Crag. 'What if Cornolli was kidnapped in the movie?'

'That's what I'm talking about!' said Test. 'Think about it – Craggan plays Cornolli mirroring Craggan. It's pure PR. What d'ya say, Penny?'

Penelope nodded. 'It could work. It's a hook.'

'Right,' said Test. 'We're on track. Now all we need is Hannah back with us. Where is that girl? Someone tell me she's found a guy with a massive schlong and run off with him.'

Penelope looked to Sergeant Petras.

'I think she is not with the nationalists,' said the sergeant. 'They already had Mister Craggan and they set him free. From what he tells me, they seem to be young and inexperienced. Perhaps they got afraid. I think they wouldn't take somebody else.'

'So where is she?' said Test.

'I have made investigations,' said the policeman. 'It seems she has many lovers in the area.'

'That's Hannah!' said Test. 'So I'm probably right – she's just rutting somewhere. She's probably on a bad pill cocktail and thinks she's back at summer camp.'

The sergeant shrugged. 'I will keep looking.'

'One more thing,' said Test. 'Who's this Theopolis guy I've been hearing about? The crusade guy. Sounds like the Greek Pope or somethin'. He famous?'

'Philotheos. He is a monk from Athos,' said the sergeant. 'A madman. He says Satan lives in the Internet and mobile phones. The people think he can do miracles.'

'Great. Can we get him?'

'I don't understand . . . '

'In the movie. We can give him a cameo. Maybe get a miracle on film. Does he do healing? Resurrections? Never mind, we can always CGI it. Does he have a problem with cameras? We could do it covert.'

'I don't think . . . '

'Somebody talk to him. Make it happen. Can't you see it? Hannah, naked, tied to a bed . . . Theopopolis performing an exorcism as Chet plays his electric mandolin in the background. Yeah! Write it. Send me the pages when you're done.'

Grace felt her mouth hanging open. She closed it.

Test clapped his hands. 'Now we're making movies!'

Stone Hut, near Sami

'Somebody's coming,' said Andreas.

'Petras?' said Kyriakos, adjusting his binoculars.

'No. That white van.'

'It's the third time this morning.'

'Do you think they know?' said Andreas. 'Is it the Special Weapons Unit?'

'Wait . . . no, it's just a guy selling potatoes,' said Kyriakos.

'We're all going to prison,' said Achilleus, sitting in an armchair and smoking. 'There are so many people looking for us now. The press, the police, movie fans. Craggan will tell them everything. It's just a matter of time. I can't *believe* you took him back!'

'What was I supposed to do?' said Kyriakos. 'I couldn't stand any more lessons about montages and close-ups. Didn't he understand we were making a hostage video, not a mini-series! Anyway, my mum was asking too many questions about the "crippled dog" we were feeding.'

'The voice of a true revolutionary!'

'*Malakas*! Did you really want to keep him? You know we would never have cut off his ears or set fire to him. We didn't think it through.'

'Maybe they'll just forget it ever happened,' said Andreas.

'Yeah, right,' said Achilleus.

'I blame Athens,' said Kyriakos. 'They should have replied to your letter and given us help. Where was "The Patriot" when we needed him?'

'He must be busy,' said Achilleus. 'It's not just us, you know. There are cells across Greece working on action plans for 1832. We're going to look stupid when they hear we let Craggan go before all the Jews were thrown out of Europe. We'll be the joke of *Filiki Eteria*.'

'It was never in our action plan anyway,' said Kyriakos.

'Did your mum notice you'd taken her sleeping pills?' said Andreas.

'Not yet. She's still asking about the dog.'

278

'What dog?'

'The dog we made up to explain all the food we've been taking from home.'

'We made up a dog?'

'Never mind the dog, *malakas*,' said Achilleus. 'Your mum might be watching you on TV if anyone finds out what we did. If Craggan can remember just a few details, Petras might be able to guess where we are.'

Somebody knocked on the door.

They froze.

The knocking came louder.

'I don't want to go to prison!' said Andreas, his voice cracking.

'Just ignore it,' said Kyriakos.

A face appeared at the window. A man in his early thirties with short, dark hair. He rubbed the grimy glass with a sleeve. He saw them.

'Zorbas! Kolokotronis! Achilleus! It's me: The Patriot – from Athens!'

They looked at each other.

'Can you let me in, guys? I'm kind of on the run.'

'Should we let him in?' said Andreas.

'Well, he's here now,' said Achilleus. 'I can't see we have much choice. Better in than out.'

Kyriakos went to the door and opened it. The Patriot darted inside and was shown to the room.

The Patriot looked around at the heavy-metal posters and old furniture. He was sweating and his clothes – black jeans, black t-shirt – were streaked with dirt. 'Thank-you, brothers. The police raided our Athens office. I was lucky to get out alive. When I saw you'd taken James Craggan, I knew I'd be safe with you: the bravest, most committed and most outrageous cell in all of *Filiki Eteria*. Where is he? Is he here?'

'Kyriakos . . . I mean Kolokotronis gave him some of his mother's sleeping pills and took him back,' said Andreas. 'He was eating too much and kept talking about movies all the time.'

'You let Craggan go?' said The Patriot.

'It's been all over the news,' said Achilleus.

'I've been running from the Judeo-foreign investors and police. I haven't had time to watch the news. Look – you have to get him back.'

They looked at each other.

'He's the key to our revolution,' said The Patriot. 'You energised the whole movement when you took him.'

'We're planning to work with Philotheos,' said Andreas. 'He's here on an anti-pagan crusade. Apparently, Jews are a kind of pagan.'

'Philotheos? No, he's insane. He'd make us look like a joke. We need to get Craggan back. How did you capture him the first time?'

'I found him under a plastic sheet,' said Kyriakos. 'I was having a piss.'

The Patriot stared.

'Are the police really chasing you?' said Andreas. 'They're chasing us, too. And the media. We might all go to prison together.'

'We'll die before we go to prison!' said The Patriot. 'They'll never take us alive! We must get Craggan back.'

They looked at each other.

'"We?"' said Kyriakos.

'Why didn't you give me a proper codename?' said Achilleus.

Private house, Allomeros

Hannah Caro opened her eyes and saw only whiteness. Was this heaven? She blinked. She turned her head and saw a light fitting. It was just a ceiling. There was a nice smell – some kind of perfume. She had a headache. A *really* bad one.

She propped herself up on her elbows and saw that she was wearing a white dress. Not her own. It was pinned at the shoulder like a Roman toga or something. Her skin shone with some kind of oil. It was the oil that smelled nice.

She was unconcerned. It wasn't the first time she'd woken up in a strange bed in a costume and covered in oil. She tried to reconstruct the last few hours. There had been the Greek guy who had come to "fix" the air-conditioning in her Winnie. There'd been the party he'd taken her to in some village. Someone had some crazy weed. A few pills . . . the vodka. It must have been the vodka.

She sat and swung her legs down to the floor. Her brain sloshed. She fought a rush of bile. Hair of the dog – there had to be something in this house. A beer would be good. A Bloody Mary, better.

Little oil-burners had been placed around the room – around the bed. The décor was nice. It looked like a woman's bedroom, not a man's. She stood uneasily and went, barefoot, in search of a drink.

The Church, Exogi

Xenomachos watched Philotheos eating a *pita*. The monk's lips shone with grease. *Tzatziki* decorated his moustache. A half-gnawed chip was lodged in his beard and his embroidered mantle was stained with a fast food cornucopia. He made grunting noises as he chewed. But it was actually happening – the anti-pagan crusade was happening.

Dozens of monks and nuns sat around them on the sun-scorched grass: brothers and sisters from the monasteries and convents of Themata, Agios Andreas, Kipouria, Atros, and Panagia on Ithaca. The brothers of Agios Athanasios has sent word that they would be arriving presently, hinting that they might also bring the reliquary of the eponymous saint's remains. All had come in answer to Philotheos' call at Sami port. Still more were arriving by ferry from the mainland and islands of Greece – a holy influx greater than Xenomachos could ever have hoped for. Many of them had mobile phones, on which they sent the message ever wider.

Local and foreign news crews – drawn by the kidnapping of James Craggan – had parked their vans close to the church and were reporting the novelty. A location scout from the movie had been sent by Test Weedle to take photographs and assess the potential for a scene in *Cornolli*.

Xenomachos watched Philotheos wipe his mouth with a sleeve and reach for a bottle of Coke. 'Brother – I think perhaps you should address them. The world is watching. There are reporters. Tell them our plan so that the whole of Orthodoxy might know.'

Philotheos dribbled. 'Yes. Yes. I will speak.'

'Here – stand on the steps of my church.'

Philotheos belched and stood to take his pulpit. Awareness rippled through the gathered monks and nuns. Camera crews jostled for position.

'Brothers and sisters in Christ!' said Philotheos. 'Thank you for hearing my prayer. And I speak of prayer only – not the telecommunications devices and Internet technologies which embrace the numerology of Satan! No – do not think me ignorant of modernity. I know all about Windows and Intel. I have made a study of these instruments of evil. Do you know, for example, that the little arrow on the screen – the one moved by the so-called mouse – is known, in English, as a "cursor"? Yes! In such a way do we curse our Lord with every process enacted by computer!'

'The crusade!' prompted Xenomachos.

'In such ways are we led to evil by the Hebrews,' said Philotheos. 'By the Sanhedrin, who killed our Lord and who control Europe through the German banking system.'

'The pagans,' muttered Xenomachos.

'But I speak to you today about something equally bad: pagans among us – worshippers of the so-called Twelve Olympians. Heathen gods. They seek to

282

fight us through politics and the age-old weapons of the Beast: logic, rationality, freedom of faith and democracy. There are many of them – more every year. And here on the island of Kefalonia, in the village of Allomeros, they have been *sacrificing* to the pagan goddess of Aphrodite.'

A murmur passed through the cassocked crowd.

'Yes – sacrificing! I ask you all: what kind of abhorrent religion places death at the centre of its rites? What evil religion would see one of god's own creations sacrificed for sin?'

'Move along,' coughed Xenomachos.

'On Sunday, we will cast this heathen deity from these shores. On Sunday, we brothers and sisters in Christ will descend upon the village of Allomeros and consecrate the ancient site. Yes! That site where the bones of a sainted martyr are thought to lay. Our combined prayers will saturate the earth and banish its heathen spirits. We will plant a cross there – a great cross of Kefalonian mountain pine that will be as a stake through the heart of pagan worship!'

A flutter of "amens" passed through the al fresco congregation.

'Mention the service!' urged Xenomachos.

Philotheos looked momentarily confused. He had been distracted by a delivery moped bringing pizza.

'*You know,*' urged Xenomachos. 'The service we discussed! Afterwards. In my church?'

Philotheos nodded. The nibbled chip was still in his beard. 'Brothers and sisters! Brothers and sisters! After we have banished the ancient gods, we will all return here to this . . . this . . . ah, very modern church and celebrate our faith together in gratitude for the prayer of brother Xenomachos that first called me here.'

Xenomachos stepped beside the monk and held up a humble hand of gratitude.

Indifference emanated from the congregation, many of whom were smug in the knowledge that their churches were many centuries older than this one at

Exogi. Xenomachos stepped down, the smile becoming stale on his features. He saw Sergeant Petras' police car parked beside the TV-station vans. He saw the policeman approaching through the massed ranks of nuns and monks.

'Sergeant,' said Xenomachos. 'May I introduce Philotheos of Athos.'

'Nice to meet you, *pappas*,' said Nikos.

The monk nodded a perfunctory greeting. He was opening a pizza box and dipping his head inside to inhale the scent of hot pepperoni.

'Listen,' said Nikos. 'I can't stop you and these other holy people from visiting the site at Allomeros—'

'I know that,' smiled Xenomachos.

'But you can't erect a cross there. You can't even pass through the new fence. It's a protected antiquity. You'd need permission from the Ministry, otherwise you'd be breaking the law.'

'You had your chance, Petras. I warned you a higher law would be invoked.'

Nikos sighed. 'People might get hurt, especially some of these elderly ones. The ground is uneven there.'

'What will you do? Arrest all of us? There will be a hundred, two hundred, brothers and sisters there. Will we all fit in your single cell in Exogi? Will you stand against the whole of Orthodoxy?'

'*Pappas* – this isn't how we do things—'

'This is the dawn of a new age Petras. Why don't you concern yourself with finding missing film actors instead? Christ is coming, but first we must eradicate the pagans. With Philotheos' leadership, I will make my church in Exogi the standard-bearer for a new golden age of faith.'

Philotheos looked up at the mention of his name. A strand of mozzarella dangled from his lower lip. 'Eh?'

Nikos walked away shaking his head. Something would have to be done. Something drastic. He went back to the police car, stepping between journalists with cameras and microphones. Everywhere, it seemed, nuns and priests were talking to the media about pagans.

'Sergeant! Sergeant!' said a reporter. 'How close are you to finding the men who took James Craggan?'

'Less close every time my investigation is put on the television by you people.'

'Sergeant! What do you think to Philotheos' crusade?'

'I think the church's previous experience of crusades should be a lesson to us all.'

'Sergeant! Sergeant! Do you believe in the Twelve Olympians?'

'It doesn't matter what I believe – only what keeps the peace in our community.'

Nikos got into the car and closed the door. Somebody knocked on the passenger window and he saw a young man wearing a heavy-metal t-shirt. The boy didn't look familiar, but he looked like a local. Nikos leaned over and rolled the window down.

'What do you want, boy?'

'Is it true you're looking for the members of *Filiki Eteria*?' said Andreas.

'What of it?'

'I'm one of them.'

Nikos studied him. He couldn't have been more than seventeen: pimply, and reeking of that insecticide deodorant they all seemed to wear.

'My codename is Kolokotronis,' said Andreas. 'The others are Zorbas and Achilleus . . . but that's actually Achilleus' real name. He's a bit tetchy about it. They don't know I'm here. I think we might be in some trouble.'

Nikos pushed open the door. 'Get in, Kolokotronis. We should talk.'

Location Shoot, near Exogi

'So you really don't remember anything about them taking you?' said Grace.

285

'Nope,' said Crag. 'I heard a car. I started to turn and it side-swiped me. That was it: instant blackout. When I woke up, I was tied to a chair.'

'And you didn't see the colour or the make of car?'

'No . . . but listen – that's all over now. It's a memory. An experience. I don't hold any grudges. I could have been killed, sure, but someone, somewhere wanted me to live. Do you know I had the crystal in my pocket the whole time? It gave me strength. I was right to go back and get it.'

'I guess.'

He put an arm around her shoulders. 'I knew *you* wouldn't give up on me.'

'I didn't really . . . '

'I felt you with me. When I was alone there. It was like you were there reassuring me.'

Grace smiled. 'I suppose we should get on with . . . '

'Yeah, yeah. Let's do this.'

Crag went to confer with his cinematographer Mario and his assistant director Mike (who had opted to stay after Tony's departure). The lighting and sound crews had already rigged the nave of beautiful Venetian-style church. The stand-in with the "melted" face was drinking water from a polystyrene cup. An extra dressed like the Virgin Mary was receiving some final touches from Make-Up. The FX guys were testing air currents to decide the best place for the smoke machine.

Granger wandered over. 'Surreal, isn't it?'

'I just don't know anymore,' said Grace. 'Three months ago, I would have said this was the biggest crock of Hollywood bullshit. Just laughable. Today, it actually kind of makes sense. I feel like the real world doesn't apply. The real world can't be lit or soundtracked. It's too unpredictable. You know what I mean?'

Granger put on a bad Bogart voice. 'Welcome to the movies, kid!'

Grace nodded towards Crag. 'How's he doing?'

'He'll be fine. Mario and Mike'll help him. He has a script to follow. Tony was losing it anyway – Test took all of his control away. I'm sure he's happy he was kicked out.'

'I suppose.'

'Can I ask? How's it going with you and that British guy?'

'How did you know . . . ?'

'It's a small island; we're a big crew. People see things and talk. It's none of my business of course . . . '

'No, it's no problem. His name's Jim. I thought he was cool. We talked about film. But it turned out he was just a liar. Maybe it's my fault . . . maybe I wasn't clear with myself about what I expected, you know?'

'It's not your fault he lied. There's never a good reason.'

'Well, he did have a pretty good reason.'

Granger put a hand on Grace's shoulder. 'Well, if you need to talk . . . '

'Thanks, Granger. Really. I appreciate it. Do you think they'll find Hannah before the media discover the truth?'

'She'll be behaving badly somewhere. That's what she does. It's all publicity in the end. That's her role. It's why she was cast. Test would be happy if the media *did* find out.'

'He's a strange one. Reminds me a lot of Mel Weitz. But at least Test seems to have actually seen some movies.'

'You think he's *seen* those titles he mentions? No way. He's seen their *numbers*. He's seen spreadsheets prepared by consultancies on what audiences like. You know how many 'buddy' movies came out after *Lethal Weapon? The Last Boy Scout* was one of the highest-paid screenplays of the early nineties because it ticked so many of the boxes established by *Weapon*.'

'Yeah. I guess posterity will tell how *Captain Cornolli* shows up on the spreadsheets.'

'Hey, it's not our call. We do our jobs and we do them well. You think Mario'll be looking for work if this movie bombs? You think Crag'll fall back

287

into obscurity? Look at some of the shit Travolta's done, but he keeps coming back. People like Mel Weitz and Test Weedle are the ones who end up eating a shotgun when the movie tanks.'

'So there is some justice in the world.'

Granger smiled. 'Maybe. Maybe. Got any plans for after the shoot?'

'Go back to LA, I guess. Do a Masters in directing. Crag says wants to stay in contact.'

'How do you feel about that?'

'I don't know yet. It's kind of weird, but . . . '

'Look – we'd better get into position. We're about ready to go.'

Crag clapped his hands. 'OK, people! Can we have the Virgin on her spot? Cue the smoke. Let's shoot this miracle . . . '

Executive Trailer, Main Set, near Sami

Test Weedle took a deep hit of the village weed and felt his brain tingle with spearmint freshness. He fumbled for the remote and pointed it at the DVD player. The big screen flickered into life: rough cuts of Hannah Caro playing her mandolin naked in a tub. Side angles. Low angles. Aerial views. Yeah, they'd have to cut those occasional glimpses of pussy, but the nipples could stay. There was more than enough here for a really hot edit. Use the mandolin itself as the censor.

Hannah, Hannah – where are you?

'Test – you really are a pervert.'

He turned. It was Audrey Hepburn again, wearing the *Breakfast at Tiffany's* dress. 'Hey! What's up, Aud?'

'*Captain Cornoll?* Seriously? What the frig, Test?'

'Hey, cut me some slack, Aud! The geeks have run it all through their computers. It's gonna do at least forty per cent over spend worldwide. Maybe more, with all this publicity. Then you've got DVDs and merch on top of that.'

'Merch, Test? Like Cornolli action figures?'

'Yeah, laugh it off, Aud. Tell it to George Lucas. Ya know how much he's made out of dolls and lunchboxes? Friggin' gazillions. Wait 'til the kids get a load of electric mandolins. It'll be the new Hula Hoop.'

'You're stoned, Test. Your cerebral processes have become scrambled by excessive quantities of THC. Your grip on reality has slipped.'

'Whoa! When did ya start talking like that? Aud? Aud?'

She was gone. Her *Tiffany* movie was overrated anyway. Fourteen mill grosses worldwide. Classic cinema, my ass.

The big screen went dark. He reached for the iPad that the location scout had delivered barely an hour ago – footage of the mad monk Philopopulous. Close-ups of the guy snarfing pizza, a french fry in his beard. His speech: mad, staring eyes and anti-Jewish shtick. All those nuns and priests dressed in black. Great visuals. Free extras!

Make it a scene! Cornolli plays to God! Something about global warming – that was hot at the moment.

He leaned forward to take his phone and toppled from the sofa to the floor. His limbs wouldn't move. The thick-pile carpet was swaying like some undersea forest. Pixar. How about an animated insert? How much did *Roger Rabbit* gross . . . ?

Hannah, Hannah – where are you?

289

The ports of Kefalonia

And still they continued to arrive at the ports of Sami, Poros, Argostoli and Fiskardo. Some even came by air from Meteora and Athos, from the plains and the mountains, from the Sporades, the Cyclades, the Dodecanese and the Argo-Saronic isles – a great tide of monks and nuns in many shades of black, from deepest the midnight dark to charcoal and hermitic faded grey.

They came old and young: the wizened abbots, the beardless novices, the shrunken and deformed. They came wearing only the soiled clothes they lived in, or resplendent in gold-embroidered mantles. Some carried standards and flags – the Holy Cross, the Greek white-and-blue, the yellow double-headed eagle of Byzantium – while others bore reliquaries of saints' remains: a finger bone, a lock of hair, a jewelled ring that breathed the scent of immortality.

Cultures mixed as oil and water. In towns along the coasts, the holy met the unholy – the football shirt beside the cassock, the beard beside the tattoo, the earnest pale face beside the buxom sun-burned cleavage. Contemplation and hedonism clashed. The chants of Orthodoxy challenged Euro-techno. The branded leisurewear of the tourist hordes was matched by the symbol of the cross.

And the black tide washed inexorably in miraculous congregation towards the town of Exogi: staging post for the crusade against the pagan site of Aphrodite at Allomeros.

No Name Bar, Exogi

Jim upended the fourth glass of ouzo and worked his tongue among the melting ice cubes for a last taste of the spirit. Ice water ran down his neck and into his polyester polo shirt. So what? It was forty degrees even at eight in the evening and the shirt looked like he'd performed an autopsy in it anyway thanks to the ham-and-ketchup *pita* he'd had for lunch.

The barman nodded to the group of tourists, fresh off the plane that day. 'They're waiting for you. They want their welcome meeting."

Jim turned to look at them. Most were a post-mortem pasty white, although a couple had managed to burn themselves in the few hours they'd been here. Only seven of them had bothered to turn up: a wheezing lard-ass, a gurning imbecile, a football-shirt bigot, a warty witch, a slack-jawed trollop, a soon-to-be cuckolded boyfriend, and an insipid HR middle manager. Standard Iliad fare. Interchangeable, really.

'Are you OK, *re*?' said the bar owner. 'You wanna drink a coffee before you talk to them?'

'Nah, I'm a professional,' said Jim. 'I can do these in my sleep now.'

He walked unsteadily over to where the tables had been pushed together and stood before the tourists. They looked back at him, seeing an unshaven young man with a lot of food down his white top and blue shorts.

'Right. Listen up,' he said. 'I'm Jim. I'll be your rep for the duration of this holiday. That means I'll be visiting your various accommodations – idiotic plural, that – at times chosen to be most inconvenient to you, namely: early morning and when you're on the beach *et cetera*. Talk to me if you want to make a complaint and I'll fill out a CC-Ex form, which will be sent to my boss in Argostoli, or thrown in the bin here to save time. Things you might want to complain about – just in case you need any ideas – could include: no kettle (very popular, that one); no basin or bath plugs; room too small; room too hot; room not clean enough; room has no view; excursions badly organised and poor value for money; resort rep bad tempered and/or flagrantly disrespectful of guests' needs . . . I'm quoting there from my most recent written warning.

'OK. Excursions. Ignore what I just said about them. The excursions offered by Iliad Holidays are quite the most exhilarating experiences you could hope to have in your entire lives. Only last week at the Melissani Cave, a woman of portly stature had a near-death encounter brought on by the incomparable beauty of the place. For only fifty euros each (non-refundable, even if you lie under the departure coach), you can pluck the very fruits of this Edenic isle as if you were Adam and Eve when the world was newly-made and all was good. Fiskardo? A veritable paradise! The Drogarati Cave? A wonderland of stalactites and stalagmites that absolutely *doesn't* smell of piss, no matter what the other tourists may tell you. I myself have been on these excursions more than a hundred times each and never become bored of them. Ask me for tickets at the end.

'Right. Something about Exogi. Frankly, there's shit-all here, as you'll have gathered. The beach is small and doubles as a public toilet. There's only a couple of bars, and they'll compete to rip you off because the mini-market costs even more. If you have any medical emergencies, which you no doubt will, there's a health centre at Sami. The local taxi drivers can take you there for about three times more than locals pay. Don't call me, though – I haven't got a mobile because Iliad Holidays are too tight to get me one!

'Finally, I'd like to welcome you all to Exogi and wish you a pleasant holiday on behalf of Iliad, the only company named after an armed conflict. Any questions?'

The seven tourists looked back at him. The warty witch raised a hand.

'We're not at school now,' said Jim. 'No need to be so formal.'

'Why do you do this job if you don't like it?' she said.

'Who *does* like their job . . . sorry, what's your surname?'

'Cleaver.'

'Yeah, that suits you. Like I said, who *does* like their job? We work for money. If it's a choice between this job or working at a sewage plant, I'll take this. Doesn't mean I have to like it. Do you like your job, Ms Cleaver?'

'I love it.'

'Really. What do you do?'

'You seem like a clever boy, Jim. Educated. Maybe you can guess.'

292

'Are you a chicken-sexer? A jockey? An astronaut? No, wait . . . something in PR.'

'My name's Morag Cleaver. I'm the Iliad Holidays general manager for the Ionian Islands. I'm Donna's boss.'

The others took a few seconds to process the reply. A couple smiled. Slack-jawed trollop giggled. Football-shirt bigot and wheezing lard-ass started to applaud.

Jim's sphincter twitched. He felt himself go pale. 'I suppose I'm in trouble now.'

'You've no idea, Jim Lad. Perhaps, first of all, you'll apologise to these guests.'

He looked at the leering faces. 'I'm very sorry.'

Morag urged more. Her eye had started to twitch.

'Sorry for my flagrant disrespect and . . . my flippant nature . . . and my general appearance.'

'Too late, Jim. You're fired.'

The tourists applauded. Football-shirt bigot cheered.

'Wha?' said Jim.

'You thought this job would be a walk in the park, didn't you? A bit of a lark over the summer? Bit of pocket money? You thought you were above it. Well, now you're out of it. Time's up. The nightmare is over. Someone else'll be taking over on Monday. You'd better be gone by then. Leave the flat in Allomeros. Leave the car keys in the office. You might as well throw your uniform away – nobody else would wear it. Gone gone gone! We've got your contact details – I'll find you if anyone chooses to pursue their legal action.'

Jim stood stunned. Nocturnal Exogi swirled abstractly at the fringes of his consciousness.

'What? No witty comments?' said Morag. 'No quotes from Aristotle?'

Football-shirt bigot laughed. 'Looks like your're out on your ear, mate.'

'He's got a first class degree,' said Morag. 'But he eats like a baby. Look at his shirt.'

They laughed. They slapped the table, They leered and grunted.

'Drinks are on me tonight,' said Morag.

They cheered.

'Oh, are you still here, Jim?' said Morag

Jim saw a flash of her being ducked and burnt at the stake. He walked numbly to the bar.

'It didn't go so good, eh?' said the owner.

'No. Quite badly. Listen – have you got any of that dodgy alcohol left? The stuff that poisoned a load of people earlier in the season?'

'There's some in the drum, but Sergeant Petras told us not to use it.'

'Do me a favour. Keep sending free shots to my new tourists there. I'll take full responsibility if the policeman comes asking. Just keep sending them shots on the house. They're English; they'll drink anything you send them.'

'Ha! I know it. Can I get *you* anything?'

'No . . . I have things to do . . . '

He wandered out of No Name and along the street to his car. Kelly and Philippa were walking arm in arm towards him: Kelly all blonde hair and bovine teats, Philippa wearing a mini-skirt that sheathed her undulating hips and made her honeyed legs look even longer. Seeing him, they giggled and shared a comment.

Great.

'Jimbo!' said Kelly. ''Ow yer doin'? Is that yer lunch on yer shirt?'

Philippa smiled, winked, licked the corner of her mouth.

'I've just done a welcome meeting. Iliad's Ionian general manager was in it. I didn't know.'

'*Shiiit!*' said Kelly. 'Morag Cleaver?'

'You know her?'

'She's famous. They call 'er the witch. I've 'eard she's a real bitch.'

294

'She fired me. I've got to be out by Monday.'

'Are yer really surprised, Jim? Yer the shittest rep 'oo ever put on a uniform.'

'Thanks, Kelly – that means a lot.'

'Leave him alone, Kel,' said Philippa. 'Can't you see he's sad?'

'He's just sulkin', the big babby.'

'*I'll* miss you, Jim,' said Philippa. 'Really. You entertained us. You were there for me when I needed you. I'm sorry if ... if you thought it was something more than it was.'

'Call me a traditionalist,' said Jim. 'Sucking someone's knob used to mean something.'

Philippa leaned in to plant a kiss at the corner of his lips. Her ponytail swung against his shoulder. Perfume rose hotly from her naked skin. He felt her tongue flick. His shorts stirred.

'No hard feelings,' she said with a wink.

'Looks like 'e's 'aving some now,' observed Kelly.

'I'll miss you Kelly,' he said. 'The apostrophe is safe as long as you're around.'

'Eh?'

'Never mind. I've got to ... I've just got to go.'

He waved and walked past them to his car: the trusty, dusty Seat Marbella. Might as well head back to the flat in Allomeros. There was a half bottle of ouzo there. Or perhaps Diogenes' bar was a better place to obliterate the evening.

Private House, Allomeros

'I just don't understand how she could have got out,' said Niki. 'We were just there in the garden!'

295

'It was as simple as walking out the front door,' said Professor Stratigakis.

'But she didn't make a sound,' said Magda.

'I know what you're both thinking,' said the professor.

'Well, couldn't it be true?' said Niki. 'We used the perfume – just like on the vase.'

'She must have left the mortal vessel and gone into the aether,' said Magda.

'She looked through the kitchen cabinets first, though,' said the professor.

'Don't you believe even a little?' said Niki.

'I want to . . . I really do.'

'Look at the evidence,' said Niki. 'The tremor, the movie, the hair I buried . . . even Xenomachos's earth-mover revealed the vase to you. It's a pattern. We prayed for it, but now you don't want to believe it.'

'All I know is that when the gods appeared to mortals, they did so unequivocally. There was never any doubt. And they didn't search the kitchen for booze.'

'That's because our predecessors truly *believed*,' said Magda. 'Maybe the gods come because they know whether we believe or not. Maybe she disappeared because she sensed you didn't have enough faith. What would make you believe?'

'We could go out and look for her. She might be walking around the village disoriented. If there's no sign of her . . . '

'She might have gone back to the site,' said Magda. 'That's where she was drawn.'

'Maybe that's what happens when you use the oil,' said Niki. 'We have no idea what's supposed to happen. I think . . . I think she came especially to fight against Xenomachos' crusade. That's why we called her, isn't it? I think she'll reappear when he comes with Philotheos and all those others and tries to plant the cross. Then we'll see the Goddess in her true divine form. Then the earth will shake.'

296

'We have to be there when they come,' said Magda. 'You're the guardian of the site, Danae. It's your responsibility.'

'I know,' said the professor. 'I've already spoken to Sergeant Petras about it. I can't stop them, but I have to do something.'

'The Goddess will speak for us,' said Niki. 'Wait and see. We've woken her. Her power is older than Xenomachos' god.'

The doorbell rang.

'Her. It must be her,' said the professor.

They went to the door and the professor switched on the exterior light.

'Ladies. Sorry to bother you at this hour,' said Sergeant Petras. 'I wonder if I might speak to you about an urgent religious matter.'

'It was the brush, wasn't it?' said Professor Stratigakis. 'You saw the brush.'

He shrugged. It was his job to notice things. A brush. A silver box of hair.

'You'd better come in.'

'There's a young lady in my car,' said the sergeant. 'I think we should all talk. Her name is Grace. She works on the movie.'

Jim's Flat, Allomeros

The Marbella crunched to a halt in the driveway. Jim sat listening to the engine tick. This old piece of crap. This skip on wheels. This automotive joke. Should he leave a bowel movement in the car for the next rep? Fill the windscreen wiper reservoir with urine? No – they'd probably just deduct any cleaning costs from his final pay cheque. And – it hardly seemed true – he had to admit he'd developed a sort of grudging fondness for the Seat. Like him, it didn't belong, was useless at its job and usually dirty.

Better simply to change out of the risible Iliad uniform, drink the rest of that ouzo and head up to Diogenes' bar for a tumbler or six of whisky. The goggle-eyed stoner would no doubt be able to provide a philosophical spin on the firing. Perhaps Grace would be there, too. He could apologise properly before leaving, if she'd let him.

He walked to the steps. The infra-red turned the spotlights on. There was a figure slumped on the floor against his apartment door. A girl with long, dark hair and long, honey-hued legs.

Again?

'Hello? Are you lost?' he said.

She stirred and brushed hair from her face. Hannah Caro.

He felt the peculiar sensation one gets when seeing a famous person in the flesh – that mental double take. It looks like her. It can't be her. It *is* her. She looks just like herself, but real and here, now, in my presence. It had been the same with Craggan, true, but Jim hadn't abused himself repeatedly to the films of James Craggan. And he hadn't just run Caro over.

His mind swirled with cinematic recollections of her naked form. That scene in *Deep Six* where she peeled off the wetsuit and rode Matthew McConaughey. The infamous bit in *Succubus* when she'd molested Ben Affleck in his sleep. Jim had actually broken a DVD player pausing that one.

'Er, are you OK?' he said, walking slowly up the stairs. 'Do you know where you are?'

'Home,' she said. The same voice as on screen.

His Iliad shorts sparked and crackled. 'I suppose you'd better come in.'

He helped her to stand and she fell against him just as Philippa had done. She wore an old-fashioned dress fastened at one shoulder, like a classical goddess. She smelled wonderful: spicy, musky, flowery.

'You got a drink?' she said.

'It looks like you've probably had enough.'

'I've never had enough.'

'I've heard that about you.'

She giggled. Her hair tickled his neck.

298

He led her to a rickety white-plastic patio chair in the corner of his kitchen. She dropped into it. Even wasted, she was gorgeous. Those full lips. Those huge, dark eyes. And there, inside the white linen folds, that body. That body. He felt a powerful urge just to run to the bathroom and masturbate furiously in the knowledge that he had touched Hannah Caro. Would she notice his brief absence?

'I'll make you some coffee,' he said. 'That's an interesting dress. Is it from the film?'

She plucked at it. 'Don't know. They put it on me. And the oil. It smells nice.'

'It does. You do. You look very . . . er, nice.'

Jim the Lothario. His hands shook as he reached for the coffee and set the kettle boiling.

Hannah Caro was fiddling with the pin at her shoulder. It pinged and the garment dropped open, revealing her breasts.

'Oops!'

Powdered coffee dusted the draining board. His eyes went telescopic. The Iliad shorts jerked. Breathe . . . must breathe.

She stood and the dress dropped round her ankles. No tan lines. Just smooth, flawless skin.

Too late to run to the bathroom? A couple more seconds and he might as well just come in his shorts and get it over with.

'You, ah, you probably shouldn't . . . ' he said.

She raised her arms above her head and started some kind of slow dance to whatever music she was hearing in her head. She was clearly oblivious to him, oblivious to her surroundings. Maybe he didn't need to go to the bathroom at all. He could just knock one out where he stood. Would she notice? Would she remember? She might even become libidinously enraged at the sight of his member and pounce on him as she had done Affleck. He nonchalantly began to undo the button at his waist. It wasn't like the chance would ever arise again.

There was rap at the door. Jim twitched and fumbled.

Four faces were at the glass: Sergeant Petras, Grace, and two other women Jim didn't recognise.

He assessed the situation. He was standing in his kitchen with his shorts half-unfastened as a Hollywood starlet danced nude before him. It probably looked sleazy. But had he *actually* committed a crime yet?

The door opened. The policeman was the first in, though clearly too distracted by the dancing nymph to begin remonstrating.

'Grace,' said Jim. 'I know this probably looks quite bad, but . . . but, honestly, she was just sitting on the stairs when I got back. She took her *own* dress off. I was making her coffee . . . you know, to sober her up.'

Grace looked down at his unfastened shorts.

He shrugged and offered an awkward smile. What else was a man to do when a starlet stripped in his kitchen?

The two other women fussed over Hannah, retrieving the dress and draping it about her again while throwing accusatory looks at Jim.

Only when Hannah was covered and seated again did Sergeant Petras turn to Jim. 'You don't need to explain. We know she was lost in the village. She has been drinking. She doesn't know where she is.'

'Yes, yes – that's what I thought,' said Jim. 'I didn't want to disturb her . . . you know: it's like how you shouldn't wake a sleepwalker.'

Grace stared at him, apparently more in pity than hatred. Pity was good. There might still be hope.

'I got fired,' he said. 'I've got to be out on Monday.'

Everybody seemed very serious. Nobody seemed particularly concerned about his job.

'Er, what's going on?' said Jim.

The policeman looked to Grace.

She nodded. 'It's quite a long story, Jim. There's a bit of a situation and, well, it looks like we'll have to work together to resolve it: me, you, the movie crew . . . some other people. But let's go to see Diogenes – he's expecting us.'

Dawn, Sunday, Exogi

The bars, the cafes, the restaurants – all were closed at this early hour. The night's detritus lay where it had fallen: half-empty bottles, cigarette butts, *pita* wrappers, vomit splatters, blood drops, oil stains and a discarded t-shirt. Cats prowled and peered from dustbin tops. A fisherman puttered along the street on his moped, the morning's catch in a basket on the back. There was no smell of baking bread.

And almost two hundred black-clad figures mingled. Silk swished. Sandals scuffed. Beards predominated. A group formed admiringly around the colossal cross that had been prepared to consecrate the pagan site. There was talk of making the walk to Allomeros a formal pilgrimage: a prayer walk. Some said they would make the journey on their knees. Others aimed to crawl. An elderly monk from the Peloponnese made it known that he would prefer to be dragged behind a mule in the manner of Saint Kraktoros of Ephesus, but a mule could not be found and a taxi was judged too untraditional for the job.

There was much discussion, too, about who would carry the cross. Xenomachos had suggested drawing lots, but Philotheos had had severe misgivings about the numerical probabilities of Satan's apocalyptic number occurring, so it was decided that four monks or nuns would take turns carrying the cross, changing over every three minutes until everyone had had a go. If there was time left at the end, the most senior monks would get a second chance.

The brothers of Agios Athanasios monastery had indeed brought the great silver reliquary of his remains: an object the size and shape of an upright coffin,

301

carried by means of two horizontal poles affixed to its sides. Some said that the nineteenth-century Patras craftsman who made it went blind and mad from the complexity of the filigree work. Certainly, it glinted splendidly in the morning sun, although its dimensions belied the relative paucity of the contents. All they really had of holy Athanasios was an unspecific thumb bone and a suspected eyebrow. The rest of him had yet to be found.

Xenomachos paced, both anxious and exultant that his grand vision was actually going to occur. True, the assembled holy throng was more interested in talking to Philotheos and seeking his blessing, but the Athonite invariably had something in his mouth. Presently, it was a stale *tiropita* baked the previous day. His beard glistened with pastry flakes. His moustache was speckled with feta cheese. Each uttered benediction was a blizzard best avoided.

'Bring the cross to the front!' shouted Xenomachos. 'It is our beacon. It will lead the way.'

There was a brief scuffle as the brothers from Lixouri challenged some brothers from Ithaca for the first go, but the cross soon passed through the inky ranks. Prayers were uttered. Three monks from one of a richer monastery at Athos took pictures on their iPhones and emailed them back to the Holy Mountain, unmindful of Philotheos' militant stand on the Internet.

'Forward!' shouted Xenomachos. 'Forward to Allomeros.'

The holy phalanx began to move. Banners and standards were raised. Censers swung and smoked. Silver aspergillums sprinkled holy water on dusty asphalt. A brother from Agios Georgios in Messina began to sing and was joined by a harmonious choir. Those who had opted to go on their knees were relegated to the rear, followed by the crawlers, and finally by the elderly monk from the Peloponnese, who had opted simply to lie face-down in the road, judging himself unworthy to join the others in pilgrimage. He would be picked up and given a plate of *souvlaki* later when the town awoke and he became a traffic hazard.

302

At the *kafenio* on the corner, a small group of old men sat waiting for the place to open. They twirled their *komboloi* and watched the procession with amused interest. It was not, after all, a typical Sunday-morning occurrence. Among them were Sergeant Nikos and Jim – the former in uniform, the latter not.

'How long do you think it'll take them to reach Allomeros?' said Jim.

'Three miles? Maybe two hours. Longer, of course for the crawling ones. We will have a coffee and follow them in one hour.'

'I suppose they'll get quite thirsty on the way.'

'We must hope so.'

'Do you really think this is going to work?'

'It is difficult to say. Normal rules do not apply to men like Xenomachos and Philotheos. They live in a different world. Look at them.'

Jim looked. The cross-carrying quartet, one at each extremity, was passing the *kafenio*. Philotheos walked at the vanguard holding an open box of sugar-dusted almond biscuits. Xenomachos nodded a smug greeting as he passed.

'They believe the devil lives in computers and phones,' said Nikos. 'They carry an eyebrow in a silver coffin. The monks don't have sex, but the priests have a dozen children each. The monks talk about Christ being poor, but they have much land in Greece.'

'You're not Orthodox, then.'

'Of course I am – I'm Greek.'

'Right.'

'Is it not the same with your church in England?'

'Not really. We only talk to God on lottery night or if our aeroplane's lost a wing.'

'Hmm.'

'Has Grace called?'

'Not yet. She will. Everything is organised.'

303

The procession continued to flow past, following the road west towards Allomeros. The kneelers and the crawlers were making very slow progress. They clearly wouldn't reach the site before nightfall. Many would probably pass out once the sun really started to lash them.

Nikos slowly shook his head. 'We will collect them later. They will be too tired to argue. Ah, here comes Gerakos, the *kafenio* owner. How do you take your coffee?'

Test Weedle squatted in the back of the white, unmarked van parked among the many other vans and trucks of the media.

'How is it?' he said. 'We got good angles? We gonna get it all?'

'It's good,' said Hans, the assistant cameraman. 'We lose a little quality shooting through this laminated glass, but we should be able to process that later. There's another camera the other side of the site so we won't miss any angles. We're set up for maximum flexibility. Here, I'll show you on the monitors.'

Hans flicked on the screens and both shots appeared. He zoomed the camera in and out.

'Great,' said Test. 'How about sound? We gonna have sound?'

'You'd need to talk to the sound guys. I know they're not using booms. I think they've planted radio mics around the site.'

'Bitchin'. Good work!'

Test stepped down from the van and went over to another. He knocked on the rear door: three short raps, a pause, then two more. The door opened. Four FX guys were crowded inside.

'How're we doin'?' said Test. 'How's Chet? He still alive in there?'

'Vital signs are good,' said one of the crew. 'He's fine. Probably just a little hot.'

'He got plenty of air? I'm already looking an insurance nightmare from the lion thing.'

304

'He's good. We can get to him any time if we need to. I think he kind of likes the challenge.'

'Course he does. He's method all the way. Good. Good. Ya got my number if there's a problem.'

Test left the van and walked over to Craggan's Winnie, which had been brought up from the Main Set near Sami. Grace was standing outside talking to Lomu.

'Guys!' said Test. 'Where's the big man? He inside porking Honee? Catching up on lost time? I don't blame him. I mean, she's old, but there's no need to teach her any new tricks. Or so I've heard. Don't quote me!'

'He's doing an interview,' said Grace.

'Yeah? Publicity – it's all good. So when are these friggin' monks due? If I'd known they were gonna walk, I would have paid for a bus.'

'That's not really the point, is it?' said Grace. 'I mean, they're not supposed to know we're filming, are they?'

'Right. Right. Yeah, that's right. I can see it now in the teaser trailer: monks as far as the eye can see. Like a field of wheat in the wind. Only black. With beards. Ya know what I mean.'

'Yeah,' said Grace.

Test winked at Lomu. 'How ya doin', Leroy? Happy to have the boss back?'

'The name's Lomu.'

'Yeah. Isn't that short for Leroy? No? Maybe I got that mixed up.'

'I think Granger was looking for you,' said Grace. 'She's over by the site somewhere.'

'OK. Right. Yeah.'

Test wandered off.

'What a tool,' said Lomu. 'You see his eyes? Man's in a different dimension.'

'You don't need to look at his eyes to know that.'

Professor Stratigakis was talking to a female reporter alongside the new fence of the ancient site.

'Professor – what do you plan to do about Philotheos' anti-pagan crusade?'

'I'm not sure I can do anything. But as guardian of the site – and as an archaeologist – it's my duty to protect this invaluable connection to our national heritage. Its secrets have still to be discovered.'

'What secrets do you mean? Like treasure?'

'For someone like me, knowledge is indeed treasure. As you know, Aphrodite was one of the Olympian deities, but little is known about her in earlier periods, such as the Mycenaean. This site might one day reveal that history.'

'And what of the Church's claim that the site contains the remains of a sainted martyr?'

'No archaeological evidence of a Christian church has been found on this site. I strongly suspect that this relatively recent rumour has been propagated by the church authorities in order to maintain some sort of claim on the site.'

'But am I correct in thinking, Professor, that the site hasn't been fully excavated? There may actually be new things to find here.'

'It's true that much more work needs to be done. If the remains of a more recent burial are found, they will – of course – be given the same care and attention as any finds. However, the site will be very seriously disrupted if these monks descend upon it and attempt to plant their cross. Archaeology is a science; it's more than just digging holes. If a martyr's bones are discovered amid a hundred scuffling feet, we may not be able to date them correctly.'

'What of Pappas Xenomachos' claim that the site is a centre of pagan worship?'

'His evidence is certainly fanciful. I might remind you that this is the same priest who campaigned against European identity cards in the belief that they might inadvertently contain the "number of the beast".'

'But do you agree that pagan worship is a danger to Orthodoxy?'

306

'A danger to Orthodoxy? Perhaps I should remind you that we enjoy a legal entitlement to freedom of religion in Greece. Look at the Muslims of Thrace, the Catholics of Syros and Tinos, even the many Jehovah's Witnesses. All are allowed to practice unmolested. Yet the Orthodox Church fears them and seeks to control them through classification and regulation. That is the real danger in this birthplace of democracy.'

The reporter smiled. 'What do you think will happen here today?'

'I think Philotheos and his "crusade" will cause significant damage to this site and to the reputation of Greece as the tolerant country that has given the world so much.'

'Thank-you, Professor.'

There was a bustle activity over by some of the press vans. The reporter's phone buzzed and she grabbed it. 'Yes. Really? OK – I'm on my way now.'

'What's happening?' said the professor.

'The procession is on the road. Excuse me – I have to . . . '

The reporter ran towards her colleagues.

Niki approached the professor. 'You were great. You said all the right things.'

'Maybe, but you know it won't make any difference.'

'Let's wait and see. I have faith in our prayers even if you don't.'

'It's not that . . . it's just this whole "Orthodoxy versus Hellenismos" thing that gets me down. We shouldn't have to fight like this.'

'Maybe we won't have to after today.'

'Maybe. How is Hannah doing?'

'Magda said she drank a lot of water. Now she's sleeping.'

'Do you still believe she's the Goddess incarnate?'

'I keep an open mind. So should you.'

Diogenes smoked contentedly in the shade of a large eucalyptus tree. He wore a wide-brimmed hat woven from palm leaves and a gaudy Hawaiian shirt that perfectly mis-matched a pair of Bermuda shorts. Two long trestle tables were set up beside him, each one laid with embroidered table cloths and supporting a bounteous offering for the approaching crusade. In the tradition of monastic hospitality, he had prepared two-hundred shot glasses of fiery *tsipouro* and ten large bowls of rose-flavoured *loukoumi* to refresh the brothers and sisters as they passed.

True, the powerful anise flavour of the *tsipouro* masked the presence of a local weed. And, yes, the gelatinous *loukoumi* contained a certain resin harvested by Diogenes himself, but neither ingredient was harmful if taken in moderation. Had he not proved as much by consuming both in immoderate quantities over the last decade or so?

He inhaled. He held it. He exhaled. The eucalyptus tree giggled and Diogenes winked at it.

Monastic chants came to him on the wind. Another hallucination? No – it was the first of the monkish procession, led by Xenomachos and Philotheos and followed by the cross bearers. Diogenes stubbed out the joint and dropped it in the breast pocket of his shirt.

'Brothers! Sisters!' he said. 'Please accept our hospitality! Take an invigorating sip of *tsipouro* to fortify your pilgrimage. Taste our local *loukoumi* for energy. Welcome! Welcome!'

Xenomachos scowled. 'We don't want your alcohol, Diogenes. You are no friend to the Church.'

But Philotheos seemed to have no such reservations. He grabbed a handful of *loukoumi*, dusting his beard with icing sugar, and followed it with three rapid shots of *tsipouro*. Others drew close, observing Philotheos, and allowed themselves also to indulge in the offering.

Diogenes came from behind his table bearing a tray for the cross bearers. 'Here, brothers! Let me bring you refreshment as you bear your holy burden.'

The monks nodded their gratitude. They offered blessings. All were red-faced and sweating.

308

'What a wonderful cross!' said Diogenes. 'Is it Kefalonian pine?'

The monks were not sure what kind of wood it was.

'Is it built to the correct Biblical proportions?' enquired Diogenes.

The monks observed that the True Cross's exact proportions were difficult to define.

Xenomachos swished towards them. 'What are you trying to do, Diogenes? This crusade will not be disrupted by you. Come, brothers and sisters! Let us march onwards to Allomeros! Brother Philotheos? Brother Philotheos, where are you?'

The Athonite stumbled from the bushes, having relieved himself in the manner of the itinerant hermit. His cassock was dusted white with icing sugar and he seemed to be wobbling slightly from the heat and the shots of *tsipouro*.

Xenomachos took him by the arm and led him to the front. The others followed him as the visionary that he undoubtedly was.

'Onwards!' shouted Xenomachos.

The chanting started again. There was another brief scuffle for the burden of the cross. The procession moved on.

Diogenes took the joint from his pocket, brushed off some lint and lit it. The trestle table was littered with empty shot glasses and spilled icing sugar. The monks had been suitably refreshed.

'This is worse than the balaclavas,' said Kyriakos.

'I'm so hot, I'm going to pass out,' said Andreas.

'It just seems wrong,' said Achilleus.

'Nobody said the revolution would be easy,' said The Patriot. 'Do you think I can just walk around showing my face? I'm a wanted man. Besides, how else do you think we're going to get close to Craggan? Just walk up to him and bundle him into a car? This way, he won't suspect a thing.'

The four of them were dressed as priests, Achilleus having driven all the way to an ecclesiastical wholesaler in Argostoli to buy cassocks and hats. The false beards were from a joke shop.

'This doesn't look anything like a beard,' said Kyriakos. 'It looks like a load of pubes on my face. Smells like it, too.'

'I told you,' said The Patriot, 'nobody is going to notice four odd-looking priests among two hundred. We'll be invisible. After we've snatched Craggan, eyewitnesses will only be able to say that "some monks did it".'

'What if we can't get close to Craggan?' said Kyriakos. 'What if they're protecting him after last time?'

'Andreas ... I mean Kolokotronis ... says they're going to film him among the monks. We can get close. We'll offer him a private blessing,' said The Patriot.

'Or maybe ask him if he wants to see some puppies in our car,' muttered Achilleus.

'I've read interviews with Craggan,' said The Patriot. 'He's very spiritual. It doesn't matter which religion. You need to improve your attitude.'

'They're coming!' said Andreas.

'Get back in the bushes until they've passed,' said The Patriot. 'We'll join the end and work our way through them.'

Xenomachos and Philotheos passed first, the latter weaving slightly and resting on Xenomachos for aid. The cross-bearers followed, beetroot-faced and sweat-stained. The straggling procession shuffled after.

'I thought Philotheos would be taller,' whispered Andreas.

'Was that a piece of pepperoni in his beard?' said Kyriakos.

Chet Braddock waited in absolute darkness. The heat was almost insufferable. The heavy clothing itched. Would the make-up run off him in the heat? There was no opportunity for touch-ups. And yet, was this not the crossover – the moment when acting and life truly became one? Where acting influenced reality rather than vice versa. One take. No rehearsal. Was it possible to get closer to life than this?

He went through the lines in his head. He'd worked on the pronunciation with Eleftheros, but the intonation, the timbre, the pauses would be all his own. In the mouth of the true actor, words became more like music. A breath, a gesture, a sounded consonant or stretched vowel – these were the tools of his art.

He manoeuvred the oxygen mask over his face and inhaled. They'd said no longer than two hours. How long had it been now? Was somebody keeping track? He could have worn a watch, of course, but that would have been out of character. Other actors might have done it – not Chet. He had foresworn underwear for the entire Cherokee picture because there was nothing to show they had worn it. He had born the chafing philosophically. It had added to the performance. Ditto the finger he'd felt obliged to amputate. Some things just had to be felt. Tony Hopkins had shot the whole of *The Edge* with a back injury and used the pain in his performance. Martin Sheen had really cut himself while drunk in the opening scenes of *Apocalypse Now*.

Soon. Soon the time would come . . .

The police car crawled around the kneelers and crawlers, some of whom had progressed barely half a mile outside Exogi and were covered in dust. The windows were up and the air-conditioning was on.

'Do you think they'll make it?' said Jim. 'Some of them look like they might die.'

'It would please them,' said Nikos. 'It would make them martyrs.'

'It's not very practical clothing they wear.'

'They are priests, not athletes.'

Jim watched a monk going on his hands and knees. Hadn't his own uniform been something of a hair shirt?

'What will you do now you have lost your job?' said Nikos.

311

'I don't know. I'd like to stay on the island, but I haven't got enough money to pay rent and there's no English teaching in the summer. I might have to stay with friends on the Peloponnese.'

'But you are happy, yes? No more tourists.'

'Happy about that, yes. But I like Exogi. I like Kefalonia. I'll miss it'

'And the girl with the long hair?'

'Philippa? The Smithson rep? Don't tell me even you've heard about it . . . ' Nikos smirked.

'She wasn't my girlfriend, you know. She has a Greek boyfriend.'

'Of course she has.'

'But she came to me when she needed consolation.'

'Women are like that. They like to play their games.'

Jim nodded sagely. This was women-talk. He was one of the guys.

They drove in silence until they reached Diogenes and his trestle tables. He was clearing all the shot glasses into boxes and smoking a joint the size of a big toe.

Nikos rolled down the window. '*Ola kala, file?*'

'The monks are refreshed,' said Diogenes. 'Philotheos especially so. I believe they are ready.'

'Do you want a lift back to Allomeros?' said Nikos.

'No, I'm OK. The sun is out. The birds are singing. All is wonderful with the world.'

Nikos smiled and closed the window. The car moved on.

'Is he all right – mentally, I mean?' said Jim. 'He's a nice guy, but . . . '

'He made his money in America – now he doesn't work. He is happy.'

'But, you know . . . the drugs, the alcohol . . . the clothes.'

'I know nothing about drugs.'

'Seriously? Do you think that was a Marlboro he was smoking?'

'I didn't see a cigarette. A man's choices are his own if nobody is hurt, no?'

'Of course. But you're a policeman . . . '

'First, I am a man. Then I am from Exogi. Then I am Greek. Then I am a policeman.'

'Right.'

The stragglers of the main procession came into view up ahead.

'Those four at the back don't look like monks,' said Jim. 'They move like teenagers.'

'They are teenagers,' said Nikos. 'It is the Kefalonian cell of the ultra-nationalist organisation *Filiki Eteria*.'

'The people who kidnapped James Craggan?'

'Yes.'

'Teenagers? Dressed as monks?'

'Yes. But they did not plan to kidnap Mister Craggan. They found him by the side of the road.'

Jim's tongue dried. His bowels gurgled. 'Really? That sounds very . . . odd.'

'Yes. Somebody must have hit him with their car.'

'That's . . . shocking.'

'I think so. Who would hit a man and leave him by the road under a plastic sheet? Only a *malakas*. You know this word?'

'Yes.'

'This *malakas* is lucky that Mister Craggan was not injured more seriously.'

'Very lucky. A lucky *malakas*.'

Nikos nodded.

'But if you know who they are and that they're disguised as priests . . . ?'

'Everything is planned.'

'OK.'

The car passed the cross-bearers. Xemomachos and Philotheos seemed to be holding each other up. Nikos accelerated, leaving a cloud of dust for the monks to walk through.

'They should be at the site in about ten minutes,' said Nikos. 'Let us hope everything is prepared.'

313

James Craggan looked at the sky. No clouds. The lighting would be very contrasty. It might be necessary to fill the frame with the monk's cassocks to minimise glare. There would be no way to choreograph them – it was pure guerrilla shooting. Just capture what he could with both cameras and see what they had for the edit.

He was dressed as Cornolli and held an electric mandolin. Grace was standing by his side.

'So I should just get in among them and mingle,' he said. 'Maybe play a few notes.'

'Yeah. Just go with it,' said Grace. 'Test wants the monks in the movie – it doesn't really matter what the context is. Apparently, Orthodox Christians make up at least ten percent of the target demographic. We'll write a script around it afterwards. Cornolli charms the monks. Cornolli accompanies the miracle. Cornolli is the Second Coming.'

'It's just a movie, Grace.'

'*Citizen Kane* is just a movie. There's no mandolin-playing Virgin in that.'

'You need to chill. I've made bad films before. What's the worst that can happen?'

'You could get kidnapped by terrorists and threatened with death?'

'They weren't really terrorists. And I'm pleased you care about my choice of projects. Be honest – you started to like me a little bit, didn't you?'

Grace blushed. 'A bit. Maybe.'

'I knew you would. There's a connection, even if you don't buy it.'

Grace's walkie-talkie crackled a query. She answered.

'They're coming,' said Granger, who was waiting further down the road.

'I'd better get in position,' said Craggan.

'Have you got your crystal?' said Grace.

He winked as he walked towards the site.

Grace had noticed the police car arrive as she was talking. The policeman was talking to Professor Stratigakis and now Jim was approaching cautiously as if Grace was an unchained lioness. He held both hands up.

'How's it going?' he said.

'Fine. I thought you'd be packing.'

'Nothing to pack, really. So what do you think? Is this going to work?'

'It's mostly *your* idea.'

'I'd drunk a lot of ouzo even before we went to Diogenes' place. It all seemed believable at the time. Are you having second thoughts?'

'It would be stupid in a movie – even *this* movie. In real life, well, it's just . . .'

'Here they are,' said Jim. 'We're about to find out.'

Xenomachos was still at the front, his face an apoplectic scarlet. Philotheos staggered sweat-bedraggled a few steps behind. The cross-bearers stooped and swayed beneath their burden. The entire procession moved with a weaving slowness that looked like intoxication or fatigue.

At the gate to the ancient site – Professor Stratigakis and Sergeant Nikos stood together.

'Stand aside!' panted Xenomachos. 'We have come to purge this place of pagan gods.'

'This is a protected archaeological site,' said the professor.

'You have no legal right to enter,' said the sergeant.

'I have told you before,' said Xenomachos. 'There is only one law: divine law. Stand aside – we will enter and plant the symbol of Christ on this unholy plot. Come, brothers and sisters! Let us breach the heathen bounds of this evil enclosure!'

The rest of the monks moved inexorably towards the site: a dark tide seeping. The chants began again. The cross lumbered on. One of the brothers

315

produced a pair of bolt cutters from the folds of his cassock and began to work on the gate's padlock.

James Craggan received word from Granger via a micro-earpiece and moved in from the periphery, mingling unnoticed among the monks. Taller than most of them, he could be easily picked out by the twin cameras following the scene from the vans. His electric mandolin glinted in the sun and he made a show of plucking at it as if his music was calling the ecclesiastical clans. Four of the monks had noticed him, however, and began to move through the throng in his direction.

Sergeant Nikos led Professor Stratigakis back, away from the influx to where a crowd of villagers, journalists and film crew had gathered. Jim was standing beside Grace.

'That's a lot of monks,' said Grace.

'Nice cross, too,' said Jim.

She looked askance at him.

'Here!' said Xenomachos, pointing to a cavity between two stretches of ancient masonry. 'Here is where we will plant the Holy Cross. Bring it closer! Forwards with the cross! Brother Philotheos – will you speak? Will you lead us in a prayer to banish pagan spirits from this site and bless it in the name of Christ? Here, here – stand on this block.'

Philotheos was aided to the slightly elevated position. He appeared unsteady and confused. His face was scarlet and shining with sweat.

The cassocked congregation fell silent.

'Brothers and sisters!' began Philotheos. 'We . . . come here today to fight against the satanic amphibian . . . '

'*Pagans*!' coughed Xenomachos.

'. . . against the satanic pagans. There is no place in Orthodoxy for human sacrifice. The old gods are dead. Jesus Christ is risen . . . '

In the unmarked vans beside the site, equipment hummed. Headphones received a translated version of hidden mic feeds. Test Weedle's face glistened in

316

the light from a monitor. 'That's our cue!' he said. 'The "risen Christ" thing. Do it now!'

The FX guys pressed buttons. Micro-earpieces crackled.

At the site, fragrant smoke began to seep from a fissure in the earth. Monks stepped back alarmed. Some fell. Some shouted. Was it seismic activity? Was it a buried terrorist device? But the smoke smelled sweet: a pleasing fragrance . . . a divine perfume.

'Behold: the ancient gods expire at the name of Christ!' cried Philotheos.

'It's the true aroma of divinity!' shouted another monk.

The loose earth began to quiver at the smoking spot. Monks parted around it.

Grace looked to Jim. The professor looked to Sergeant Nikos.

'Tell me you're getting all this!' said Test in the white van.

And the soil lifted, as if a door into the earth was being opened. A skeletal hand emerged, raising a what appeared to be a coffin top. There was a flash of dusty embroidered material. A reclining figure sat and revealed itself: a pale, parchment-skinned mummy wearing an ornate mitre and magnificent bishop's mantle. The beard was long and white. The fingernails were yellowed. The eyes were sunken, yet vital.

Philotheos dropped to his knees. 'The sainted martyr! He comes to hear our prayer!'

Monks gaped. Nuns stared. Incredulity fought faith. They looked to each other. They looked to Philotheos furiously crossing himself.

'See!' cried a young brother from Kefalonia. 'See his missing thumb! It is holy Athanasios discovered at last. He reveals himself to us at our time of need!'

'No!' said another brother. 'It is Saint Nektarios of Sami. I recognise him from the frescoes. Yes! Yes! It is he! His bones were lost and now they are found. Praise Christ!'

'No!' shouted a portly monk from Patras, 'it is Saint Gregory of Kerkyra who made a pilgrimage of these islands. I have read of it!'

'It is Saint Methodius!' claimed an Abbess from Meteora. 'I saw this in a vision!'

'It is the prophesied resurrection of Saint Nikephoros!' came another voice.

'It's Saint Chet of Braddock,' murmured Jim. 'Methodios actor.'

Grace jabbed him in the ribs.

Chet began his memorised oration, but his words were lost in the clamour. Nobody was listening. A minor scuffle had broken out between the monks of Agios Athanasios and Agios Georgios over who the risen saint actually was. A nun stepped backwards into the excavated trench and dragged a fellow sister with her. A cohort of monks from Zakynthos used the opportunity to wrestle the cross from the brothers of Agios Nektarios, who were reluctant to give it up at this, their moment of glory.

Xenomachos watched the scene descending into chaos. He felt lightheaded. Perhaps the heat. Perhaps that ill-advised shot of *tsipouro* offered by Diogenes. He felt his bowels gurgling and realised with sudden horror that . . .

'Can you smell that?' said Grace.

'The aroma of divinity?' said Jim.

A number of monks ran quickly to the bushes surrounding the site. Others were not able to make it and squatted where they stood. Philotheos appeared to be in the throes of a major bout of dysentery.

Chet stood anciently resplendent amid the defecating masses. Had anyone said "cut"?

Xenomachos sought Sergeant Nikos out among the crowd and strode angrily, albeit wetly, towards him

'You! You, Petras, and this pagan witch. You are behind this sabotage!'

'I've no idea what you're talking about, *pappas*.'

'The *tsipouro* and *loukoumi*. The movie people. I can see what you have done.'

'You took Diogenes' hospitality quite freely. The movie people are entitled to be here.'

'I am not a fool!'

'I believe the film footage of your "crusade" will tell quite a different story. Look at what you have created.'

Xenomachos looked back to see the cross topple to the ground as monks squabbled over it. Philotheos was kneeling before Chet, who had placed a hand on his head and appeared to be conducting a blessing.

'You will be punished in Hell for this!' hissed Xenomachos.

'I suspect I won't be alone,' smiled Nikos, peering over the priest's shoulder at the debacle.

In among the mêlée, four of the monks were making their way ever closer to the bewildered figure of James Craggan, who continued to strum his mandolin in the certain knowledge that the edit and script re-writes would make everything right. Maybe a voiceover.

'Mister Craggan – I am a big fan of your movies,' said The Patriot.

'Thank-you, brother,' said Craggan. 'Although I'm surprised that you've seen any.'

'*Kung Fu Tyrant*. "Now ya got lead poisoning!"'

'That's right. What about you other brothers? Do you like my movies, too?'

'They've taken a vow of silence,' said The Patriot. 'Listen – we would like to bless you.'

'That's very kind, brother.'

'Would you like to walk over there a little to where the vans are parked? The smell here is rather bad.'

'I should really stay here on the ancient site for a little longer.'

The Patriot took his arm. 'Let's walk over there.'

Lomu appeared beside them. 'There a problem here?'

'The brother wants to bless me,' said Craggan with a grin.

Lomu reached over and jerked The Patriot's false beard off.

'What are you doing, *re*?' said The Patriot. 'You don't just pull a monk's beard off!'

'You ain't no monk. You're that ultra-nationalist who's runnin' from the police.'

'What? *What?*'

'You're comin' with me,' said Lomu. 'The policeman wants to talk you.'

The Patriot turned to the others with wild eyes. 'Now we fight, brothers! Now we fight for 1832!'

They stepped back.

'Brothers! For the revolution!' cried The Patriot.

They stepped back further.

'Cowards!'

He tried to run and found himself immediately in a neck-lock as unyielding as the trunk of an oak tree.

'Struggle, asshole, and see what happens to your spine,' said Lomu.

'Easy, Lomu,' warned Craggan.

Nikos approached and handcuffed The Patriot's wrists behind his back. 'I will take this person from you.'

'There are others!' said The Patriot. 'There's a cell here in Sami. There they are! Those cowards walking away there . . . '

'I see only monks among monks,' said Nikos

'They're in disguise! There – the ones with the pubic-looking beards! One of them is wearing Nike trainers.'

'I can't see them,' said Nikos. 'Let's go to my car. There are people who would like to talk to you.'

They walked among multitudinous monks: monks squatting, monks praying, monks arguing over the cross, monks clustered around Chet to receive a blessing from whichever saint they thought he was. Philotheos appeared to be unconscious.

'You know,' said Jim. 'If any of this does appear in the film, people will say it's ludicrous.'

'It *is* ludicrous,' said Grace.

'How about you let me buy you a drink at Diogenes'? I'll be gone tomorrow.'

'You're really leaving the island?'

'I don't have much choice. I'm basically the worst rep that ever lived. Just one drink?'

'I suppose I could do that.'

Grace waved to Craggan and indicated she was walking into the village.

They passed Professor Stratigakis and Niki.

'Coming for a drink?' said Grace.

'Maybe later,' said the Professor. 'I need to see this place cleaned up.'

'I'm really sorry about the mess they've made,' said Grace.

'The biggest mess is how stupid they've made themselves look. I think Xenomachos won't be saying much more about pagans when this is publicised. I'll be surprised if they let him keep his church.'

'Well, see you later,' said Grace. She took Jim's arm and they walked up the hill towards Diogenes' bar.

'So what do you think?' said Niki. 'Was the Goddess here today?'

The professor looked at the cassocked shambles. She smiled. 'One thing we know about the Goddess – whatever form She takes, She's always made fools of men.'

Post season

Honee d'Angelo did not stay with James Craggan for the duration of the shoot. She left the island very soon after meeting an elderly Greek shipping magnate while shopping in Argostoli. Her current whereabouts are unknown.

Lomu continued as James Craggan's personal bodyguard and driver, becoming popular in his own right after appearing briefly as a hitman in Craggan's later release *Kung Fu Tyrant 2: Lead Poisoning.*

Mel Weitz capitalised on the publicity around *Captain Cornolli* by selling the script he had bought from Grace. He got $250,000 dollars for it at auction. His wife divorced him shortly afterwards, having discovered his secret relationship with his receptionist.

Granger stayed with Lustre Productions and was promoted to unit director on a subsequent production. She remains an efficient and very diplomatic resource.

Mr Twyford, the secret tourist, was transferred from Europe to the Middle East and currently resides in a Saudi Arabian prison on charges of theft. The British government is lobbying to reduce his sentence from amputation to ten years' imprisonment.

Morag Cleaver drove her car into the sea after leaving Exogi on the evening that Jim was fired. Later, in hospital, she claimed that she had soiled herself and crashed because she was being chased by an alien spacecraft. Her continued employment with Iliad Holidays is under disciplinary review, following seventeen separate accusations of bullying and nineteen of excessive drinking.

Donna was promoted to acting general manager for the Ionian Islands and was allowed to keep Argostoli as her base. The first thing she did was to reject Exogi and Tripa as resorts for the following season. The beds were subsequently taken by Golden Holidays.

Philippa remains the Smithson rep for Exogi and Sami. She got engaged to her boyfriend Christos, but continued to cheat on him whenever they had an argument.

Kelly was rewarded for her season in Exogi with a posting to Florida the following year. She took her Greek boyfriend Yiannis with her and left him shortly afterwards when he cheated on her.

Tony Brass's career was not harmed at all by his brief association with *Captain Cornolli*. He went on to direct the critically acclaimed film about British astrophysicist Stephen Hawking: *Wheels of my Mind.*

Kyriakos surprised his friends with his sudden and earnest intention to become a monk. He is currently a novice at the Evangelistrios monastery of Mount Athos, where he occasionally meets monks who had been at Exogi on that fateful day. Few like to talk about it.

Achilleus went on to study Politics and History at Thessalonika University. He started a black metal band called *Holy Shit* and they enjoyed moderate success playing live in the city.

Andreas failed most of his subjects at school and was accepted into the police training academy.

The Patriot was very publicly prosecuted as an example of extremist political thought and sent to prison for eight years, reduced to six months after his wealthy politician father paid a massive bribe to the judge. He currently works as a tour guide in the historic Peloponnesian town of Nafplio.

Hannah Caro went directly back into rehab after *Cornolli* wrapped. In her next movie, she played Aphrodite opposite Anthony Hopkins' Zeus and Colin Farrell's Apollo. Her scandalous affair with the latter made her an even hotter proposition.

Chet Braddock appeared in *The Olivetti Diaries* and *Master Po* using a hand double. He was nominated for an Oscar for his role as chimney sweep in Martin Scorcese's *Soot*, but lost out on the day to teen-pop sensation Chucky Feinstein, whose role as a bullied male cheerleader had the biggest opening weekend of the year. Chet remains a dedicated spokesmen for the digitally challenged.

Niki, with her friend Magda, continues to worship Aphrodite. She is still a language teacher at the small school in Exogi and still has teenage boys abusing themselves at her attractiveness.

Professor Stratigakis published a celebrated paper on pre-classical Aphroditic cults and drew funding from a German university to properly excavate the site at Allomeros. Subsequent finds there persuaded the Ministry to invest in a properly secure enclosure.

Xenomachos was temporarily suspended from duty pending an investigation into his vandalism of the ancient site and bringing the Church into disrepute. In an event that many thought symbolic, his beloved pre-fabricated church was struck by lightning the following winter and melted in the fire. When he announced plans to send his oldest daughter Andriana to a convent, she ran away from home to become a model in Athens. His wife is pregnant again.

Philotheos returned to his hermit's existence on the Holy Mountain. He is occasionally seen by pilgrims: stalking the rocky wastes with a box full of sugared treats or an energy bar scrounged from a hiker. He continues to eschew technology and retains an abnormal fear of amphibians.

Penelope continued as the head of publicity for Lustre Productions for only six more months after leaving Greece. She then set up a private practice specialising in "problem celebrities".

James Craggan returned to his glory days and made a series of poorly reviewed but lucrative sequels to his old action movies, directing three of them himself. In a move that surprised many in Hollywood, he than announced his retirement and set up a charitable foundation for orphans.

Test Weedle suffered what his doctors called an "extreme psychotic episode" shortly before returning to Hollywood. It was thought to be caused by excessive use of a toxic narcotic compound found in certain local weeds. His belief that he is Mickey Rooney persists and he is under observation at a specialist facility somewhere in California.

Diogenes continues to live a life of ease and contentment with his cat Socrates and his cannabis plants. His bar remains a haven for all those who find reality too tedious to bear.

Sergeant Nikos Petras was offered a promotion for his work in capturing the *Filiki Eteria* mastermind and in locating the missing Hollywood stars. He turned down the offer, choosing to stay in Exogi and work among his own people. He spends his time smoking and maintaining a network of adulterous relationships.

Grace Willetts returned to Los Angeles and completed her Masters in directing at UCLA. She kept in touch with James Craggan and worked on two of his action pictures for experience before accepting a job with an indie production company. She never spoke or wrote to Jim again, but thought occasionally about that summer and the relationship that never quite started between them.

Jim left Kefalonia with a backpack and headed for the Peloponnese. His intention was to seek experience. Nobody seems to know what happened next, or where he might be now.

Captain Cornolli's Mandolin School remains unreleased.

About the author

Tom Fynn is a freelance writer. He once worked as a holiday rep in Greece, but was fired after six weeks. His final written warning gave the reasons for termination as:

1. Taking guests on the wrong transfer coach.
2. Not giving departure times to guests.
3. Not giving a good service to guests.
4. No photograph on notice boards.
5. Negative and carefree attitude.

tom.fynn@yahoo.co.uk